THE CHURCH OF THE BIBLE

J. RIDLEY STROOP

Gospel Advocate Company
P.O. Box 150
Nashville, Tennessee 37202

The Church of the Bible
Gospel Advocate Reprint Library Edition, 2001

© 1962, J. Ridley Stroop

Published by Gospel Advocate Co.
P.O. Box 150, Nashville, TN 37202
www.gospeladvocate.com

ISBN: 0-89225-521-8

TABLE OF CONTENTS

INTRODUCTION

There are approximately two hundred and fifty churches in the United States. Each of these claims to be the church of the Bible or the true church. Some make the claim exclusive of all other churches, while others make the claim conjointly with other churches. The former make the divisive condition that exists among religious people very evident. The latter attempt to veil the ugliness of the situation by their pronouncement that one church is as good as another. This veil, however, becomes exceedingly thin when it is examined in the light of the realities of the situation. Each of these churches has its own distinctive teaching which represents its own selection, adaptation, and evaluation of some Bible teaching, with its own deletion and its own addition of religious ideas of human origin. Thus, the members of each church are united by means of a common doctrine, are influenced in their thinking by common preferences and prejudices, and are separated from those of other churches by a peculiar loyalty to their own creed and membership. Hence, it appears that the claim that "one church is as good as another" is an unconscious rationalization by which the speaker assures himself that his church is not inferior to the others and justifies the tenets peculiar to his church by putting all churches in the same class. If this statement were an actual conviction of the people who make use of it, if they actually believe that "one church is as good as another" with the implication, of course, that all are right, where is their justification for dividing the Lord's people into parties or factions in the face of our Lord's plea for unity. And if the people of the respective churches believe one to be as good as another, what is the justification of the rivalry that exists among them that on some occasions rises to a pitch that presents an unchristian ugliness?

And furthermore, if it were true that one church is as good as another, this provides no evidence that all are right. In reality it is a case of churches "measuring themselves by themselves and comparing themselves with themselves" as was practiced by the individual Christians at Corinth (II Cor. 10:12). And I am persuaded that the results are the same. Paul told these Christians that they were "without understanding," and the result was that they commended themselves. Since such a practice, measuring the unknown by the unknown, will always leave us without understanding, we can never discover the true church by this method. We can never be sure that we have found the church that Jesus said he would build without an authentic description of it, and that can be found only in the Bible. Any church today that has departed from the practices followed by the church of New Testament days or is teaching for doctrine that which was not taught by Jesus and his apostles has no right to the claim of being the true church.

From this it naturally follows that any church today that finds it necessary to turn to any source other than the Bible in an effort to sustain the validity of its teaching admittedly has no right to the claim of being the church of the Lord which he purchased with his own blood. Any effort to validate religious teaching, not found in the Bible through the avenue of oral traditions, is recognized by all who are aware of the ease with which man's thinking is modified by environmental factors as well as by his own fleshly desires as being wholly untrustworthy if not preposterous. If Jesus did not trust the apostles whom he had taught personally and who had witnessed his crucifixion and resurrection to make known the gospel to the people until they had received the Holy Spirit to guide them (John 14:26, Acts 1:4, 2:4), how can one believe that God would have us trust teaching that has been handed down through more than fifty generations subjected to the influences of human wisdom with its conflicting religious ideas as well as the radical social and cultural changes of a rapidly developing civilization? Furthermore, any claim to apostolic succession or to any other continuum of specially inspired power is without foundation. In fact, all such claims are not only without scriptural support but are nullified by the character and lives of those by whom such claims are made. These circumstances and conditions make it evident that the only reliable source from which to learn of the true church is the Bible. Then with a fervent prayer that we may extricate ourselves from the blinding influence of our own preconceived notions of the church, let us in humility and child-like faith seek earnestly to know the church as it is revealed in the Bible. Reader, this means you, regardless of which church you call yourself a member.

WHAT IS THE CHURCH?

If we are to get the true picture of the church of the Bible, it is important that we have the Bible meaning of the word "church." Since the meaning of a word is determined by its use, if we are to secure the Bible meaning of the word "church," it is necessary that we become acquainted with the word as it is used in the Bible. Since the Bible is a translated book, it is necessary for us to examine the original language in which it was written and ascertain the usage of the word that is represented in our translated book by the word "church." The word used in the original was "ekklesia." This is the word that Jesus used that is translated "church" in his statement, "Upon this rock I will build my church" (Matt. 16:18). So when we learn the meaning of the word "ekklesia" as it is used in the original text, we will know the meaning of the word "church" as it is used in the Bible. Then let us turn to the Bible and learn the meaning of the word "ekklesia" as it was used by the inspired writers.

The word "ekklesia" was used to speak of a riot in the city of Ephesus. Here is a description of the occasion. Demetrius, the silversmith, called the craftsmen together and told them that Paul's preaching was endangering their trade and also threatening to cause their great goddess Diana to be deposed from her magnificence. "And when they heard this, they were filled with wrath, and cried out, saying, Great is Diana of the Ephesians. And the city was filled with the confusion: and they rushed with one accord into the theatre, having seized Gaius and Aristarchus, men of Macedonia, Paul's companions in travel" (Acts 19:28-29). "Some therefore cried one thing, and some another: for the assembly (ekklesia) was in confusion; and the more part knew not wherefore they were come together. And they brought Alexander out of the multitude, the Jews putting him forward. And Alexander beckoned with the hand, and would have made a defence unto the people. But when they perceived that he was a Jew, all with one voice about the space of two hours cried out, Great is Diana of the Ephesians" (Acts 19:32-34). After quieting the multitude the town clerk in part said, "For indeed we are in danger to be accused concerning this day's riot, there being no cause for it: and as touching it we shall not be able to give account of this concourse. And when he had thus spoken, he dismissed the assembly" (or ekklesia) (Acts 19:40-41). The word "ekklesia" was added in the quotations above to show that it is the word that was used in the original text and was translated "assembly." From this record it is clear that the word "ekklesia" was used to speak of a multitude or concourse of people in the state of riot.

On this same occasion the town clerk also said to the multitude, "If therefore Demetrius, and the craftsmen that are with him, have a matter against any man, the courts are open, and there are proconsuls: let them accuse one another. But if ye seek anything about other matters, it shall be settled in the regular assembly (or ekklesia) (Acts 19:38-39). Here again we find the word "ekklesia" translated "assembly" and used to speak of what was evidently a sort of town meeting.

The following quotations show still another use of the word "ekklesia." "For first of all, when ye come together in the church (ekklesia), I hear that divisions exist among you; and I partly believe it" (I Cor. 11:18). "I thank God, I speak with tongues more than you all: howbeit in the church (ekklesia) I had rather speak five words with my understanding, that I might instruct others also, than ten thousand words in a tongue" (I Cor. 14:18-19). "But if there be no interpreter, let him keep silence in the church" (or ekklesia) (I Cor. 14:28). "And if they would learn anything, let them ask their own husbands at home: for it is shameful for a woman to speak in the church" (or ekklesia) (I Cor. 14:35). In each of these cases the word "ekklesia" is used to speak of a religious gathering.

From these three cases, and these are the only occasions where the word "ekklesia" is used with this literal meaning; (we shall examine its figurative usage later) it is evident that it means "a gathering" or "an assembly" without any indication whatsoever of the nature of the assembly and without any implication whatsoever of any particular type of organization. These qualities must be shown by the context. It was used to refer to a riot at Ephesus, a town meeting or a political meeting at Ephe-sus, and religious meetings at Corinth. Thus, it is clear that any gathering of people, whether religious, political, or even criminal in purpose, may be called an "ekklesia."

The meaning of the word "ekklesia" given in Thayer's Greek-English Lexicon is in full agreement with the meaning which we have derived from New Testament usage. Here is Dr. Thayer's definition, "A gathering of citizens called out from their homes into some public place; an assembly" (pp. 195-196). This does not say what kind of citizens or people, what purpose for which they have gathered, what place or character of place in which they are gathered, nor what arrangements or organization pertains. Since the word "ekklesia" means an assembly if or when the word "church" is used to translate it, the word "church" must mean assembly. It can mean nothing more or nothing less.

Now that we have learned the literal meaning of the word "ekklesia" as it is used in the New Testament, let us consider its figurative use. In his speech Stephen identified Moses in this manner, "This is he that was in the church (or ekklesia) in the wilderness" (Acts 7:38). From the context we see that Stephen's phrase, "ekklesia in the wilderness," has reference to the people of Israel. It is also clear from the context that he was not speaking of the people of Israel gathered in a literal assembly, people who had been called out from their homes into a literal gathering or concourse, but rather of a people who had been called out from among the people of Egypt who were bound together in a common interest and worked together toward a common goal. Although some of these people were religious and at Mount Sinai when the law was being given, all of them pledged themselves to keep the law; the fact that they were spoken of as an "ekklesia" has no reference whatsoever to their religious status. As we have seen the literal meaning of the word "ekklesia" is assembly. Its figurative use can include no more.

A similar use has been made of the word "ekklesia" in speaking of the people who have accepted the gospel and become followers of the Lord Jesus Christ. It does not mean that these people have been called out of their homes to a public meeting, but that they have been called out from their sinful ways of living with their diverse selfish interests and conflicting desires into a unity of interests, a unity of purpose, a unity of life. Of course, the word does not indicate that the change was religious in nature, nor that this was a religious body of people, but rather that they have been called out from diverse interests and ways into a common interest. In the word "ekklesia" there is no designation whatsoever of the nature of the assembly nor of the character of its organization. Since the word "church" is used in our Bible to translate the word "ekklesia," it must convey the same idea and nothing more. Therefore, the word "church" as it is commonly used in the Bible to refer to God's people simply makes known the fact that as individuals through faith in God they have been turned from their devious paths to a common way of life, dedicated to the same cause and guided by the same teaching. In fact, "church" is a group designation of God's people just as "Christian" is the individual designation, nothing more. Thus it is unmistakeably clear that the word does not depict the church as an organization or a body politic with any special power or authority over individual Christians.

It is regrettable that the translators of our Bible, it seems for some reason, thought that they knew a better way to express what the inspired writers were saying on this matter than they did; or did they want to make the writings say a little more than its authors intended? Regardless of what purpose or influence was responsible for the act we are confronted here with a very strange situation. They translated the word "ekklesia" according to its regular meaning by the word "assembly" in all cases where the assembly referred to was not religious or was not believed to be religious in nature, but where the assembly to which it referred was thought to be religious in nature they translated it by the word "church." The word "church" is from "kuriakon" which means "the Lord's house" which is from "kurios" meaning "Lord or Master" which is from "kuros" meaning "power." (Webster's dictionary). Is it not strange indeed that the translators rejected the word used by inspiration and substituted a word from the same language with a different meaning? "Kuriakon" is never used in the New Testament; neither is any form of it used to refer to God's people. So one might say that the word "church" is not in the New Testament at all. I know of no explanation of this matter, and this has not been called to your attention to impugn the motive of these great men but rather to impress a correct understanding of the Bible teaching in the hope that it will help us in having the proper conception of the church.

It may be that the translators were only seeking to impress those who accepted the gospel with their obliga-

tion to live holy lives by reminding them that they be-
longed to God by using the word "church." However,
this word with its specialized religious meaning has either
encouraged or given rise to specialized ideas in regard to
God's people that would never have arisen from the use
of the word "assembly." Unfortunately, the church has
come to be thought of as an institution through which
those who are members enjoy God's blessings as they
would secure to themselves advantage through membership in any of a wide variety of human organizations.
Judging from the way many people who call themselves
Christians are living today, they have put their trust in
their relationship to the church rather than in their relationship to Christ. They seem to think of the church as an
institution with the power to save instead of looking to
Jesus as the Savior. Their hope is in the fact that they are
members of a church which they believe to be the church
of the Bible and not in the fact that they are followers of
the Lord Jesus Christ. Their concern is church membership, not living for Christ. They have substituted church-
anity for Christianity. They seem to have attributed the
power of salvation to the church and to have led people
to believe that they will be saved by virtue of membership
in the church as an institution. Sometimes in their prayers
Christians thank God for the church and speak of it as
"the blood bought institution which the Lord purchased
with his own blood." This is a misrepresentation of the
truth.

The Lord did purchase the church with his own blood
(Acts 20:28), but he did not buy an institution. Nowhere

does the Bible ever speak of the church as an institution, either universally or locally. Never is there an implication of such. It is true that Jesus shed his blood to redeem or to buy men back from their wicked way of living, but they were bought back as individuals. They were also purified as individuals. They were sanctified as individuals. They were reconciled as individuals. The blessings and promises are received through Christ, not through the church as an institution. People are members of the church because they are Christians, not Christians because they are members of the church. People become members of the church of the Bible by becoming Christians and can become such in no other way. In fact there is not one word of instruction on how to become a member of the church, and there is no record in the Bible where anyone was ever invited to become a member of the church. The conditions of church membership were never stated in the Bible as such. All such talk is the language of Ashodod and has caused more confusion in the religious world than it has done good. When a person hears the gospel, the good tidings of the love of God and of the promise of eternal life through the Lord Jesus Christ, and believes it with that reality that makes it effective in changing his mind from that of an enemy to that of a friend and turning him away from his own way of living to accept Jesus as his Lord and God's teaching as revealed through Christ as his guide to a life that will please God and obeys the truth, being baptized into Christ for the remission of his sins, he has been reconciled, redeemed, purified, and sanctified. He has became a follower of Christ, a Christian, and is therefore one of the assembly of Christians. He is what man calls a member of the church. This should make the matter clear. Every Christian, every follower of Christ is a part or a member of the church and every true member of the church of the Bible is a Christian.

Someone may ask, "But is it not true that after one has heard, believed, and obeyed the gospel God must add him to the church?" The answer to this question is "No, this is not true." The person might ask further, "But have I not heard preachers tell people to believe, to repent of their sins, to confess Christ as Lord, and to be baptized into his name and God would add them to the church?" The answer to this question is "Yes." At least many people have had an opportunity to hear it. What is the explanation of this? It is simply that the preacher does not mean exactly what he is saying. If you will question him about the matter, you will soon see that this is the case. This is an allusion to the closing statement of the second chapter of Acts as given in the King James Translation. "And the Lord added to the church daily such as should be saved" (Acts 2:47). It is to be regretted that frequently this scripture has been used carelessly. An examination of the context will easily reveal the fact that the writer was not speaking of an act that God would perform to make one a member of the church after he had completed his obedience to the gospel, but that he was referring to the whole process of conversion through the power of the gospel as being the work of the Lord. Surely since the gospel is the power of God unto salvation, there is no reason to believe that God must add a personal supplement. The same writer refers to the progress of the gospel, thus "and believers were the more added to the Lord, multitudes both of men and women": (Acts 5:14) "and much people was added unto the Lord" (Acts 11:24). Here we see that those who became Christians are spoken of as being added unto the Lord. Now since Paul makes it plain that people who became Christians were baptized into Christ (Rom. 6:3) (Gal. 3:27) (I Cor. 12:13), certainly no other act was necessary to add them to the Lord.

There is another statement of how one becomes a Christian that makes the matter doubly clear. Everyone that has any acquaintance with Bible teaching knows that God's people, Christians, they that are Christ's, are spoken of as God's children (I Jno. 3:1) and that they call upon him as father (I Pet. 1:17) and also that their coming into that relationship is spoken of as a birth (Jno. 3:5). This means that one who becomes a member of God's family does so by a process that resembles a birth. Therefore, as is true of the physical birth, when the process is completed the whole matter has been accomplished. When a child is born into a family, he is a member of the family, nothing more is necessary. The father of the family does not have to "add" him to the family. In fact, through the process of begetting and birth, the father has already added him to the family. This is just what happens in the divine family when one is begotten by the incorruptible seed, the Word of God (I Pet. 1:23) and is born of the water and the Spirit (Jno. 3:5), he is a mem-

ber of God's family. He is one of God's children, he is a
Christian, he is a member of the church. There is nothing
more for God to do to make him such. There is nothing
more that God can do to make him such for it is already
done. This should make it clear that what makes a person
a Christian makes him a member of God's family and
what makes a person a Christian makes him a member of
the church. The very instant that a person has completed
that which purified him he is a member of God's family,
the church.

QUESTIONS ON LESSON 1

1. What word did Jesus use that is translated church?
2. Show from its use in the Bible that "ekklesia" means "assembly."
3. To what kinds of assemblies does it refer?
4. How does Thayer define "ekklesia"?
5. Give two examples of "ekklesia" used figuratively.
6. Of what is there no designation in the word "ekklesia"?
7. By what reasoning is it evident that the word "church" means "assembly"?
8. Then just what does the word "church" indicate?
9. Distinguish between church and Christian.
10. What does the word "church" not show the church to be?
11. Show that there is no reason for the word "church" having ever been used in the New Testament.
12. What unfortunate thinking has grown out of the use of the word "church" that would not have arisen from "assembly"?
13. What has this led people to substitute for Christianity?
14. What false conception of church membership has grown out of the matter?
15. What did the Lord purchase with his blood and what did he not purchase?
16. How have Christians been purchased?

17. How do people become members of the church of the Bible?
18. Of what is there not one word of instruction in the Bible?
19. What was no one ever invited to do?
20. Detail what one has done who has been reconciled, redeemed, purified, and sanctified.
21. Is it true that after one obeys the gospel that God adds him to the church?
22. To what was the writer referring in Acts 2:47 by the expression "added to the church"?
23. What other expression was used in Acts to give the same idea?
24. Show from the figure of "a birth" how God adds one to the church.

WHAT IS THE CHURCH? (Continued)

A failure to understand that the word "church" as it is used in the Bible means "assembly" and nothing more, that the church of the Bible is made up of Christians and nothing else, and that it includes all of the Christians and nothing less has permitted another tragic error in Bible interpretation as a result of an exaggerated emphasis in the opposite direction. Instead of exalting the church as an institution and debasing Christ, it has led to exalting Christ relatively and virtually discrediting the church, insisting that one can be saved, that one can be a Christian without being a member of the church. The church seems to be considered a sort of missionary institution for those who are interested in such, but that membership in the church is wholly unnecessary to one's salvation.

As one error frequently leads to another, this case is no exception. Those who thus consider the church a sort of religious adjunct and not the natural cumulative result of children being born into the family of God through the power of the gospel, have been led into the fearful mistake of changing God's order of things. God, through the Lord Jesus Christ and the apostles, guided by the Holy Spirit, has made known unto man the way of holiness, revealing to him the great privilege of purifying his soul in his obedience to the truth, instructing him that this is

19

accomplished when a believer repents and is baptized unto the remission of his sins (Acts 2:38), thus calling on the name of the Lord (Acts 22:16) and becoming a Christian, one of the great group of Christians, the church. However, those who suffer from a distorted concept of the church and would remove it from its normal place in God's order of things and yet retain it on Bible authorization, have found it necessary to have part of God's instruction to man apply to the salvation of his soul and the other part to becoming a member of the church, thus, making an unnatural division in man's obedience to the truth for the purification of his own soul. These two activities of the believer which constitute his obedience to the truth, repentance and submission to baptism, combine to show that he truly believes Jesus Christ to be the Son of the living God. Repentance, changing his mind or attitude from that of an enemy to that of a friend and causing him to turn away from following his own lusts, is evidence that he is moved by the love of God. To be moved to such a change by the love of God, one must know God and know God's love for him. Since the story of God's love is the gospel story, the story of the Christ and him crucified, this change shows one's faith in Christ to be real with respect to the love of God. Being baptized into Christ, pantomiming the death, the burial, and the resurrection of Christ, not only indicates one's faith in Christ as the sacrifice for sin, but also that he accepts him as his Lord by this obedience to him. Thus, repentance and baptism together make it evident that the believer has not merely turned away from himself, but that he has been redeemed, bought back from his own way to follow God's way and at the same time, through the same obedience he has been purified. From this we should be able to see that both of these activities, repentance and baptism, are essential to the salvation of the believer's soul. To remove baptism from man's obedience to the truth declaring it to be unnecessary to the salvation of the soul and announcing it as a mere ordinance of church membership is a fearful disorganization of God's order of things. This change also removes baptism from its meaningful relationship and divests it of its real significance, reducing man's obedience to it as a testimony of his faith in God's goodness to a mere meaningless form with no objective manifestation of his faith in Jesus' sacrifice for sins, or of his submission to God's instruction.

Surely these two grave distortions of the teaching of the Bible that have grown out of the institutional concept of the church with their disastrous results are sufficient to warn us against any practices that would encourage such a concept. When some people have been led, either consciously or unconsciously, to attribute to the church as an institution the power to save, putting their trust in church membership instead of trusting in the Lord Jesus Christ and being content when their practices are such as appear to justify honorable church membership, it is a serious matter. Also, when others are permitted to think of the church as an institution that is wholly unnecessary to the salvation of a man's soul, that one can be saved without being a member of the church, and resulting in a dissection of Jesus' teaching through the apostles to those who seek the forgiveness of their sins and a nullification of the teaching on baptism by declaring it an ordinance of church membership, it is a serious matter. Since both of these grow out of a misconception of the church, there can be no doubt that this misconception of the church is a serious matter. In fact, this institutional concept of the church has given rise to more disagreement, confusion, and division in the religious world than any other misunderstanding of the sacred scriptures. Further evidence of this will be seen in the lessons that follow.

Some one may ask the question, "Is there not any sense in which the word 'institution' may be used to speak of the church? Do not the definitions of the word as given in our dictionaries justify its application to the church?" The answer to these questions is "Yes." It may be used to speak of the human aspect of the church as a body of people who have subscribed to the same teaching and whose efforts are aimed at a common goal. However, the implication that all of the blessings enjoyed by those who participate in the relationship are the direct result of its establishment and operation, is unsound and misleading when speaking of the church. It is true that our dictionaries show the application of the word institution to the church as being correct; but we should not lose sight of the fact that the definitions given in our dictionaries are merely a compilation of the accepted usage of the term being defined, no more or no less, whether the use is founded in truth or in error. Even though speaking of the church as an institution can be justified by the use of the term in society, its usage has certainly been shown to be without Bible authorization, as well as dangerously misleading.

Why not speak of Bible things in Bible terms, as some religious people claim to do, especially when other terms are misleading and confusing? Why not speak of the church as the assembly and why speak of it as an institution when the Bible never speaks of it as such? Why not speak of when the church began to be built which implies that the gathering of people into the assembly of Christ is continuing instead of speaking of when the church was established which suggests the beginning of an organization or an institution impowered to provide for man's spiritual needs? The New Testament speaks of hearts being established (Heb. 13:9, James 5:8), the law being established (Rom. 3:31), the will being established (Heb. 10:9), and Christians being established (Rom. 16:25; I Thess. 3:2, 13; II Thess. 2:17, 3:3; I Pet. 5:10); but never a word about the establishment of the church. Why not invite people to come to Jesus (Matt. 11:28) accepting him as Lord, rather than pleading with them to become members of the church when such terms were never used in New Testament days? Why not speak of people becoming obedient to the faith (Rom. 15:18), or obeying the gospel (II Thess. 1:8), or obeying the word (I Pet. 3:1), or the truth (Rom. 2:8), rather than joining the church or becoming a member of the church of which act the Bible says never a word?

Why is this change proposed? Is it to meet legal demands? Is it to comply with technicalities? Certainly not. It is demanded by the principle of expediency. It is to put the emphasis where the New Testament puts it. It is to keep people aware of their vital relationship with God and the Lord Jesus Christ and conscious of their personal obligations to them as the real source of their spiritual blessings. This is to keep people aware of the fact that the power unto man's salvation is from God through the gospel and not a power delegated to the church. It is the privilege and obligation of the church, of them that are Christ's, to make this power known to the world through their own living and teaching. "Ye are seen as lights in the world, holding forth the word of life" (Phil. 2:15-16). In no other sense does the church have any control of the power. No other privileges or powers relative to the salvation of man are given into the hands of the church.

It is hoped that these statements will not be misunderstood. They should not be taken in any sense that would detract from the importance of the glorious work of the church. It is to be a glorious church (Eph. 5:27), not as an organization or an institution with special powers, but rather because it is a body of redeemed, purified and sanctified people whose purpose it is to show forth the light of the gospel through their lives. May God bless everyone who has entered into this sacred relationship to seek earnestly and prayerfully to do his part.

Since the most threatening danger among religious people today, especially in this country at this time of material prosperity and growing popularity of the church along with a considerable increase in self-indulgence, is the expanding emphasis upon the need for church relationship or church membership to the sad neglect and a growing ignorance of the vital relationship that must exist between the Christian and Christ, this matter should be given prayerful attention. All need to recognize that without this relationship and its moving influence in the life of an individual he cannot be a Christian—he is only a church member. He has only attempted to join himself to a group of God's people, but has failed to become united with Christ. His religion is formal or nominal with his hope largely based upon church ritual and church relationship. And as strange as it may sound this threatening situation is to be found even among those religious people who teach church membership to be unnecessary. Since these conditions exist, it is most important that we be made aware of the Bible emphasis upon our relationship to Christ which in turn gives spirit and meaning to our church relationship.

We have seen earlier in this lesson that the real addition of Christians is to the Lord not to the church (Acts 5:11, 11:23). The Bible never speaks of baptism as a manner or means of becoming a member of the church, but rather as the way of coming into vital relationship with Christ. In the commission, the apostles were told, "Go ye therefore, and make disciples of all the nations, baptizing them into the name of the Father and of the Son and of the Holy Spirit" (Matt. 28:19). On the day of Pentecost the people were told, "Repent ye, and be baptized everyone of you in the name of Jesus Christ, unto the remission of your sins" (Acts 2:38). Of the people of Samaria we are told, "For as yet it was fallen upon none of them: only they had been baptized into the name of the Lord Jesus"

(Acts 8:16). Of the people of the household of Cornelius, "And he commanded them to be baptized in the name of Jesus Christ" (Acts 10:48). Of the twelve at Ephesus, "And when they heard this, they were baptized into the name of the Lord Jesus" (Acts 19:5). Paul wrote to the Galatians, "For as many of you as were baptized into Christ did Put on Christ" (Gal. 3:27). To the Romans, "Or are ye ignorant that all we who were baptized into Christ Jesus were baptized into his death?" (Rom. 6:3). To the Corinthians, "For as the body is one, and hath many members, and all the members of the body, being many, are one body; so also is Christ. For in one Spirit were we all baptized into one body, whether Jews or Greeks, whether bond or free; and were all made to drink of one Spirit" (I Cor. 12:12-13); and "But he that is joined unto the Lord is one spirit" (I Cor. 6:17). It is true that when one is baptized in or into the name of Christ or into Christ "calling on his name" (Acts 22:16), his sins are remitted (Acts 2:38) and he is pledged or "joined to the Lord," he is a Christian and, consequently, one of the total group of Christians, and, therefore, a member of the assembly or church. He was not baptized into the church in order to reach Christ nor to receive his blessings, but he was a member of the church because he had been baptized into Christ and had received his blessings.

One might ask was not Paul saying that we were baptized into the church when he said, "in one Spirit were we all baptized into one body," since he wrote to the Colossians, "and he is the head of the body, the church"

(Col. 1:18), and to the Ephesians, "as Christ also is the head of the church, being himself the Saviour of the body"? (Eph. 5:23). It is true that these quotations show unmistakeably that the body of Christ and the church of Christ are made up of the same people and that everyone who is a member of his body is also in the church, being a Christian; but the word "church" has particular reference to their group relationship while the word "body" signifies a close personal relationship with Christ. This is implied by the fact that no New Testament writer ever speaks of a Christian as "a member of the church," but Christians are spoken of as "members of the body." This connotation is further supported by the fact that the statement, "In one Spirit were we all baptized into one body," was preceded by a statement which relates the body very closely to Christ: "For as the body is one, and hath many members, and all the members of the body, being many, are one body; so also is Christ" (I Cor. 12:12). Later in the same discussion Paul also wrote, "Now ye are the body of Christ, and severally members thereof" (I Cor. 12:27); and when using the same figure on another occasion he wrote, "So we, who are many, are one body in Christ, and severally members one of another" (Rom. 12:5). Also when urging the Corinthians to flee fornication Paul wrote, "Know ye not that your bodies are members of Christ? shall I then take away the members of Christ, and make them members of a harlot? God forbid" (I Cor. 6:15).

Christians are spoken of as "babes in Christ" (I Cor. 3:1). Never "babes in the church." Paul declared, "If any man is in Christ, he is a new creature" (II Cor. 5:17), not "If any man is in the church, he is a new creature." Christians are said to be "alive unto God in Christ Jesus" (Rom. 6:11), not "in the church." In claiming his Christian status Paul wrote, "If any man trusteth in himself that he is Christ's, so also are we" (II Cor. 10:7). Similarly he expressed the Christian status of others, "And if ye are Christ's, then are ye Abraham's seed, heirs according to promise" (Gal. 3:29). He never pointed to church membership as an evidence of their good standing. Paul wrote that Christians were made a heritage in Christ (Eph. 1:10-11), and "To wit, that the Gentiles are fellow-heirs, and fellow-members of the body, and fellow-partakers of the promise in Christ Jesus through the gospel" (Eph. 3:6). The heritage was never declared to be in or through the church. Speaking of Christian relationships we are told, "Nevertheless, neither is the woman without the man, nor the man without the woman, in the Lord" (I Cor. 11:11). "A wife is bound for so long time as her husband liveth; but if the husband be dead, she is free to be married to whom she will; only in the Lord" (I Cor. 7:39). "No longer as a servant, but more than a servant, a brother beloved, specially to me, but how much rather to thee, both in the flesh and in the Lord" (Philem. 16). "All my affairs shall Tychicus make known unto you, the beloved brother and faithful minister and fellow-servant in the Lord" (Col. 4:7). "Even as ye learned of Epaphras our beloved fellow-servant, who is a faithful minister of Christ on our behalf" (Col. 1:7). The expression used is always "in the Lord" or "of Christ," never "in or of the church." Paul declared, "I have therefore my glorying in Jesus Christ in things pertaining to God" (Rom. 15:17), and "for we are the circumcision, who worship by the Spirit of God, and glory in Christ Jesus, and have no confidence in the flesh" (Phil. 3:3), and admonished, "But he that glorieth, let him glory in the Lord" (II Cor. 10:17). From these statements it is clear that Christians should glory in the Lord and not in the church as an institution.

Paul did write to the Ephesians, "Unto him be the glory in the church and in Christ Jesus unto all generations for ever and ever" (Eph. 3:21). The expression "in the church" used here evidently means "in the lives of the Christians or people of the church." As suggested by this statement to the Corinthians, "For ye were bought with a price: glorify God therefore in your body" (I Cor. 6:20). This is made even clearer from these exhortations, "And whatsoever ye do, in word or in deed, do all in the name of the Lord Jesus, giving thanks to God the Father through him" (Col. 3:17), and "If a man suffer as a Christian, let him not be ashamed; but let him glorify God in this name" (I Pet. 4:16); and these statements of fact, "They therefore departed from the presence of the council, rejoicing that they were counted worthy to suffer dishonor for the Name" (Acts 5:41), and "Men that have hazarded their lives for the name of our Lord Jesus Christ" (Acts 15:26). From these quotations it is also clear that all Christian work, as well as Christian teaching, is to be done in the name of the Lord Jesus and not in the name of the church.

Furthermore, we are told that grace is given to us in Christ, not in the church (Eph. 1:6, I Tim. 1:14, II Tim. 1:9, 2:1), and that redemption is in Christ Jesus, not in the church (Rom. 3:24, Col. 1:13-14). We are also told that "There is therefore now no condemnation to them that are in Christ Jesus" (Rom. 8:1), that salvation is in Christ Jesus (II Tim. 2:10), that God gave unto us eternal life in his Son (I John 5:11). As Paul declared, "Blessed be the God and Father of our Lord Jesus Christ, who hath blessed us with every spiritual blessing in the heavenly places in Christ" (Eph. 1:3).

Also, when Paul warned the Galatian Christians against accepting circumcision as a part of the gospel, he declared to those who had done so, "Ye are severed from Christ . . . ye are fallen away from grace" (Gal. 5:4). He did not say they were severed from the church or had fallen away from the church. We are also instructed, "That God was in Christ reconciling the world unto himself" (II Cor. 5:19), not that God was in the church doing so. Surely, this is sufficient to make it unmistakably clear to all who will reasonably consider that the Christian's vital relationship must be with Christ, that no church as an institution has been made custodian of spiritual things, or in any sense impowered to impart spiritual blessings. Even the spiritual gifts of the first century were through individuals and not through the church (I Cor. 12:4-11). The only power that the church has, or has ever had, is not an institutional power but power as an assembly of God's people as new creatures through the gospel. It is the power of the gospel, the power that will change the hearts of those who believe the gospel and also the lives. It is the power that will bring people to Christ, that will lead them to be baptized into Christ and that will bring Christ into them.

Reader, do not put your trust in any church regardless of its name or its claim. Do not rest your hope of glory upon church membership. It is unsafe. Paul has declared, "Christ in you, the hope of glory" (Col. 1:27). All that you can hope for from any church is the teaching of the gospel as it was revealed through the Lord Jesus Christ, and an encouragement to give it a place in your heart and to open your life to the indwelling of Christ, remembering that unless Christ dwells in you your hope of glory is without foundation. "Try your own selves, whether ye are in the faith; prove your own selves. Or know ye not as to your own selves, that Jesus Christ is in you? unless indeed ye be reprobate" (II Cor. 13:5).

Do you teach or preach to others? If so, may I beg you to seek prayerfully an understanding of the true Bible concept of the church and restore the proper balance of emphasis to Bible teaching, recognizing that the church is the product of Christianity, not the author; that the power to save souls does not reside in the church but in the gospel of our Lord Jesus Christ; that Christ and not the church is the need of the world. Preach Christ more and the church less. Seek to cause men's faith to stand in the power of God and not in the wisdom and the maneuverings of men. Cease to preach the church and preach Jesus as Lord.

QUESTIONS ON LESSON 2

1. What grave error has been made in the opposite direction from the one discussed in lesson 1 by the failure to understand that the church is an assembly?
2. Describe the fearful disorganization of God's order of things that has resulted from the doctrine that church membership is not essential to salvation.
3. What do true repentance and baptism show?
4. What does making baptism a mere ordinance of church membership do for it?
5. Re-state the two grave distortions of Bible teaching that have grown out of the institutional concept of the church.
6. In what sense may the word, "institution," be used to speak of the church and with what meaning should it not be used?
7. What words that are applied to the church are pointed out as not being Bible terms?
8. What reasons are given for returning to the use of Bible terms?
9. What power has not been delegated to the church?
10. Why is the church a glorious church?
11. What is the most threatening danger among the religious people of America today, and what has it caused people to fail to do?
12. Give evidence from the Bible that the real addition of Christians is to the Lord, not to the church.
13. What do the words, "church" and "body" signify?
14. Give further evidences from the Bible that our vital relationship is with Christ, not the church.
15. All Christian work should be done in what name and not in what name?
16. Show that no church as an institution has been made custodian of spiritual things or has been empowered to impart spiritual blessings.
17. What is the only power that the church as the assembly has, and how only can it be imparted?
18. What is the Christian's hope of glory?
19. The lesson closed with what special appeal to preachers?

THE NAME AND BUILDING OF THE CHURCH

In view of the emphasis that has been put upon the fact that there is one church, in the face of the existing situation of the large number of churches, it is natural that the question will be asked, "Which is the one church?" or "What is the name of the one church?" These two questions could be taken to imply that THE ONE CHURCH can be identified by its name. This is not true. The one church of the Bible can be identified only by the nature of the people. Are they God's people? If not, then it is not God's church. But they claim to be God's people. A claim does not make it so. If they have been redeemed (bought back from following their own ways), purified (obeyed the truth, I Pet. 1:22), sanctified (dedicated to the service of God), and reconciled to God having enthroned in their hearts Jesus as Lord to obey him implicitly, they are God's people. If not, then they are not God's people, neither are they the one church, neither are they a part of it.

But what is the name of the church of the Bible? The answer: it has no name. That is right. It has no name. Many religious people have tried to give it a name, and some have insisted that there is only one scriptural name of the church. God has not named it. This fact implies that God designed that the church as such occupy a secondary place in his plan for man's redemption with the primary power residing in the gospel of Christ. The church has been designated in several ways by those who wrote by inspiration. More than any other the word, "church" or "churches," (speaking locally) has been used with the context showing its characterization. Among other designations are the church of God (Gal. 1:13), the church of the Lord (Acts 20:28), the churches of God (I Cor. 11:16), the churches of Christ (Rom. 16:16), and churches of the saints (I Cor. 14:33). There is little grounds, however, for these being called "names." A name identifies an object from all other objects. When a person uses several names they are called aliases, and are used to hide the identity. Surely this is not true of the church, but these were just different ways of speaking of God's people. A Christian of the first century could speak of the body of people of which he was a part as the church of God, the church of Christ, the church of the saints, etc., because they were all indicating the same people. Often the expression varied but from the context it was evident that the expression used was that which referred to God's people. That was all that was necessary then and should be all that is necessary today.

In fact there was just one assembly, one church. Why should there be any particular designation other than that which showed it to be God's church by some term that would relate it to God or Christ or holiness? The people at that time made their mistakes, had their misunderstandings, and were probably lacking in agreement on some of the details of God's teaching, but they had not become such apparently that they wanted to promote their peculiar doctrine by taking a different name or a different brand. Paul wrote, "Only, as the Lord hath distributed to each man, as God hath called each, so let him walk. And so ordain I in all the churches" (I Cor. 7:17). It was a practice in all of the churches. "But if any man seemeth to be contentious, we have no such custom, neither the churches of God" (I Cor. 11:16). "For God is not a God of confusion, but of peace. As in all the churches of the saints, let the women keep silence in the churches: for it is not permitted unto them to speak; but let them be in subjection, as also saith the law" (I Cor. 14:33-34). "Whether any inquire about Titus, he is my partner and my fellow-worker to you-ward; or our brethren, they are the messengers of the churches, they are the glory of Christ" (II Cor. 8:23). From these statements we see that Paul's teaching was the same in all churches or congregations. There was no need for special designation, for any church to distinguish itself from other churches so it was only necessary to indicate that they were God's churches or made up God's church or assembly. When religious people began to press their own interpretations of God's teaching to the extent that they refused to work with others, and wanted to propagate their own peculiar doctrine, then they were in need of a name to represent them. In other words, each church name has become a sort of brand or trade-mark for a particular kind of religion or one having its own characteristic emphasis.

The churches of the western world seem to have developed through individual adaptation, motivated either by the desire to conform more closely to the Bible teaching than the other churches of the community or to secure for themselves greater religious freedom than that which was offered by the other churches. Many of those of the former class have sought to give evidence of their zeal for the truth by adopting or adapting some Bible designation of the church as the name of their church, while others have used a modification of some Bible term that in part characterizes their form of church organization or government or their characteristic religious procedure, while still others have accepted the name of some outstanding religious leader. However, in most cases, there have been so many doctrinal modifications that most church names have virtually lost their significance and only serve as a group identification and the process of adaptation of church doctrine under the influence of individual desires continues. The irony of the whole situation lies in the fact that this motley array of names which probably stands as the most universal monument to human pride and conceitedness to be found in the entire world has been erected and is being maintained by the people whose redeeming characteristic must be humility. It is a picture of rugged individualism, rather than that of a submissive people. They have been guided by their own desires instead of the wisdom of the God whom they claim to serve. They are walking in the ways of men instead of becoming imitators of the Christ whom they claim to love.

The Building

Since we have seen that the church is the assembly, it follows that the building of the church must partake of the nature of the building of an assembly. Let us first consider the building of an assembly in the literal sense. People must be gotten together if there is to be an assembly. When people have been caused to leave their homes and to come together in a public place, regardless of the nature of the occasion, they constitute an assembly, therefore, getting people to come together is building an assembly. How is it done? Announce a ball game, a dance, a picnic, a political speaking, a funeral or a church service in any average community and several persons will attend. Who will make up the crowd or assembly in each case? And why? The ones who come will be those who have an interest in what the occasion has to offer to them and will come because it is valued more highly than what they would be doing otherwise. Thus when people are offered something of a public character that is more attractive to them than their private affairs at the time, they will be brought together and in this manner an assembly is built.

It is evident to everyone that people come to a meeting or a gathering only when there is something there of interest to them or when there is some value there—social, political, economic, religious, or otherwise—that attracts those people sufficiently that they come together in that assembly. Hence the nature of the building of the ekklesia, the church, or the assembly, must be similar in character. Thus it is evident that that which brings the church together or builds it or causes it to be must be that which will interest people, that which will be recognized as having personal value, that which will attract people so that they will leave the various types of lives that they have been living and come together with common interests, hopes, and expectations of blessings through the promises that Jesus has made. This is to say that the foundation upon which any assembly or meeting of a group of people is based must be something that is shown to be of personal value to the individuals who come to make up the church. In fact, it must be recognized as being of great personal value in order to turn people away from their way to Jesus' way and to sustain them in it.

With this thought in mind, let us consider Jesus' statement relative to the foundation upon which he would build his church or his assembly. His statement is, "Upon this rock I will build my church" (Matt. 16:18). To what did Jesus refer? Some say he referred to Peter; others to Peter's confession, the great fact that Jesus was the Son of the living God. Which is correct? First let us observe that that upon which one builds is a foundation and that in speaking of a material building, rock was not only the most common material used, but the most solid and the best; and that the word, "rock," applied figuratively in speaking of the foundation of anything other than a material building conveys the idea of solidarity or soundness or full support for that which rests upon it. Second let us bear in mind the fact that Jesus was speaking of building a church or an assembly. Third, let us recall the fact that the foundation of an assembly is that which provides interest and offers values that are personally attractive to individuals. With these in mind, now which of the two, Peter or the great truth that Jesus Christ is the Son of the living God, could become a solid rock foundation upon which an assembly could be built? Which would support values that would become so strongly personal that they would lead people to leave their own selfishness and to come out from the ways of the world, to crucify the flesh with the lust thereof and to make up that sanctified assembly, that glorious church? Would it be Peter or would it be that great truth which supports all of the hopes and promises of the gospel?

It is evident that when Jesus said, "Upon this rock I will build my church," he was referring to the cardinal fact which gives meaning and value to his teaching and to his promises. Consequently, it must have referred to the truth which Peter expressed and not to Peter. You remember the connection. Peter had confessed Jesus Christ to be the Son of the living God. It is the accepting of that fact that brings people together into a church, an assembly, or an ekklesia. If he is not the Son of God, the promises go for nought. If his teaching does not have that foundation to rest upon in the minds of people, his teaching has little attraction. So the foundation is that which gives meaning, that which brings people together; it is that which establishes with them the promises that will make them willing to leave all other things even at a sacrifice and turn and accept the teachings of Christ.

Further in keeping with this, Paul declared to the

Corinthians, "For other foundation can no man lay than that which is laid, which is Jesus Christ" (I Cor. 3:11). This is a part of his discussion of building a church. The foundation is Jesus Christ, or Jesus the anointed, or Jesus as the Son of God. In writing to the Ephesians Paul said, speaking of their being built into the church, "Being built upon the foundation of the apostles and prophets, Christ Jesus himself being the chief corner stone" (Eph. 2:20). Here Paul is referring to the work of the apostles and prophets in giving to these people the foundation of the church, in pointing to Jesus as that which made meaningful the work of the apostles and prophets as the prophets pointed to Christ and the apostles delivered the teaching that Christ had given. (Whether these prophets were New Testament prophets or Old Testament prophets, their work supported the same teaching.) Also, Paul wrote, "Seeing that Jews ask for signs, and Greeks seek after wisdom: but we preach Christ crucified, unto Jews a stumbling block, and unto Gentiles foolishness" (I Cor. 1:22-23). The teaching that he preached to bring people to the church or assembly, the teaching that he preached to establish with them values that would cause them to turn away from their former ways and accept Christ to become a part of the assembly, was Christ crucified or Christ the Son of God.

In the second chapter of Acts we find the record of Peter's preaching on the day of Pentecost. His emphasis was the same. After having clearly and forcefully taught that those people had crucified the Christ and that he had been raised from the dead, Peter urged, "Let all the house of Israel therefore know assuredly, that God hath made him both Lord and Christ, this Jesus whom ye crucified" (Acts 2:36). In the record of Philip's work, we are told, "And Philip went down to the city of Samaria, and proclaimed unto them the Christ" (Acts 8:5), and when the Ethiopian Eunuch asked him about the prophecy of Isaiah, we are told, "And Philip opened his mouth, and beginning from this scripture, preached unto him Jesus" (Acts 8:35). (See also Acts 17:18, Rom. 1:4, Acts 9:22, Acts 8:12, Acts 11:20.) These statements and much other teaching in the New Testament show unmistakably that the church is founded upon, or the assembly is built upon, the great truth that Jesus Christ is the son of God, and not upon Peter.

QUESTIONS ON LESSON 3

1. How only can the church of the Bible be identified?
2. Describe God's people who make up his church.
3. Show that the church of the Bible did not have a name and did not need one.
4. What does this imply?
5. What designations of the church have been used in the Bible?
6. What is the purpose in using several names for the same person?
7. How should a Christian today be able to speak of the group?
8. Why were church names unnecessary in first century and why necessary now?
9. What are our church names today?
10. Tell how our present church names originated?
11. Wherein lies the irony of our church names situation of today?
12. The building of the church must partake of the nature of the building of what?
13. What must be the character of its foundation?

14. State the two conflicting interpretations given to Jesus' statement, "Upon this rock I will build my church."
15. Give the reasoning presented to show that Jesus was speaking of the truth that he was the Christ.
16. Give evidence from the epistles and also from Acts that the fundamental truth taught to bring people into the assembly was Jesus is the Christ.
17. Show that Jesus could not have been referring to Peter in his statement.

NAME AND BUILDING OF THE CHURCH
(Continued)

Not only do the statements at the close of the preceding lesson show that without mistake the Bible teaches that Jesus is the foundation upon which the church is built, a recognition of Jesus as the Son of God being the foundation truth of the assembly, but the very nature of the church, the assembly, demands that he be the foundation. What was there in Peter, a poor fisherman from Galilee with his evident personal instability, that could have served as a foundation for such an assembly; that could have offered to people that which would have brought them together leaving the things of the world which they had learned to love, to dedicate their lives to a cause which was without foundation? One might object that it was not the person of Peter to which Jesus referred but the teaching that Peter was going to teach. But this could not be the case for in this sense many others are included in the foundation, for Paul tells the Christians that they were "built upon the foundation of the apostles and prophets" (Eph. 2:20). Thus in this sense, Peter was only one among many. Also what was said to Peter about binding and loosing was said to others, "Verily I say unto you, What things soever ye shall bind on earth shall be bound in heaven; and what things soever ye shall loose on earth shall be loosed in heaven" and "Whose soever sins ye forgive, they are forgiven unto them; whose soever sins ye retain, they are retained" (Matt. 18:18 and John 20:23).

Furthermore, if the church was to be built upon Peter to whom Jesus was speaking directly, why should he express this fact in the third person in the very middle of his direct conversation with Peter instead of continuing his second person address? All other ideas are expressed in the second person. Why did he not say, "Thou art Peter, and upon thee will I build my church?" He used the direct second person form in telling Peter of the part that he was to have in the matter, "I will give unto thee the keys of the kingdom of heaven: and whatsoever thou shalt bind on earth shall be bound in heaven; and whatsoever thou shalt loose on earth shall be loosed in heaven" (Matt. 16:19).

In reality the idea that Jesus was going to build his church or assembly upon Peter is not only out of harmony with the nature of the situation and contradictory to the Bible teaching, but has for its only semblance of support the distortion of a language technicality. It is hardly reasonable to make "petros" and "petra," which are used in Matthew 16:18, refer to the same thing or person as would have to be true if Peter were the foundation. Then Jesus would be saying in meaning, "Thou art Peter and upon 'this' Peter I will build my church." Also, we have Paul referring to Christ as the spiritual rock and making use of a form of the same word, "and did all drink the same spiritual drink: for they drank of a spiritual rock (petras) that followed them: and the rock (petra) was Christ" (I Cor. 10:4). Futhermore, if Peter held such a place of honor and power in the church, why did he act as he did at Antioch? "For before that certain came from James, he ate with the Gentiles; but when they came, he (Peter) drew back and separated himself, fearing them that were of the circumcision" (Gal. 2:12). Why should some coming from James and whatever happened among the circumcision have caused him who occupied such a high place to change? And why did James take the lead in settling the question about circumcision of the Gentiles (Acts 15:13-21)? James also seems to have been given a sort of special attention by Paul when he returned to Jerusalem from the third missionary journey as shown in this statement: "And the day following Paul went in with us unto James; and all the elders were present" (Acts 21: 18).

The question is sometimes raised, "When was the church established?" which implies that the querist is thinking of the church as an institution. However, we shall ignore the non-Biblical wording and consider it as intending to ask when did the church begin or when did Jesus begin to build his church or assembly. Since Jesus declared to Peter, "Upon this rock I will build my church (or assembly)," it is evident that it was to be done after that statement was made; for Jesus said "I will build." Also there are three terms used in this quotation that contribute to the answer of the question. "Build" suggests the construction of a building. "Upon this rock" implies that he is speaking of the building of the superstructure not including the foundation. "Assembly" indicates the nature of what he was to build. Since the actual house is not built until the foundation is laid the foundation must be laid for this assembly before it could be built. And since the foundation upon which it was to be built was the great truth that Jesus Christ was the Son of God the assembly could not be built until the evidences of this truth were fully provided. And since the assembly was to be made up of people from all nations the evidences must be universally sufficient—sufficient to cause the truth to be realistically accepted, to cause those who believe it to enthrone Jesus in their hearts as Lord and to discard all ideas from other sources that were in conflict with his teaching.

It is true that prior to the time of Peter's confession definite proof had already been given to the disciples that he was the Christ. In fact, John's testimony (John 1:29-35), together with one day's visit with Jesus (John 1:39-40), led Andrew to testify when he found his brother, Simon, and brought him to Christ, "We have found the Messiah (which is, being interpreted, Christ)" (John 1:41). However, it is clear from the incident that followed Peter's confession that although he had confessed the great truth to be a fact, he had not given the fact that controlling place in his thinking that showed a recognition of its real meaning. The record says, "From that time began Jesus to show unto his disciples, that he must go unto Jerusalem, and suffer many things of the elders and chief priests and scribes, and be killed, and the third day be raised up. And Peter took him, and began to rebuke him, saying, Be it far from thee, Lord: this shall never be unto thee. But he turned, and said unto Peter, Get thee behind me, Satan: thou art a stumbling-block unto me: for thou mindest not the things of God, but the things of men" (Matt. 16:21-23). Peter had not made this fact or truth a personal conviction, for a fact fully accepted makes all ideas that conflict with it untenable for by it they are shown to be false. Peter failed to respect Jesus' announcement, which was evidently made in all seriousness, as a teaching of divine truth, but acted upon ideas that he had accepted from another source of which action Jesus said, "Thou mindest not the things of God but the things of men."

In this we see that Peter had a faith that was sufficient to confess Jesus as Lord and evidently sufficient to cause him to do many other things, but not realistic enough to provide that "simplicity and purity toward Christ" that would lead him to accept Jesus' teaching even when his own ideas were to the contrary. Peter did not yet have the faith of Abraham, for on three separate occasions Abraham readily accepted God's teaching when his ideas were in direct conflict with it (Gen. 15:1-6, Gen. 17:15-21, Gen. 22:1-9). He did not have the faith that prepared him to accept all of Jesus' teaching as divine and to give it the place of honor and respect that it must have in the hearts of those who make up the true church. Unfortunately, there are many people today who, like Peter on this occasion, have confessed Jesus to be the Christ and who would probably contend for the fact, but who have never given the great truth that realistic personal value in their thinking that enthrones his teaching in their hearts and makes the teachings of men untenable. In view of this experience of Peter, how can honest sincere people become so blinded as to believe that a faith that only confesses Jesus to be the Christ is sufficient to save one's soul, and how can a preacher who is moved by a love for the souls of men be so forgetful as to exalt the formal verbal confession of Christ by stating that the only question he has a right to ask is, "Do you believe that Jesus Christ is the Son of God?" Confession with the mouth is not unto salvation unless "with the heart man believeth unto righteousness," or unless he has a faith that causes him to think God's thoughts and to walk in God's ways.

Although many evidences that Jesus was the Son of God had been given before the time of Peter's confession, many others were to follow. That which was the greatest was yet to come. It was the resurrection of Jesus from the dead. We are told that Jesus "was declared to be the Son of God with power, according to the spirit of holiness, by the resurrection from the dead" (Rom. 1:4); that "he first by the resurrection of the dead should proclaim light both to the people and to the Gentiles" (Acts 26:23); and that God "according to his great mercy begat us again unto a living hope by the resurrection of Jesus Christ from the dead" (I Peter 1:3). Surely the foundation was not completed until Jesus was raised from the dead. And further, Paul described the gospel that he preached to the Corinthians and by which they would be saved in these words: "That Christ died for our sins according to the scriptures; and that he was buried; and that he hath been raised on the third day according to the scriptures" (I Cor. 15:3-4); and he wrote the Romans thus, "If thou shalt confess with thy mouth Jesus as Lord, and shalt believe in thy heart that God raised him from the dead, thou shalt be saved" (Rom. 10:9-10). Since the gospel was and is God's power unto salvation (Rom. 1:16), the power by which people became Christians, and therefore a part of God's assembly, the church, it is inconceivable that the church that Christ was to build could have begun before the basic facts of the gospel had become facts. Therefore, there can be no doubt that the building of the church was begun after the resurrection of Christ.

Furthermore, the church or assembly could not be built until the truth that Jesus is the Christ was preached to the people, for until this was made known there was no great personal value to cause them to accept Jesus as Lord and to bring them together into a common way of life. Then if we can ascertain when this was first preached and accepted, we shall know without question when the church began. Let us review the New Testament record of preaching.

John the Baptist preached, "Repent ye; for the kingdom of heaven is at hand" (Matt. 3:2) and that the people "should believe on him that should come after him, that is, on Jesus" (Acts 19:4). Jesus' preaching is described with the same words, "Repent ye; for the kingdom of heaven is at hand" (Matt. 4:17). When the twelve were sent forth they were told, "As ye go, preach, saying, the kingdom of heaven is at hand" (Matt. 10:7). When the seventy were sent they were instructed, "And say unto them, the kingdom of God is come nigh unto you" (Luke 10:9). None of these preached to the people Jesus as the Christ. Even after Peter confessed him to be the Christ, Jesus charged his disciples "That they should tell no man that he was the Christ" (Matt. 16:20). Also when he was transfigured before Peter, James, and John we are told, "And as they were coming down from the mountain, Jesus commanded them, saying, Tell the vision to no man, until the Son of man be risen from the dead" (Matt. 17:9). We also find that the apostles were not given the commission to preach the gospel until after the resurrection (Matt. 28:19-20, Mark 16:15-16). Also during the forty days while Jesus was giving evidence of the resurrection he gave them the commission and during this time also "He charged them not to depart from Jerusalem, but to wait for the promise of the Father, which, said he, ye heard from me; for John indeed baptized with water; but ye shall be baptized in the Holy Spirit not many days hence" (Acts 1:4-5); and just before his ascension he added, "But ye shall receive power, when the Holy Spirit is come upon you: and ye shall be my witnesses both in Jerusalem, and in all Judaea and Samaria, and unto the uttermost part of the earth" (Acts 1:8). They were not to be his witnesses, they were not to preach Jesus as the Christ until they had received the power. This they received on Pentecost about ten days later (Acts 2:1-3).

In the record that follows we are told that the apostles began preaching Jesus as the Christ, the Messiah through whom the Jews looked for the fulfillment of the promise made to Abraham. Those who believed the good tidings and were made aware that the great blessings of God were to be bestowed through the one whom they had rejected and crucified "said unto Peter and the rest of the apostles, Brethren, what shall we do" (Acts 2:37); and "And Peter said unto them, Repent ye, and be baptized every one of you in the name of Jesus Christ unto the remission of your sins; and ye shall receive the gift of the Holy Spirit. For to you is the promise, and to your children, and to all that are afar off, even as many as the Lord our God shall call unto him. And with many other words he testified, and exhorted them, saying, Save yourselves from this crooked generation. They then that received his word were baptized: and there were added unto them in that day about three thousand souls" (Acts 2:38-41). Here we have the brief account of the beginning of the ekklesia, the assembly, the church. The great truth that Jesus was the Christ began to be preached by those who had been instructed and prepared to do so, and those who believed it and came to recognize the great personal value of God's love and promise through him were called out from their devious unholy ways of living to accept him as Lord, being redeemed, purified, sanctified, and reconciled, and were members of the blood-bought assembly or church.

Remember also that it was not until after his resurrection from the dead, that he started his workmen on the construction or the building of the church. It was not until after his ascension that the apostles began to preach

Jesus as the Christ and to gather the assembly or church together on that foundation. You recall that he instructed the apostles to remain in Jerusalem, after giving them their commission, until they received the power from on high, until they were more fully qualified to do the work he wanted done. We are also acquainted with the fact that on the day of Pentecost when that power had been received, they immediately began their work of building. They began to do what? They began to preach that Jesus Christ was the Son of God and those who truly believed that teaching became a part of that congregation, that assembly, coming together with the apostles who had already believed. Consequently, the building of the church was begun. In Acts 2:36 we see that it was preached to those people that the same Jesus whom they had crucified had been made Lord and Christ, and they were told to know that assuredly. Those who believed that, those who accepted him as Lord and Christ, those who were willing to look to him as their ruler, were the ones who became the church or the assembly. In Acts 2:41 we have the statement that those who received the word became a part of the church. In Acts 5:14 we are told that both men and women were added to the Lord. Thus the assembly or church that Jesus was to build had its beginning on the first Pentecost after his resurrection from the dead.

QUESTIONS ON LESSON 4

1. Why could Peter not be the foundation?
2. Why could Peter's teaching not be what Jesus was speaking of?
3. Did what Jesus said about binding and loosing mean that he would have a power other apostles did not have?

4. What change in language construction shows that he was not speaking of Peter as the foundation?
5. What is the only semblance of support for the teaching that Peter was to be the foundation?
6. If "petros" and "petra" both refer to Peter what was the meaning of Jesus' statement?
7. Where does Paul use the same word, "petra," to refer to Christ?
8. Give other evidences that Peter was not above the other apostles.
9. What does Jesus' statement show about the time the church began to be built?
10. What implies that Jesus is speaking of building the superstructure not including the foundation?
11. What must be done to provide the foundation before the church could be built?
12. Give evidence that some proof that Jesus was the Christ had been given before this time?
13. Show by Peter's experience that followed this occasion that he did not have the faith of Abraham.
14. Who today are like Peter at that time?
15. How have some preachers exalted the formal verbal confession?
16. Confession is unto salvation only when?
17. Through what was Jesus declared to be the son of God with power?
18. What did Paul preach as the gospel or power of God unto salvation?
19. Then what must have happened before it could be preached and the church actually begun?
20. What shows the church was not begun before Jesus' ascension?
21. When was this gospel with the full evidence that Jesus was the Christ preached?
22. Describe the beginning of the church.

LESSON 5

THE CHURCH AND THE KINGDOM

Unfortunately many of the preachers and teachers of the twentieth century have emphasized the church but have given little attention to the kingdom. This has led to a misunderstanding of both the church and the kingdom and has led some Bible students to declare that they are one and the same. It is true that they are very similar in nature and closely related, but they are not the same. The word "church" and the word "kingdom" cannot always be used interchangeably. This confusion has resulted from the failure to identify them as two separate things. This is the same trouble that many people have in distinguishing between what are commonly called "true twins." They have not become thoroughly acquainted with them and consequently have overlooked the marks of their individual identity. Since we have discussed the identity of the church along with the Bible use of the word "church" in preceding lessons, now we shall consider the Bible use of the word "kingdom" in the same way with the hope of clarifying the Bible concept.

First these observations seem to be in order. (1) The word "kingdom" is commonly used to designate a territory or domain over which a king rules or reigns. Therefore the use of the word "kingdom" implies the presence of a king and the use of the word "king" indicates the existence of a kingdom. The use of the word "throne" also suggests the presence of a kingdom and a king. (2) The Bible does not provide us with an analytical description of the kingdom just as it does not furnish us with a detailed picture of the church. Therefore it will be necessary to derive the true concept of the kingdom from the usage of the word in the Bible as we have in the case of the church. (3) The "kingdom of heaven," the "kingdom of God," and the "kingdom of Christ" may be used interchangeably (Matt. 10:7, Luke 9:2, Eph. 5:5).

The first use of the word "kingdom" referring to God's rule over men is found in his appeal through Moses to the people of Israel at Mount Sinai. "Now therefore, if ye will obey my voice indeed, and keep my covenant, then ye shall be mine own possession from among all peoples: for all the earth is mine: and ye shall be unto me a kingdom of priests and a holy nation" (Exod. 19: 5-6). The use of the word here certainly implies that God is ruler and suggests the nature of the people over whom he desires to rule, "a kingdom of priests and a holy nation," a people who maintains holiness and who worships him. From this it is clear that God's rule over men has been expressed in terms of the kingdom concept from the days of the descendants of Jacob. Hence "the kingdom of God" can rightfully be applied to the people over whom God ruled at that time.

The next use of this concept in the Bible record is expressed in the term "king" and God himself is the one who used it. This occurred more than four hundred years after God had appealed to these people to be unto him "a kingdom of priests and a holy nation." During this time God had cared for them in the wilderness, fought for them in the conquest of Canaan, given them the land for an inheritance and raised up saviors or deliverers, who were called judges, who saved them out of the hand of the nations round about. When the people of Israel asked for a king and Samuel who was then judge prayed to Jehovah about the matter, "Jehovah said unto Samuel, Hearken unto the voice of the people in all that they say unto thee; for they have not rejected thee, but they have rejected me that I should not be king over them" (I Sam. 8:7). It is also apparent that some of the people during the period of the judges recognized this relationship of God to them, although it was not referred to by the word "king" or "kingdom." When God so wondrously raised up Gideon, one of the judges, and saved the people of Israel from the Midianites and the Amalekites "Then the men of Israel said unto Gideon, Rule thou over us, both thou, and thy son, and thy son's son also; for thou hast saved us out of the hand of Midian. And Gideon said unto them, I will not rule over you, neither shall my son rule over you: Jehovah shall rule over you" (Judg. 8: 22-23).

God told Samuel to give the people a king, but he did not relinquish his rule over them. He charged Samuel to make known to the people the nature of the kingdom with the burdens and sufferings that it would bring, but in his mercy extended them the privilege of continuing their former relationship with him. "If ye will fear Jehovah, and serve him, and hearken unto his voice, and not rebel against the commandment of Jehovah, and both ye and also the king that reigneth over you be followers of Jehovah your God, well: but if ye will not hearken unto the voice of Jehovah, but rebel against the commandment of Jehovah, then will the hand of Jehovah be against you, as it was against your fathers" (I Sam. 12:14-15). The first king, Saul, failed to meet the conditions imposed; consequently, David was made king over Israel. Although he failed in many things, the faithfulness of David's efforts led God to promise "And thy house and thy kingdom shall be made sure for ever before thee: thy throne shall be established for ever" (II Sam. 7:16). However, because of the wickedness of King Solomon, David's son, ten tribes of the people of Israel were taken away from the house of David, and later because of the unfaithfulness of the kings who reigned upon the throne of David and the people who remained under their rule, they were taken away into Babylonian captivity. During this period of captivity those who had been subject to the throne of David while Babylon was in the height of her glory as a world power, God made known to her king, Nebuchadnezzar, by a dream that was interpreted by Daniel, that the time would come when the God of heaven would set up a kingdom which should never be destroyed, but should stand forever (Dan. 2:44).

From the record of the New Testament it is unmistakeably clear that the faithful Jewish people fully believed that the God of heaven would set up a kingdom, and also that the king over that kingdom would be of the seed of David. It is also apparent that it was spoken of in terms of the one who was to come rather than the kingdom that was to come. At the time of Jesus' birth we are told that the wise men asked "Where is he that is born King of the Jews? for we saw his star in the east, and are come to worship him" (Matt. 2:2). When the chief priests and scribes of the people were asked where the Christ should be born, they said, "In Bethlehem of Judea: for thus it is written through the prophet" (Matt. 2:5). This teaching was even accepted among the Samaritans. While Jesus was talking with the Samaritan woman at Jacob's well, "The woman saith unto him, I know that Messiah cometh (he that is called Christ): when he is come, he will declare unto us all things" (John 4:25). These quotations leave no doubt that the teaching concerning the coming kingdom had become widely known and generally accepted, that it was founded in the teaching of the prophets, that the one who was to come as ruler, the king, was spoken of as "the Christ" or "the Messiah," and that they knew that the king, the Christ, or the Messiah to come was to be of the seed of David by the question asked when they were contending over the identity of Jesus. "Hath not the scripture said that the Christ cometh of the seed of David, and from Bethlehem, the village where David was?" (John 7:42).

There is much other evidence that the Jews strongly expected the kingdom of the Christ or the Messiah to come. At the coming of John we are told "And as the people were in expectation, and all men reasoned in their hearts concerning John, whether haply he were the Christ" (Luke 3:15). "And this is the witness of John,

when the Jews sent unto him from Jerusalem priests and
Levites to ask him, Who art thou?" (John 1:19). "And
they asked him, and said unto him, Why then baptizest
thou, if thou art not the Christ, neither Elijah, neither the
prophet?" (John 1:25). When Jesus began to gather his
disciples about him, of Andrew, who was one of the first,
we read, "He findeth first his own brother Simon, and
saith unto him, We have found the Messiah (which is
being interpreted, Christ)" (John 1:41). When Philip
became his disciple we are told "Philip findeth Nathanael,
and saith unto him, We have found him, of whom Moses
in the law, and the prophets, wrote, Jesus of Nazareth, the
son of Joseph" (John 1:45), and "Nathanael answered
him, Rabbi, thou art the Son of God; thou art King of
Israel" (John 1:49). Later in Jesus' ministry, when it was
known that the Jews sought to kill him, he continued to
speak openly without interference, some of the people of
Jerusalem asked "Can it be that the rulers indeed know
that this is the Christ?" (John 7:26).

Not only had the people of Jesus' day, especially the
Jews, been taught of God's blessings to them in terms of
the coming kingdom and were already looking for the
coming of the kingdom, but also the preaching of both
John the Baptist and Jesus was concerning the kingdom.
"And in those days cometh John the Baptist, preaching in
the wilderness of Judea, saying, Repent ye; for the kingdom of heaven is at hand" (Matt. 3:1-2). "Now after
John was delivered up, Jesus came into Galilee, preaching
the gospel of God, and saying, The time is fulfilled, and
the kingdom of God is at hand: repent ye, and believe in

the gospel" (Mark 1:14-15). "And Jesus went about in all Galilee, teaching in their synagogues, and preaching the gospel of the kingdom," (Matt. 4:23). "But he said unto them, I must preach the good tidings of the kingdom of God to the other cities also: for therefore was I sent" (Luke 4:43).

Many of Jesus' parables were teachings about the kingdom (Matt. 13:9, Matt. 13:24, Matt. 13:44, Matt. 13:45, Matt. 13:47, Matt. 13:52, Matt. 18:23, Matt. 20:1, Matt. 22:2). When the disciples asked Jesus why he spake to the multitudes in parables, "He answered and said unto them, Unto you it is given to know the mysteries of the kingdom of heaven, but to them it is not given" (Matt. 13:11). It is clear from these things that Jesus' work was to make known the mysteries of the kingdom. Jesus also made it clear that "This gospel of the kingdom shall be preached in the whole world for a testimony unto all the nations; and then shall the end come" (Matt. 24:14).

Not only did Jesus preach the good tidings of the kingdom and explain to his disciples the mysteries of the kingdom, but this great truth was made to dominate their thinking and to control their daily living. They were taught to pray "Thy kingdom come" (Matt. 6:10). Jesus informed the twelve and charged them "As ye go, preach, saying, The kingdom of heaven is at hand" (Matt. 10:7). When the seventy were sent forth they were to preach "The kingdom of God is come nigh unto you" (Luke 10:9). Not only did the disciples pray for the kingdom to come and preach the coming of the kingdom, but the matter was so realistic they became concerned about the places that they should occupy in the kingdom. On different occasions they contended over the matter of who was greatest (Mark 9:33-34, Luke 22:24). They asked Jesus, "Who then is greatest in the kingdom of heaven?" (Matt. 18:1). Places of greatness were even requested of the Lord. "Then came to him the mother of the sons of Zebedee with her sons, worshipping him, and asking a certain thing of him. And he said unto her, What wouldest thou? She saith unto him, Command that these my two sons may sit, one on thy right hand, and one on thy left hand, in thy kingdom" (Matt. 20:20-21). It seems that the disciples set the time for the kingdom to come at least once. "And as they heard these things, he added and spake a parable, because he was nigh to Jerusalem, and because they supposed that the kingdom of God was immediately to appear" (Luke 19:11). Their enthusiasm for the kingdom seems to have reached its climax as they entered the city of Jerusalem. "And many spread their garments upon the way; and others branches, which they had cut from the fields. And they that went before, and they that followed, cried, Hosanna; Blessed is he that cometh in the name of the Lord: Blessed is the kingdom that cometh, the kingdom of our father David: Hosanna in the highest" (Mark 11:8-10).

It is clear that the disciples held an erroneous concept of the kingdom. They were expecting an earthly kingdom. However it is just as evident that their conviction relative to the coming of the kingdom had been established beyond any doubt. It seemed to remain unchanged by the crucifixion, burial, resurrection, and appearances of Jesus, for on the eve of his ascension they asked, "Lord dost thou at this time restore the kingdom to Israel?" (Acts 1:6).

Although those who were to be Jesus' apostles confidently expected the kingdom that had been promised to be an earthly kingdom, it is clear that upon receiving the Holy Spirit on the day of Pentecost, which qualified them for the work of apostles by guiding them into all the truth, they had come to understand that it was a spiritual kingdom. This was made clear by the apostle Peter. "Brethren, I may say unto you freely of the patriarch David, that he both died and was buried, and his tomb is with us unto this day. Being therefore a prophet, and knowing that God had sworn with an oath to him, that of the fruit of his loins he would set one upon his throne; he foreseeing this spake of the resurrection of the Christ, that neither was he left unto Hades, nor did his flesh see corruption. This Jesus did God raise up, whereof we all are witnesses. Being therefore by the right hand of God exalted, and having received of the Father the promise of the Holy Spirit, he hath poured forth this, which ye see and hear. For David ascended not into the heavens: but he saith himself, The Lord said unto my Lord, Sit thou on my right hand, Till I make thine enemies the footstool of thy feet. Let all the house of Israel therefore know assuredly, that God hath made him both Lord and Christ, this Jesus whom ye crucified" (Acts 2:29-36). This change in their understanding of the nature of the kingdom, however, did not change the basic theme of their preaching.

They preached the gospel of the kingdom, making known the mysteries of the kingdom which had been revealed unto them. This pattern was also followed by those who were taught by the twelve apostles and also Paul, who was made an apostle later.

You will note that sometimes their preaching the kingdom is expressed by saying that they preached the Christ or preached Jesus, just as in former days the Jews referred to the coming of the kingdom as the coming of the Christ or the Messiah. They preached the Christ on the day of Pentecost (Acts 2:22-36), in Solomon's porch (Acts 3:13-26), before the Jewish council (Acts 3:8-12), and Steven preached the Christ as recorded in Acts chapter seven. The preaching of Philip is spoken of in terms of both Christ and the kingdom. "And Philip went down to the city of Samaria, and proclaimed unto them the Christ" (Acts 8:5). "But when they believed Philip preaching good tidings concerning the kingdom of God and the name of Jesus Christ, they were baptized, both men and women" (Acts 8:12). "And Philip opened his mouth, and beginning from this scripture, preached unto him Jesus" (Acts 8:35). Of Paul's preaching it is said, "And he entered into the synagogue, and spake boldly for the space of three months, reasoning and persuading as to the things concerning the kingdom of God" (Acts 19:8), "And now behold, I know that ye all, among whom I went about preaching the kingdom, shall see my face no more" (Acts 20:25), "And when they had appointed him a day, they came to him into his lodging in great number; to whom he expounded the matter, testi-

fying the kingdom of God, and persuading them concerning Jesus, both from the law of Moses and from the
prophets, from morning till evening" (Acts 28:23), "And
he abode two whole years in his own hired dwelling, and
received all that went in unto him, preaching the kingdom
of God, and teaching the things concerning the Lord
Jesus Christ with all boldness, none forbidding him"
(Acts 28:30-31). Speaking of the preaching among the
Corinthians Paul wrote, "We preach Christ crucified" (I
Cor. 1:23) and "For I determined not to know anything
among you, save Christ Jesus, and him crucified" (I Cor.
2:2).

What are we told about this kingdom which was
preached by Jesus and the apostles? It is different from
other kingdoms. "Jesus answered, My kingdom is not of
this world: if my kingdom were of this world, then would
my servants fight, that I should not be delivered to the
Jews: but now is my kingdom not from hence" (John
18:36). From this it is clear that Jesus' kingdom is not
of human origin and neither does it employ human methods of operation common to the kingdoms of men. We
also learn that Jesus' kingdom was temporal in nature;
that is, his particular reign had a beginning and ending.
John, Jesus, and others preached that the kingdom was at
hand and Paul wrote, "Then cometh the end, when he
shall deliver up the kingdom to God, even the Father;
when he shall have abolished all rule and all authority
and power. For he must reign, till he hath put all his enemies under his feet" (I Cor. 15:24-25). It is clear that he
shall reign until time shall be no more; until all human

kingdoms and powers have been destroyed. Thus of the kingdom over which the seed of David reigned, there should be no end in the sense in which man thought of such.

Just as there is a temporal kingdom, we also learn that there is an eternal kingdom and we shall see from the quotations that follow that they are not only separate and distinct, but are different in character. Paul made it clear that the Christians of his day, those who had accepted Jesus as Lord, were in the kingdom of Christ, when he wrote "Who delivered us out of the power of darkness, and translated us into the kingdom of the Son of his love" (Col. 1:13). Being in the kingdom of the Son of his love, Paul also wrote "The Lord will deliver me from every evil work and will save me unto his heavenly kingdom" (II Tim. 4:18). He thus indicated that there was another kingdom. Also in exhorting the disciples at Lystra, Iconium, and Antioch, he declared in regard to those who were in the kingdom of Christ, "That through many tribulations we must enter into the kingdom of God" (Acts 14:22). They had already entered into one kingdom, but were yet to enter into the other. In writing to Christians, those who were in the kingdom of Christ, Peter urged, "Wherefore, brethren, give the more diligence to make your calling and election sure: for if ye do these things, ye shall never stumble: for thus shall be richly supplied unto you the entrance unto the eternal kingdom of our Lord and Saviour Jesus Christ" (II Pet. 1:10-11). They were in the temporal kingdom but were seeking an entrance into the eternal kingdom.

In Jesus' description of the judgment scene (Matt. 25:31-46) he makes clear the line of demarcation between the temporal and the eternal kingdom. He said, "Then shall the King say unto them on his right hand, Come, ye blessed of my Father, inherit the kingdom prepared for you from the foundation of the world" (Matt. 25:34), "And these shall go away into eternal punishment: but the righteous into eternal life" (Matt. 25:46). Since there can be no doubt that those who were faithful as Christians in the kingdom of Christ were among those who were on the right side of the judgment seat and were invited to inherit the kingdom and went away into eternal life, it is clear that they had not been in the eternal kingdom prior to this time. Paul wrote to the Christians at Rome, "The Spirit himself beareth witness with our spirit that we are children of God: and if children, then heirs; heirs of God, and joint-heirs with Christ; if so be that we suffer with him, that we may also be glorified with him" (Rom. 8:16-17) and James wrote, "Hearken, my beloved brethren; did no God choose them that are poor as to the world to be rich in faith, and heirs of the kingdom which he promised to them that love him?" (Jas. 2:5). These statements show that Christians, those who were in the kingdom of Christ, were heirs, and Jesus' description shows their coming into their inheritance and entering into eternal life.

QUESTIONS ON LESSON 5

1. What misplaced emphasis introduces this lesson?
2. To what misunderstanding has this led? Why?

3. How only can one get the true concept of the kingdom?
4. Where is the word "kingdom" first used to refer to God's rule over men?
5. When did God speak of his being king over his people?
6. Which one of the judges showed that he knew that God was king in his day?
7. How did God still hold rule over the kingdom?
8. What promise did God make to David about the kingdom?
9. Tell how God revealed the fact that he would set up a kingdom.
10. Give evidence that the people confidently expected a kingdom.
11. What did John and Jesus preach about the kingdom?
12. About what was Jesus teaching in many of his parables?
13. Why did he teach in parables?
14. Show that the thought of the kingdom controlled the daily living of his disciples.
15. When did the twelve change their concept of the kingdom from earthly to spiritual?
16. Show that the preaching of Christ and the kingdom were the same.
17. Show that the kingdom preached by Jesus and the apostles was a temporal kingdom.
18. Show that there was an eternal kingdom that is different.
19. State the line of demarcation shown by Jesus in the judgment scene.

THE CHURCH AND THE KINGDOM
(Continued)

It is also clear that there is a marked difference between the people in the respective kingdoms. Those in the temporal kingdom, the kingdom of Christ which was to come, were human beings in the flesh who had accepted the good tidings of the kingdom as we have already seen, but in regard to the eternal kingdom Paul declared, "Now this I say, brethren, that flesh and blood cannot inherit the kingdom of God; neither doth corruption inherit incorruption. Behold I tell you a mystery: We all shall not sleep, but we shall all be changed, in a moment, in the twinkling of an eye, at the last trump: for the trumpet shall sound, and the dead shall be raised incorruptible, and we shall be changed. For this corruptible must put on incorruption, and this mortal must put on immortality. But when this corruptible shall have put on incorruption, and this mortal shall have put on immortality, then shall come to pass the saying that is written, Death is swallowed up in victory" (I Cor. 15:50-54). He also wrote, "Or know ye not that the unrighteous shall not inherit the kingdom of God? Be not deceived: neither fornicators, nor idolaters, nor adulterers, nor effeminate, nor abusers of themselves with men, nor thieves, nor covetous, nor drunkards, nor revilers, nor extortioners, shall inherit the

kingdom of God" (I Cor. 6:9-10). After listing the
works of the flesh, he wrote, "Of which I forewarn you,
even as I did forewarn you, that they who practice such
things shall not inherit the kingdom of God" (Gal. 5:21).
He also wrote, "For this ye know of a surety, that no
fornicator, nor unclean person, nor covetous man, who is
an idolater, hath any inheritance in the kingdom of Christ
and God" (Eph. 5:5). Since Paul in these statements
speaks of the inheritance of the kingdom, he is evidently
speaking of the eternal kingdom. And since he writes
these statements to people who are in the temporal kingdom as warning, it is apparent that they can become such
and fail to inherit the eternal kingdom. In his explanation
of the parable of the tares, Jesus seems to set forth the
change that will take place when he delivers up his
kingdom to the Father. "The Son of man shall send forth
his angels, and they shall gather out of his kingdom all
things that cause stumbling, and them that do iniquity,
and shall cast them into the furnace of fire: there shall
be the weeping and the gnashing of teeth. Then shall the
righteous shine forth as the sun in the kingdom of their
Father. He that hath ears, let him hear" (Matt. 13:
41-43).

It is true that the eternal kingdom is sometimes spoken
of as "the eternal kingdom of our Lord and Saviour, Jesus
Christ" (II Pet. 1:11). However, the teachings of the
Bible make it clear that it is different in nature from the
temporal kingdom. This teaching about the two kingdoms
is a very important teaching but one that has been frequently overlooked. This oversight has allowed people to

believe that since they are in the kingdom of Christ here, they will be in the eternal kingdom and will enjoy the eternal blessings. What has already been said shows this to be an ill-founded conclusion, but there is much more that could be said. Jesus declared, "Not everyone that saith unto me, Lord, Lord, shall enter into the kingdom of heaven; but he that doeth the will of my Father who is in heaven" (Matt. 7:21). Also "For I say unto you, that except your righteousness shall exceed the righteousness of the scribes and Pharisees, ye shall in no wise enter into the kingdom of heaven" (Matt. 5:20). He also said, "Suffer the little children to come unto me; forbid them not: for to such belongeth the kingdom of God. Verily I say unto you, Whosoever shall not receive the kingdom of God as a little child, he shall in no wise enter therein" (Mark 10:13-15, Luke 18:16-17). "Verily I say unto you, Except ye turn, and become as little children, ye shall in no wise enter into the kingdom of heaven. Whosoever therefore shall humble himself as this little child, the same is the greatest in the kingdom of heaven" (Matt. 18:3-4). Certainly this object lesson leaves no doubt that those to whom the kingdom of heaven will belong, those who are the rightful heirs, and those who will inherit the kingdom of God, are those who are truly humble, receive his teaching with complete submission, and those who with simplicity of heart seek to follow his teaching implicitly. The failure to maintain this humility and simplicity was what Paul had feared among the Corinthians. "But I fear, lest by any means, as the serpent beguiled Eve in his craftiness, your minds should be corrupted from the simplicity and the purity that is toward Christ" (II Cor. 11:3).

May we give further consideration to the kingdom that was promised which we have found to be a temporal kingdom, over which the seed of David, the Christ, is to reign as king until the kingdom is delivered up to the Father. We have also found that Jesus, the seed of David, was made king "both Lord and Christ" after his ascension (Acts 2:29-36), as was announced by Peter on the day of Pentecost and therefore this kingdom had its actual beginning at that time. This is a logical conclusion and fully in harmony with the concept of the kingdom as it is commonly held by most of the religious people of today. However, Jesus made a statement that seems to remove some of the former rigidity of the idea. "And being asked by the Pharisees, when the kingdom of God cometh, he answered them and said, The kingdom of God cometh not with observation: neither shall they say, Lo, here! or, There! for lo, the kingdom of God is within you" (Luke 17:20-21). This statement reveals the fact that the kingdom of God was not regional, but personal; that it was not the rule over the people within certain boundaries, physical or otherwise, but the controlling influence in the hearts of individuals. There are other Bible teachings that make it plain that of those who have been translated into his kingdom, only those who have received the kingdom as little children and have allowed God or Christ to rule in their hearts, being led by his Spirit, may hope for a place in the eternal kingdom and the blessings of eternal life. To the Colossians Paul wrote, "Christ in you, the

hope of glory" (Col. 1:27); to the Galatian Christians
"My little children, of whom I am again in travail until
Christ be formed in you" (Gal. 4:19); to the Corinthians
"Try your own selves, whether ye are in the faith; prove
your own selves. Or know ye not as to your own selves,
that Jesus Christ is in you? unless indeed ye be reprobate"
(II Cor. 13:5).

We are told that when John, who was filled with the
Holy Spirit from his mother's womb (Luke 1:15), came
in the way of righteousness (Matt. 21:32), preaching
"Repent ye; for the kingdom of heaven is at hand" (Matt.
3:2), "Then went out unto him Jerusalem, and all Judea,
and all the region round about the Jordan" (Matt. 3:5).
"He saw many of the Sadducees and Pharisees coming to
his baptism" (Matt. 3:7). The preaching of John had
wrought such marked religious changes among the Jews
that Jesus had this to say about the situation: "And from
the days of John the Baptist until now the kingdom of
heaven suffereth violence, and men of violence take it by
force. For all the prophets and the law prophesied until
John" (Matt. 11:12-13). "The law and the prophets were
until John: from that time the gospel of the kingdom of
God is preached, and every man entereth violently into
it" (Luke 16:16). These statements portray the excited
enthusiasm with which the Jews generally received John's
message of the coming kingdom and the fulfillment of
the promise through the law and the prophets. As Jesus'
statement suggests, they had turned away from the law
and the prophets and put their hope in the good tidings of
the kingdom and sought of John to know what they ought

to do (Luke 3:10-14).

However, this is not quite all of the picture. When Jesus bore witness of John and supported it by quoting the prophecy which he fulfilled, we are told "And all the people when they heard, and the publicans, justified God, being baptized with the baptism of John. But the Pharisees and the lawyers rejected for themselves the counsel of God, being not baptized of him" (Luke 7:29-30). The Pharisees and the lawyers, the leaders of the Jewish people, rejected the preaching of John which was "the counsel of God." After the death of John the multitudes of the common people still looked for the coming of the kingdom and as Jesus multiplied his miracles, they were convinced that he was the one that would be king. "Jesus therefore perceiving that they were about to come and take him by force, to make him king, withdrew again into the mountain himself alone" (John 6:15). On the other hand the Pharisees and lawyers rejected Jesus just as they had rejected John. Jesus depicted to them the ugliness of their behavior by contrasting them with the publicans and the harlots. "Verily I say unto you, that the publicans and the harlots go into the kingdom of God before you. For John came unto you in the way of righteousness and ye believed him not; but the publicans and the harlots believed him: and ye, when ye saw it, did not even repent yourselves afterward, that ye might believe him" (Matt. 21:31-32).

Jesus also warned the Jewish leaders of the terrible influence that they were having upon others. "But woe unto you, scribes and Pharisees, hypocrites! because ye shut the kingdom of heaven against men: for ye enter not in yourselves, neither suffer ye them that are entering in to enter" (Matt. 23:13). This should remind us of the fearful responsibility of leadership and the terrible damage of false leadership. In another statement Jesus pointed out to these people just what they had done to accomplish such dire results. "Woe unto you lawyers! for ye took away the key of knowledge: ye entered not in yourselves, and them that were entering in ye hindered" (Luke 11:52). How did they take away the key of knowledge? They blinded others, who respected their leadership, by acting in such a way as to make it appear worthless. A recognition of the personal value offered is the key that unlocks the storehouse of knowledge. Without it, knowledge becomes meaningless. Because they had rejected the kingdom by rejecting John and also rejecting him, Jesus said to the chief priests and elders, "Therefore say I unto you, The kingdom of God shall be taken away from you, and shall be given to a nation bringing forth the fruits thereof" (Matt. 21:43). By this statement Jesus indicated that those who received the blessings of the kingdom would be those who received the kingdom within themselves, within whose hearts Jesus would reign as king.

Jesus also made it plain that in rejecting this kingdom they would also fail to enter into the eternal kingdom. "And I say unto you, that many shall come from the east and the west, and shall sit down with Abraham, and Isaac, and Jacob, in the kingdom of heaven: but the sons of the kingdom shall be cast forth into the outer darkness:

there shall be the weeping and the gnashing of teeth" (Matt. 8:11:12). "There shall be the weeping and the gnashing of teeth, when ye shall see Abraham, and Isaac, and Jacob, and all the prophets, in the kingdom of God, and yourselves cast forth without. And they shall come from the east and west, and from the north and south, and shall sit down in the kingdom of God" (Luke 13:28-29).

The following expressions have given rise to confused thinking relative to the beginning of the kingdom and the relationship of those who were baptized of John to the kingdom. "And from the days of John the Baptist until now the kingdom of heaven suffereth violence and men of violence take it by force." "The publicans and the harlots go into the kingdom of God before you." "Ye shut up the kingdom of God against men." "But if I by the Spirit of God cast out demons, then is the kingdom of God come upon you." Since it has already been shown that the promised kingdom over which the seed of David should reign had its formal beginning when Jesus was made "both Lord and Christ" shortly after his ascension; we shall now consider the relationship of these people to the kingdom. Let us briefly recall the circumstances that led these people into this relationship. They were strongly in expectation of the coming kingdom or the coming Messiah. John, who was of priestly lineage, and whose parents walked in all the commandments and ordinances of the Lord blameless (Luke 1:6), and who seemed to have received full recognition as a prophet, proclaimed that "the kingdom of heaven was at hand." They believed John's message including his testimony that Jesus was the one to come. They were baptized for the remission of their sins; they sought to live according to his instructions that they might bring forth fruits worthy of repentance. They believed on him who was to come after. In short, they had accepted the counsel of God and were seeking to follow it, the very counsel that their leaders rejected. They had accepted God's rule in things that pertained to the kingdom insofar as they had been revealed and were waiting for Jesus to be proclaimed king that they might be completely subject to him. Certainly such a state of affairs justified the declaration that they had entered violently into the gospel of the kingdom or into the kingdom as far as it was possible.

The readiness of the twelve disciples of John, whom Paul found at Ephesus, to be baptized into the name of the Lord Jesus according to Paul's teaching (Acts 19:1-7) provides us with an example of just what has been described. Surely the publicans and harlots who had followed this course were entering into the kingdom of God before the chief priests and scribes who rejected the ministry of John. And surely insofar as their behavior hindered others from accepting John, it was reasonable to say that they had shut up the kingdom of heaven against men. In fact, the people who believed John and accepted the gospel of the kingdom had come into a new relationship with God comparable to that of Abraham when he believed the gospel that was preached to him. Although we have no statement that definitely expresses the evaluation of this status of John's disciples, we do have one relative to some of Jesus' disciples and since there was no apparent difference in their relationship to the kingdom, along with the likelihood that John's disciples became disciples of Jesus, it is reasonable to assume that the statement was applicable to both. When the seventy returned to Jesus rejoicing that the demons were subject to them, he referred to the authority which he had given to them and said, "Nevertheless in this rejoice not, that spirits are subject unto you; but rejoice that your names are written in heaven" (Luke 10:20). This certainly implies that at that time they were heirs of the promise as was Abraham of whom it is said that he will "sit down in the kingdom of God" (Luke 13:29).

Since Paul rebaptized some of John's disciples (Acts 19:1-7), some people have sought to establish the date, time, or circumstance that would require rebaptism of those baptized of John's baptism. First may we observe that it would be the same as for those baptized with the baptism of repentance on becoming Jesus' disciples, and in both cases it would be when they learned that it was God's will that they be baptized into the name of the Lord Jesus as was the case of those whom Paul rebaptized. In fact, their former teaching and commitment had obligated them to do as much. Just as was true in the case of Abraham, who believed God and whose faith was reckoned to him for righteousness before he was given the instruction relative to circumcision, that same faith demanded that he comply with that teaching when it was given to him from Jehovah.

Today some people become very much concerned about the baptism of the apostles. The idea is generally accepted that they were baptized with the baptism of repentance, some by John, but since there is no record of their being baptized again in water and since some of John's disciples were rebaptized, some have sought to give a peculiar validity to the baptism administered by John personally that was not attained by those who were baptized of John's baptism later. For this there seems to be no scriptural support whatsoever and why should one be concerned about the baptism of the apostles unless they are seeking to enforce the practice of baptism as a mere technicality in which case it would be absolutely worthless. The people of the twentieth century evidently did not live during the time when the counsel of God was to accept the baptism of John and to those who truly believe that Jesus is the Christ, it is surely enough for them to know that Jesus, through his inspired apostles, taught people to be baptized into the name of the Lord Jesus for the remission of their sins and of this there can be no doubt with those who believe the Bible. It was enough for those who had been baptized of John's baptism.

Now that we have examined the Bible use of the word "kingdom" and in former lessons the Bible use of the word "church" it is hoped that we are in position to discover the relationship between the two concepts. The only place in the New Testament record where the two concepts are used in successive sentences is the record of what Jesus said to Peter following his confession. "And I also say unto thee, that thou art Peter, and upon this rock I will build my church; and the gates of Hades shall not prevail against it. I will give unto thee the keys of the kingdom of heaven: and whatsoever thou shalt bind on earth shall be bound in heaven; and what soever thou shalt loose on earth shall be loosed in heaven" (Matt. 16:18-19). From these two statements many people have concluded that the church and the kingdom are the same and that the words may be used interchangeably. This conclusion is without scriptural foundation. In fact the multiple use of the word "kingdom" shows this to be impossible. The church could not be the same as two kingdoms that are so different in nature. Neither is the meaning conveyed by the word "church" the same as that which is conveyed by either use of the word "kingdom." Surely no one would consider the church to be the same as the eternal kingdom. Consequently we shall proceed with a comparison of the church with the temporal kingdom.

We have already learned from a former lesson that the word "church" as it is used in the Bible means assembly—nothing more and nothing less. Speaking religiously, it denotes a body of people called out from the ways of sin and dedicated to the service of God. There is no implication whatsoever of organization, power of control, or promises of divine benefits, but the word "kingdom" as it had come to be known to the people of the first century embodied all of these. The people had been taught and had fully accepted the idea that God would raise up a king whose rule they should accept and whose power would provide for those in his kingdom blessings for which they could hope from no other source. It is true that they applied the concept to earthly things and hoped for a material kingdom, while Jesus was speaking of heavenly things and applying the concept in a spiritual kingdom. However this erroneous application did not distort the concept. The word "kingdom" designates a relationship which demands the recognition of authority and provides assurances to those who give it. This is the case in the Christian relationship. A Christian accepts Jesus as Lord, ruler, and king following his teaching implicitly and looking to him for the blessings that have been promised. On the other hand, the word "church" or more accurately, the word "assembly" makes no direct reference to man's vital relationship with God, but rather has exalted the human side of Christianity and attributed to the church privileges and powers which have never been granted to it and which practice has blinded people to the gospel of Christ leading them to put their trust in the church and not in Christ and to comply with the teaching of the church of which they are members rather than with the teaching of Christ. The gospel that was preached in the first century was the gospel of the kingdom not the gospel of the church. The mysteries that were made known to the apostles, and through them to others, were the mysteries of the kingdom, or the mystery of Christ, and not the mystery of the church. Insofar as we have record Christ used the word "church" only two times and in each case he was simply referring to a body of people. The apostles always used it after the same fashion. It is clear that the word "church" is used only in a limited sense to designate God's people while the word "kingdom" represents the Christian's relationship to God.

QUESTIONS ON LESSON 6

1. What is the difference between the people of the temporal and the eternal kingdom?
2. Show that there are those in the temporal kingdom that will not be in the eternal kingdom.
3. Failure to understand this teaching of two kingdoms has allowed people to come to what ill-founded conclusion?
4. Who will be the rightful heirs of the eternal kingdom?
5. Where did the promised or temporal kingdom have its beginning?
6. What did Jesus say that shows the kingdom not to be regional but personal?
7. What shows the enthusiasm with which people received John's preaching the gospel of the kingdom?
8. Who rejected John and Jesus and what contrast is made between them and the common people?
9. How did the scribes and Pharisees shut up the kingdom of God?
10. How did the lawyers take away the key of knowledge?
11. How did Jesus show that if they rejected this temporal kingdom they would fail to enter the eternal kingdom?
12. Describe what had happened to the people that accepted John that shows their relationship to the kingdom.
13. The new relationship of those who had accepted John was comparable to that of whom?
14. What did Jesus say about his disciples that showed their relationship to the promise?
15. Why think this applicable to John's disciples?
16. To what had the acceptance of John committed his disciples?
17. Is there any difference between John's baptism when administrated by John and by others?
18. Why does the baptism of the apostles have no particular bearing on our baptism today?
19. What is the only place in the New Testament record where the concepts of church and kingdom are used together?
20. Show that the two words cannot be used interchangeably.
21. Compare the meaning of church and kingdom when refering to temporal kingdom.

LESSON 7

THE ORGANIZATION OF THE CHURCH

Basic Relationships

This is the topic about which there has been much misunderstanding, that has given rise to many misinterpretations of Bible teaching, and in turn has led to a multitude of conflicts in religious thinking, resulted in much strife and numerous divisions. The seriousness of the situation is portrayed especially in the fact that many of the divisions caused have been among those people that have been most zealous in their efforts to comply with the Bible teaching in every way. When a misunderstanding of a Bible concept causes divisions where there had been no division causing strife by misguiding one's zeal for the truth, it is surely time to carefully and prayerfully re-examine the concept and to make correction where correction is due to be made.

This is a difficult thing to do. Changing a concept is changing one's thinking; changing your thinking is changing you. This can be done only where one loves the truth more than he loves himself, and where one puts more value upon his soul than upon his personal pride. It can be done only by those who are willing to re-evaluate the concept in terms of background information instead of judging background information by ideas that have already been accepted and frequently applied as standards of measure. It will be done only by those who are not too conceited to consider that they could possibly be wrong or too lazy to re-think the matter. Can you do it? Will you do it?

First let us recall the fact that at no place in the Bible record is there given a fully detailed description of the organization of the church. This subject as many others was never formally presented but the information must be gathered from a variety of statements made by different writers under different conditions. None of the authors of the books of the New Testament ever seems to have had an occasion for writing such a description in full (This is true of many other matters such as the resurrection, judgment, etc.) but made a few statements here and there where an occasion arose that made them appropriate or necessary to the understanding of those to whom they were writing. A failure to recognize the fact that the gospel has been revealed by dealing with natural living experiences, and never through complete analytical description, has given rise to the practice of substituting a part for the whole which has resulted in fearful distortions, misinterpretations, and misunderstandings. This is because different people have adopted different parts and consequently have concepts of the same thing that vary widely. This practice naturally makes us like the blind men who went to see the elephant. (Each naturally examined a different part and had a different concept of the elephant). Our concept or picture is determined by our contact. May God bless our efforts to extend our contact

with his revelation sufficiently to secure the true picture
of church organization.

Next let us recognize the fact that we have selected
the part of the picture that we have substituted for the
whole picture in this matter of church organization as we
have in many other cases (how to become Christians,
etc.) because it fits harmoniously into the rest of our
religious system of thought: lending support to other
religious ideas and justifying, or at least permitting,
certain personal practices to which we have become
accustomed. In other words, it has been selected on the
basis of our personal bias which has resulted from the
combined influences of our learning and our past experiences in our association with relatives and friends. Therefore, it should not be surprising that such substitutions
vary widely and thus provide unquestionable evidence
that the majority of the substitutions are in error.

Let us also remember that the word "church" has a
two-fold application in its Bible usage. It is employed
to designate God's people universally and also used to
speak of the local congregation. This dual use of the
term has given opportunity for difference in emphasis
but does not imply a dual organization. Some religious
people have concerned themselves more with the organization of the universal church and others with that of the
local congregation. The former have ignored the Bible
description and gone beyond any scriptural authorization
or implication relative to offices and authorities in the
universal church, while the latter have lost sight of the
Bible description of the universal church and overdrawn

the authorities and powers of the local congregation. The effect has been as though the universal church has no organization. Therefore, it is important that all re-examine the Bible teaching for a true picture of the organization of the church of the Bible, and where necessary re-order our thinking and actions to harmonize with it. Surely all who accept the Bible as their guide in religious matters would agree that the present day organization of the church should be made to conform to the Bible plan insofar as instruction is given; that all parts of the organization both universally and locally must be maintained in their proper relationships and working effectiveness to the end that the church may fulfill its purpose. Surely the wisdom of God has provided what is best since lack of organization, over-organization, or otherwise improper organization can impede the progress or hinder the effectiveness of God's people, the church.

Since, as we have seen, the word "church" as it is used in the Bible means assembly of the called out, and nothing more, the word certainly offers little or no definite indication of the nature of the organization of the church. At most it suggests people who have been called out from their individual ways of living to a particular manner of life by something that has been recognized by each one as having personal value. This demands a mutual interest, a common purpose, and a wholehearted cooperation. Thus it is evident that our understanding of the organization of the church must be obtained from Bible statements about the church, or the people that make up the church, in regard to the relationships that existed and to the activities of those who shared these relationships.

One might ask is there an organization of the universal church? Yes, there certainly is; and it will be honored and respected and followed by all who are worthy of a place in it. It was divinely given to accomplish a divine purpose. In its very nature it demands that every individual Christian exalt Christ, humble himself and respect his brother. It is such as removes one's pride and self-seeking and encourages the spirit of humble service. It requires that one exalt Christ instead of man. May God bless our effort to understand and fill us with his Spirit that we may fully accept and follow his plan of church organization.

What is the divine organization of the church of the Bible as revealed in the Bible? Here is the record. "And he put all things in subjection under his feet, and gave him to be head over all things to the church, which is his body, the fulness of him that filleth all in all" (Eph. 1:22-23). "For he must reign, till he hath put all his enemies under his feet" (I Cor. 15:25). "For the husband is the head of the wife, as Christ also is the head of the church, being himself the saviour of the body. But as the church is subject to Christ, so let the wives also be to their husbands in everything" (Eph. 5:23-24). "And he is the head of the body, the church: who is the beginning, the firstborn from the dead; that in all things he might have the preeminence" (Col. 1:18). "And he gave some to be apostles; and some, prophets; and some, evangelists; and some, pastors and teachers; for the perfecting of the saints, unto the work of ministering, unto the building up of the body of Christ: till we all attain unto the unity of the faith, and of the knowledge of the Son of God, unto a fullgrown man, unto the measure of the stature of the fulness of Christ: that we may be no longer children, tossed to and fro and carried about with every wind of doctrine, by the sleight of men, in craftiness, after the wiles of error; but speaking truth in love, may grow up in all things unto him, who is the head, even Christ; from whom all the body fitly framed and knit together through that which every joint supplieth, according to the working in due measure of each several part, maketh the increase of the body unto the building up of itself in love" (Eph. 4:11-16). "Let no man rob you of your prize by a voluntary humility and worshipping of the angels, dwelling in the things which he hath seen, vainly puffed up by his fleshly mind, and not holding fast the Head, from whom all the body, being supplied and knit together through the joints and bands, increaseth with the increase of God" (Col. 2:18-19). "Now ye are the body of Christ, and severally members thereof. And God hath set some in the church, first apostles, secondly prophets, thirdly teachers, then miracles, then gifts of healings, helps, governments, divers kinds of tongues. Are all apostles? are all prophets? are all teachers? are all workers of miracles? have all gifts of healing? do all speak with tongues? do all interpret?" (I Cor. 12:27-30). "Wherefore, putting away falsehood, speak ye truth each one with his neighbor: for we are members one of another" (Eph. 4:25). "Speaking one to another in psalms and hymns and spiritual songs, singing and making melody with your heart to the Lord; giving thanks always for all things in the name of our Lord Jesus Christ to God, even the Father; subjecting yourselves one to another in the fear of Christ" (Eph. 5:19-21). From these statements it is clear that Christ is the head of the church, and the church is subject to him: that the church is his body, and he is head of the body; that the body is made up of many members, who are also members one of another.

From the record of the activities of the church of the first century we find a few other terms used. For the word "pastors" (or shepherds) "overseers" (or bishops) is used (Phil. 1:1, I Tim. 3:2) and also "elders" (Acts 11: 30). That these words are generally interchangeable is shown in Acts 20:28 where Paul told the elders of the church at Ephesus that they had been made overseers (or bishops) and to shepherd (or tend) the flock exercising the oversight (I Pet. 5:2). Another word used in our translation is "deacon" (Phil. 1:1, I Tim. 3:8-12). Also, the Bible record shows that elders were appointed in every local church or congregation. Paul left Titus on the island of Crete to "set in order the things that were wanting, and appoint elders in every city" (Titus 1:5). While on the first missionary journey, Paul and Barnabas "appointed for them elders in every church" (Acts 14:23).

This is the Bible picture of the organization of the church. It is evident to everyone that it is the result of piecing together statements made to different people on different occasions. It is not as complete and exact in describing the participants mentioned nor the powers allocated as some might wish, but it is all that is given other than possible implications through the record of activities within the church. This in itself should suggest the minor place occupied by church organization as it is generally thought of. But let us examine what we have and be sure that every fact is given its full meaning.

A careful inspection of the picture of church organization as presented in the statements given above forces one to the recognition of the fact that the dual use of the word "church" does not imply two separate organizations. There is but one church with one mission and, therefore, one organization or plan through which to accomplish that mission. Christ was given a place above all rule, authority, and dominion, and was made head over all things to the church. He is the head of the body. This figure is always used to refer to the universal church and certainly implies a universal organization. When Jesus said, "Upon this rock I will build my church," (Matt. 16: 18) he was speaking of the universal church. When he said, "Neither for these only do I pray, but for all them also that believe on me through their word; that they may all be one," (John 17:20-21) he was praying for the unity of the universal church. When Paul spoke of the "church of the Lord which he purchased with his own blood," (Acts 20:28) he was talking of the universal church; and when he wrote of the church as "the house of God, which is the church of the living God, the pillar and ground of the truth" (I Tim. 3:15), he was writing of the universal church. Also, we should observe that the only listings of special places of service, commonly referred to as offices in the church, are the two given above (Eph. 4:11, I Cor.

12:28). It is clear that both of these statements are made with reference to the universal church; thus, it is obvious that the organization of the local congregation is an integral part of the organization of the universal church and must contribute to its effectiveness, being subservient to it in every way.

It is true that elders were appointed "in every city," (Titus 1:5) "in every church," (Acts 14:23) but we should not overlook the fact that their work, like the others mentioned above, was "for the perfecting of the saints, unto the work of ministering, unto the building up of the body of Christ" (Eph. 4:12). It is natural that they were appointed in local congregations and that their work for the most part would be among the people of their respective congregations. It is also natural that their interest, helpfulness, and guiding influence should reach out to all Christians as they had opportunity and also to people who were not Christians as far as they had the privilege. It is also apparent that their ultimate goal was not the building up of the local congregation but the building up of the body of Christ.

This should in no wise be taken to mean that elders of different congregations may club together after any fashion and constitute a controlling body to direct the efforts of the congregations into a common work. It rather seeks to suggest that the Christian relationship gives rise to mutual interests, mutual helpfulness and cooperative effort in building up the body of Christ.

As we continue our study of the organization of the church, may we do so with complete awareness that like any other organization it is in essence a system of relationships, relationships that determine obligations and privileges. Therefore, a proper understanding of the relationships that are comprehended in the organization of the church will provide the only sound basis for correctly judging the activities that are required by it or are permitted under it. So we now set ourselves to the task of understanding the relationships that are shown by Bible teaching to be included in the organization of the church.

The most basic and comprehensive relationship in the organization of the church is stated from both points of view in these words "Christ also is the head of the church" and "the church is subject to Christ" (Eph. 5:23-24). This leaves no doubt that Christ is the ruler over the church and that the church is to obey him. It is clear that the word "church" is being used in the universal sense. It is also clear from an earlier lesson that the church is not an institution but an assembly of individuals who have been reconciled, redeemed, purified, and sanctified. Therefore, the relationship described in the statement that "Christ is the head of the church" is an individual relationship. Christ is the head, the ruler, and the lord over each Christian who is worthy of the name and, thus, is head over all. This direct relationship between each individual Christian and Christ is given further emphasis by Paul's use of the human body to illustrate it (Rom. 12:4-5; I Cor. 12:12-27). Christ is head and ruler over each Christian who is a member of his body, the church, as the human head controls the members of the human body. If Christ is not your head, ruler, and Lord, if you are not in subjection to him, and if you are not making an honest, sincere effort to follow his teaching faithfully you are unworthy of a place in the relationship and consequently unworthy of your membership in his church or assembly.

This basic relationship certainly leaves no doubt that Christianity is primarily individual, that every person in the church is directly responsible to Christ the head, and that every Christian must give an account to him. This means that Christ's teaching is supreme and every decision of right and wrong is the prerogative of each individual Christian. This also means that no one in the church, individual or otherwise, not even the church en masse, has been given the power to make the slightest modification of Christ's teaching or to forcibly impose any decision upon any individual Christian.

The individual character of Christianity is not only shown by this most fundamental relationship in church organization, but also by the very nature of the Bible teaching itself. We have already seen that Christians are redeemed, purified, sanctified, and reconciled as individuals; that the church, the assembly, was purchased as individuals; that people become Christians as individuals. To become a Christian one must believe, repent, confess Christ to be his Lord, and be baptized into Christ individually. Nobody can do it for him. A Christian must worship God individually. He may worship with other Christians in a congregation or church, but he must worship individually. His presence in a congregation does not mean that he is worshipping God. Worship is individual participation and the acceptability of the worship is not in terms of the congregation but in terms of the individual. I doubt that there are many occasions when a congregation worships, but what there are some individuals in the congregation whose worship is not acceptable to God. Worship is the expression of an attitude or a feeling, the attitude of reverence or the feeling of praise. Without this attitude there can be no true worship. The attitude must be that of the worshipper. We have stressed the importance of attending worship, and some have been careful to see that the worship activities of the congregation conform to Bible instruction and example, but little concern has been shown for the individual's effectiveness in worship and little instruction has been given on the personal character of worship. Remember, reader, the vital question to you may not be, do you attend worship, nor does the worship consist of the right activities, but it may be do you worship, do you honor and praise God from the heart.

Not only do people worship individually, but the work of the church is accomplished by individual effort. It can be done in no other way. To be sure, individuals can work together, but the actual work of the church must be done by individuals. The greatest work of the church, to be the light of the world, must be accomplished through Christian living, and this must be done by individuals. Likewise, helping the poor, visiting the sick, encouraging the downhearted, and every other work of the church is the work of individuals. And since Christians are to be judged as individuals, we would do well to awake to the fact that we will be judged by what we do individually and not by what is accomplished by the church or congregation where we worship. If the congregation is doing wonderful things, it means that individuals are doing wonderful things, and the most important question to you is "What are you doing?" We should never forget that there is no such thing as congregational righteousness, but when we stand before God in judgment that each one shall give an account for the deeds that he has done in the body, whether they be good or whether they be evil.

Certainly it is helpful and encouraging here to have the privilege of working with a congregation of people, where a great deal is being accomplished, but unless we are encouraged by it and participate in it, we will not share in the eternal blessings because of it. Christianity is collective in character only in the sense of Christians working together and being helpful to each other in maintaining a personal holiness and in promoting the gospel for the good of the community and the good of the world. Every activity of the church is for the benefit of individuals, both those toward whom it is directed and those who are participating in the activity. The church exists for the individual, not the individual for the church.

All of this is accentuated by the fact that the New Testament teaching is not written to congregations on a congregational basis but to individuals who make up the church. This statement is made with a full consciousness that many of the letters in the New Testament are addressed to churches but an examination of the teachings will show that they are directed to individuals. The Corinthian letter, for example, was not written calling for group action but for individual action. It was written to teach Christians individually the things that they ought to do. May we return to the Bible emphasis on individual Christianity.

The second basic relationship of the church organization has already been suggested in the comparison with the human body. Christians are not only subject to Christ as members of the human body are subject to the head but they have that relationship to each other as do the members of the human body. This certainly implies the obligation of every member to cooperate with every other member in every way that he can to accomplish the work of the body, the church. It is also important that we not overlook the fact that in Paul's letters to the Romans and Corinthians, he is using this parallel to the human body to speak of the universal church. He is not speaking of the local congregation. However, since the local congregation is a part of the universal church, certainly cooperation within the local congregation is included. In reality, in the very nature of the case, since it offers greater opportunity for cooperation, a failure to meet the obligation there would stand out as a more glaring weakness.

Paul also gave the early Christians to understand that the cooperation indicated must extend into the field of personal helpfulness. This was not only shown by pointing out the care exercised by the members of the human body one for another, but by the expression that shows the Christian relationship to be most intimate. Paul declared that Christians are members one of another (Rom. 12:5 and Eph. 4:25). Unfortunately, this relationship of a Christian to other Christians has not become very real with a very large number of people. Can it be possible that this is the result of the strong emphasis that has been placed upon the importance of church membership to the neglect of Bible teaching on membership in the body of Christ or the relationship of Christians one to another?

QUESTIONS ON LESSON 7

1. What shows the seriousness of an incorrect concept of the organization of the church?
2. Why is it difficult to change a concept?
3. Only under what circumstances and how can this concept be changed and by whom?
4. How must the true concept of the church be acquired?
5. What practice has given rise to erroneous concepts?
6. How have we selected the part of the concept that we have substituted for the whole?
7. Describe two false concepts of church organization that have resulted from difference in emphasis on the two uses of the word church in the New Testament.
8. Why is the matter of church organization so important?
9. What does the dual use of the word Church not imply relative to organization?
10. How must our understanding of the organization of the church be obtained?
11. In its very nature, what does the universal organization of the church demand?
12. Summarize the scriptures from which we must get our picture of the basic organization of the church.

13. List the other terms that are used in the record of the activities required by the organization.
14. What is suggested by the back discussion of church organization in the New Testament?
15. Does the church have more than one organization?
16. Give Bible statements which applied or referred to the universal church.
17. To whom should the helpfulness and guiding influence of elders reach?
18. Instead of implying combined controlling power of elders, what does it suggest?
19. The organization of the church is in essence a system of what?
20. What will provide the only sound basis for correctly judging the activities required by the organization?
21. State the most basic relationship in the organization of the church in the words of Paul.
22. Show that this statement is describing an individual relationship.
23. What figure did Paul use that further emphasizes this individual relationship with Christ?
24. Since this relationship is individual, what responsibility does it impose and what privilege does it provide?
25. Give Bible teachings the very nature of which show Christianity to be individual in character.
26. Show that Christian worship is individual.
27. What may really be your most important question about worship?
28. Show that the work of the church is accomplished by individuals.
29. Christianity is collective in character only in what sense?
30. To whom is the New Testament teaching written?
31. What is the second basic relationship of the church organization?
32. What is the obligation implied by this relationship and what is the extent of the obligation with reference to people and also activities?

THE ORGANIZATION OF THE CHURCH

Special Relationships

Besides the two basic relationships in church organization, the Christian's relationship to Christ, the head, and the Christian's relationship to fellow Christians; there are also what might be called special relationships among Christians or particular works to be accomplished. There are only two statements in the New Testament that present any sort of enumeration or listing of these relationships or functions. One is found in Ephesians 4 and the other in I Corinthians 12 and both have been quoted earlier in the discussion. The one given in Ephesians names apostles, prophets, evangelists, pastors, and teachers. The other, found in I Corinthians, lists apostles, prophets, and teachers followed by a number of the special powers or spiritual gifts. The two enumerations can hardly be said to be parallel in content. This may be explained by the fact that they were not made to the same people under the same circumstances. We must not forget that these statements as well as most others in the New Testament were made directly to people of that day under the circumstances that existed at the time and generally dealing with a definite problem situation. This statement made to the Corinthians, for example, was part of a discussion of the problem situation among them due to spiritual gifts and naturally gave emphasis to that which was especially pertinent to the situation. The statement made to the Ephesians seems to have been made under circumstances that were less strained and appears to be more generally descriptive. Consequently, we shall follow it in our consideration of the special relationships or works in the church.

What place was occupied by the apostles as a body of men in the organization of the church? What ecclesiastical powers did they have? And, by what authority did they exercise them? We have learned that the apostles were told, "Tarry ye in the city until ye be clothed with power from on high" (Luke 24:49). Also, "But ye shall receive power, when the Holy Spirit is come upon you: and ye shall be my witnesses both in Jerusalem, and in all Judea and Samaria, and unto the uttermost part of the earth" (Acts 1:8). We learn in Acts 2 that the apostles received the power that was promised and began immediately to use it for the purpose indicated, to be witnesses for Christ. To anyone, however, who will read the New Testament record carefully, anything that resembles ecclesiastical power among the apostles and anything that resembles lordship is exceedingly difficult to find. The power was to qualify these men to render a service which is briefly described, "Ye shall be my witnesses." In all of the New Testament record, there are only three references made to the authority of an apostle. Two are made by Paul in the second Corinthian letter and in each case the reference is followed immediately by the words,

"Which the Lord gave for building you up, and not for casting you down" (II Cor. 10:8, II Cor. 13:10). The third is in the first Thessalonian letter: "We might have claimed authority (or been burdensome) as apostles of Christ" (I Thess. 2:6). It is true that Paul asked the Corinthians, "Shall I come unto you with a rod, or in love and a spirit of gentleness?" (I Cor. 4:21) that in his second letter he wrote, "To spare you I forebare to come to Corinth" (II Cor. 1:23), but it is also true that in the first case Paul was dealing with those who were puffed up and set against the gospel and that the second statement was followed by these words "Not that we have lordship over your faith, but are helpers of your joy" (II Cor. 1:24). It is also evident that there was an occasional miracle such as the death of Ananias and Sapphira that was punitive in effect; but they were the exception and were evidently to serve the same purpose as the other miracles, to support the truth of the gospel. It is very clear that this was the purpose to be served by their power. It is also in order to observe here the fact that when Peter was exhorting the elders among the Christians of some of the provinces of Asia Minor he appealed to them as a fellow-elder and not as an apostle (I Pet. 5:1).

From the New Testament teaching it is clear that the apostles had no teaching of their own. Neither was there any hint of their inclination to depart from God's teaching, which had been delivered unto them. They taught, they encouraged, they exhorted people to do the will of God. James urged, "But be ye doers of the word, and not hearers only, deluding your own selves" (Jas. 1:22), and

Paul exhorted, "Be ye therefore imitators of God, as beloved children" (Eph. 5:1) and "Be ye imitators of me, even as I also am of Christ" (I Cor. 11:1). The apostles appealed to Christians instead of threatening them.

It is also very apparent from the New Testament record of the apostle's activities that they never considered themselves, nor functioned, as any sort of ecclesiastical board with special powers of management. To be sure, occasionally when special problems arose, the early Christians turned to the apostles. Those who had announced the gospel, those who had supported it by the working of miracles, would be the ones to whom they would naturally turn under such circumstances, but in the record of such occasions there is no indication that they thought of themselves as having exclusive powers or being a separate body with the exclusive right to settle matters of question or to direct the activities of the church in accord with definitely organized plans. We find no evidence that they assumed any such authority. Instead, there is every reason to believe that they thought of themselves as qualified leaders and teachers among those who received the gospel and made up God's church or assembly. There has never been a record of the work of men with such exalted privileges and powers that has been so completely lacking in show of authority as is true of the apostles of our Lord. Their work in the early church is always shown to be cooperative in character and never dictatorial. When the murmuring arose among the Grecian Jews against the Hebrews because of their widows being neglected (Acts 6:1-6), we see that the apostles asked the multitude of the disciples to select the men that were to be set over the work. These were appointed by the apostles and blessed through prayer and the laying on of hands. When the people who were scattered abroad from Jerusalem by persecution went everywhere preaching the word, there is not the slightest intimation that the apostles remaining in Jerusalem sought to manage, plan, direct, or dictate, to those who went preaching (Acts 8). Neither do we have any suggestion that the apostles told them where to go, but when they learned that the people of any place had received the gospel, they went to encourage and aid the work by bestowing upon them the Holy Spirit (Acts 8:14). When Saul of Tarsus became an apostle, he was not sent to the other apostles for instruction, nor for authorization, but he went away into Arabia, returned to Damascus and apparently preached the gospel for three years before he saw one of the other apostles (Gal. 1:17, 18). Neither is there anything in the record that reveals any jealousy on the part of the twelve because of this new apostle or the great work that he was doing. Neither did they feel called upon to send out and check on the matter even though they had never been told that Saul had been appointed an apostle. Never did they seem to pass any judgment upon Paul's work until he discussed his work with them at least fourteen years after he began (Gal. 2:1-10).

When dissension was started at Antioch by men from Judea and Paul and Barnabas with others were sent to Jerusalem about the matter, the record shows that the apostles at Jerusalem did not think of themselves as an ecclesiastical board with any manner of dictatorial power over the church. Neither did the brethren at Antioch think of them after that fashion for they were not sent to the apostles only but "unto the apostles and elders about this question" (Acts 15:2). This certainly means that they were sent to the leaders among the disciples at the place from which those who started the erroneous teaching had come. We also learn that the apostles and elders did not consider themselves an exclusive class for we are told, "And when they were come to Jerusalem, they were received of the church and the apostles and elders, and they rehearsed all things that God had done with them" (Acts 15:4) and it is also evident that the matter was discussed with the church and that the church concurred in the decision and in the action that was followed. "Then it seemed good to the apostles and the elders, with the whole church, to choose men out of their company, and send them to Antioch with Paul and Barnabas; namely, Judas called Barsabbas, and Silas, chief men among the brethren; and they wrote thus by them, The apostles and the elders, brethren, unto the brethren who are of the Gentiles in Antioch and Syria and Cilicia, greeting: Forasmuch as we have heard that certain who went out from us have troubled you with words, subverting your souls; to whom we gave no commandment; it seemed good to us, having come to one accord, to choose out men and send them unto you with our beloved Barnabas and Paul, men that have hazarded their lives for the name of our Lord Jesus Christ. We have sent therefore Judas and Silas, who themselves also shall tell you the same things by word of mouth. For it seemed good to the Holy Spirit, and to us, to lay upon you greater burden than these necessary things: that ye abstain from things sacrificed to idols, and from blood, and from things strangled, and from fornication; from which if ye keep yourselves, it shall be well with you. Fare ye well." (Acts 15:22-29). In the handling of this matter we see no sign of dictatorial management or control, but rather the cooperative effort of apostles, elders, and other Christians to work together as brethren to show forth the light of the gospel among the people of that day. Not only did the brethren in Jerusalem have a part but the message was sent to the brethren at Antioch not just to the elders as rulers.

It is true that in speaking of the work of Paul, Silas, and Timothy, we are told, "And as they went on their way through the cities, they delivered them the decrees to keep which had been ordained of the apostles and elders that were at Jerusalem" (Acts 16:4). This evidently has reference to the action of the apostles and elders together with the church discussed above, for Paul makes it plain that he received nothing from the apostles at Jerusalem "They, I say, who were of repute imparted nothing to me" (Gal. 2:6), and we know that this decision with respect to the Gentiles was nothing new. It is also natural that Paul would make this decision known in the name of the leaders of Jerusalem to show that there was unity in the matter, and that the teaching that had been circulated from Jerusalem insisting that the Gentiles be circumcised and keep the law of Moses was not sound.

Not only is there no reason to think of the apostles as

an ecclesiastical body to rule over the church or in any sense to be considered the earthly head of the church, but also there is no justification for thinking of any one of the apostles as being the earthly head of the church and certainly no reason to consider Peter so. It is true that Jesus said to Peter "I will give unto thee the keys of the kingdom of heaven" (Matt. 16:19). But in his statement to the other apostles and elders at Jerusalem, Peter reveals what Jesus referred to in this statement. "And when there had been much questioning, Peter rose up, and said unto them, Brethren, ye know that a good while ago God made choice among you, that by my mouth the Gentiles should hear the word of the gospel, and believe" (Acts 15:7). It was Peter's special privilege to be the first to preach the gospel to the Gentiles as well as to the Jews. It is also true that Jesus said to Peter "And whatsoever thou shalt bind on earth shall be bound in heaven; and whatsoever thou shalt loose on earth shalt be loosed in heaven" (Matt. 16:19). But this was not true of Peter only, for Jesus said the same thing identically to the other apostles. "And if he refuse to hear them, tell it unto the church: and if he refuse to hear the church also, let him be unto thee as the Gentile and the publican. Verily I say unto you, What things soever ye shall bind on earth shall be bound in heaven; and what things soever ye shall loose on earth shall be loosed in heaven" (Matt. 18: 17-18). "Whose soever sins ye forgive, they are forgiven unto them; whose soever sins ye retain, they are retained" (John 20:23). So regardless of what Jesus meant by binding and loosing, this was not a special privilege or power granted to Peter alone.

Not only is there no evidence that Peter was the head of the church, but Jesus makes it plain that no one of the apostles was to be such. When the mother of James and John came to Jesus with the request that "My two sons may sit, one on thy right hand, and one on thy left hand, in thy kingdom" (Matt. 20-21), we are told that the other ten were moved with indignation. "But Jesus called them unto him, and said, Ye know that the rulers of the Gentiles lord it over them, and their great ones exercise authority over them. Not so shall it be among you: but whosoever would become great among you shall be your minister (diakonos); and whosoever would be first among you shall be your servant: even as the Son of man came not to be ministered unto, but to minister, and to give his life a ransom for many" (Matt. 20:25-28). In thus assuring the ten that James and John would not be granted such places, he also made it clear that among his people there would be no such authority exercised, and among the twelve there would be no such preeminence given to anyone.

Although the apostles were never constituted an ecclesiastical body to rule the church, neither were they endowed with managerial power either collectively or individually, this should not be taken to mean that they did not occupy an exalted place. In fact, the place as ruler would have been far below the place they were given and managerial power would have been feebleness in comparison to what they used. They were entrusted with "the power of God unto salvation"—the gospel and were endued with that Spirit that humbled them before God causing them to know that the real power for accomplishing their mission was not through managing people but through changing them by the word of God. They recognized as Paul wrote "But we have this treasure in earthen vessels, that the exceeding greatness of the power may be of God, and not from ourselves" (II Cor. 4:7). Jesus gave recognition to their greatness in his promise, "Verily I say unto you, that ye who have followed me, in the regeneration when the Son of man shall sit on the throne of his glory, ye also shall sit upon twelve thrones, judging the twelve tribes of Israel" (Matt. 19:28).

Having seen that the apostles were given no organizational control over the church or assembly, let us next consider the prophets in the church, in the universal church, a people who had a special work to do in building up God's people. Of the prophets we are told very little. We are told of prophets that came down from Jerusalem to Antioch among whom was one named Agabus, who foretold the coming of the great famine (Acts 11:27-28). We also learn that there were prophets and teachers in the church at Antioch of whom seven are named, including Barnabas and Saul (Acts 13:1). Also, "And Judas and Silas, being themselves also prophets, exhorted the brethren with many words, and confirmed them" (Acts 15:32). The Ephesian Christians were told that they were "built upon the foundation of the apostles and prophets, Christ Jesus himself being the chief corner stone" (Eph. 2:20). And later, in speaking of the mystery of Christ, they were told, "It hath now been revealed unto his holy apostles and prophets in the Spirit; to wit, that the Gentiles are fellow-heirs, and fellow-members of the body, and fellow-partakers of the promise in Christ Jesus through the gospel" (Eph. 3:5-6). This suggests that the work of the prophets, as well as that of the apostles, was the making known of the mystery of Christ and the building up of the saints. Since only a few religious people, comparatively, have attempted to retain a place in church organization for the prophets and since consequently, there has been little conflict over the matter, it is unnecessary at this time to give further consideration to their place in the early church.

The next people that were listed as having a special relationship or work in the church were the evangelists. In regard to these men our record is extremely limited. We are told that on returning from the third missionary journey Paul and his company visited with "Philip the evangelist, who was one of the seven" (Acts 21:8). This is the Philip that preached in Samaria and also to the Ethiopian Eunuch and while on that journey "to all the cities till he came to Caesarea" (Acts 8:40). The only other mention of an evangelist in the New Testament record is as follows: "But be thou sober in all things, suffer hardship, do the work of an evangelist, fulfill thy ministry" (II Tim. 4:5). From these two records it appears reasonable to conclude that an evangelist is a preacher of the gospel or, as the word from which it is translated is defined, "A bringer of good tidings." Since there has been no special effort to assign to the evangelist any special organizational power, we shall not pursue the matter further.

QUESTIONS ON LESSON 8

1. Besides the two basic relationships, what special relationships or functions are named?
2. Tell of the power given to the apostles before they began their work.
3. For what work was this power to qualify them?
4. What are the only Bible statements that refer to authority of apostles?
5. How did Peter appeal to the elders of Asia Minor?
6. How did the apostles work with people?
7. What did the apostles never consider themselves?
8. How did the apostles think of themselves?
9. Give, carefully, evidences that the apostles' work was always cooperative and never dictatorial.
10. What is referred to in saying that Paul and companions "delivered the decrees"?
11. Why would Paul give this teaching as from the apostles and elders?
12. What did Jesus mean when he said, "I will give unto you the keys of the kingdom of heaven"?
13. Show that the privilege of binding and loosing was not given to Peter alone.
14. How did Jesus show that no one of the apostles would be the head of the church?
15. What does the New Testament teaching show to be the work of the prophets in the church?
16. What are we told about the evangelists in the church?

LESSON 9

THE ORGANIZATION OF THE CHURCH

Special Relationships (Continued)

We have considered the place of the apostles, the prophets, and the evangelists in the preceding lesson. To these Paul added "some pastors and teachers." Since these are named together with "some" applied to both, it seems to imply a close relationship or similarity in their work. This is also suggested by Paul when he says bishops should be "apt to teach" (I Tim. 3:2) and "Be able both to exhort in the sound doctrine and to convict the gainsayers" (Titus 1:9). We might also note that in the listing given in I Cor. 12:28, we find the word "teachers" but no mention of pastors. However we have the word "teachers" when there is no apparent reference to pastors or bishops. There were teachers in the church at Antioch (Acts 13:1). Paul was appointed a teacher (I Tim. 2:7, II Tim. 1:11). Aged women were to be teachers (Titus 2:3). Christians should all become teachers (Heb. 5:12), but the use of the word in Eph. 4:11 may refer to special endowed teachers as is suggested by its use in I Cor. 12:28 along with special gifts and a similar listing of the activity of teaching in Rom. 12:6-8. Since there has been no organizational capacity indicated, and since the record gives no information relative to such, we shall

110

not discuss the matter further. We shall give our attention rather to the place of "pastors."

The word that should have been used in this place is "shepherds." This is the only case in the New Testament record where the Greek word used by Paul here is ever translated anything but "shepherds." It has been shown in the preceding lesson that this word is used to speak of the same people that are called bishops, overseers, and elders. Of these terms probably the one that is most commonly used among us is "elders," so in this discussion we are concerned with the place of the elders and the organization of the church and shall make use of this word generally in referring to the people in this relationship except where clarity requires exactness in the ideas being expressed.

If we are going to understand the place and the work of the elders of the church of the Bible, we must not overlook the fact that we are dealing with a relationship and that the relationship must be considered in its entirety. In the former studies of the subject, this has not been done too well. We must not forget that all parties to a relationship have their privileges as well as their obligations, and their obligations as well as their privileges. To stress obligations on one side or privileges on the other, is to distort the picture of the relationship and will result in misunderstanding. In dealing with a relationship in which all parties are deemed of equal rank, there is little likelihood of being unfair, but in cases where the relationship involves people who are thought of as being of different rank, we appear to have a tendency to emphasize the privileges of those to whom we impute superiority and the obligations of those who are given a lower rank. For example, in handling the Bible teaching relative to the parent-child relationship, a great deal has been said about children obeying their parents, but little about parents not provoking their children to wrath. Also the teaching "Wives, be in subjection unto your own husbands, as unto the Lord" (Eph. 5:22) has been strongly preached, but the instruction "Husbands, love your wives, even as Christ also loved the church, and gave himself up for it" (Eph. 5:25) has been seldom mentioned. Such a practice obscures the picture, distorts the teaching, and inclines some wives to be resentful. There is no wife worthy of the name who will not respect the teaching to obey her husband, if at the same time, the husband is taught to fulfill his obligations to his wife. In the relationship of the elders to the church and the church to the elders, people have preached long and loud "You must obey the elders," but they have had little to say about the obligations of the elders to the assembly of God's people. We should not lose sight of the fact that such careless or dishonest handling of the Bible teaching tends to breed disrespect. Neither should we overlook the fact that when one fails to fulfill his obligation in any relationship as best he can, he has no right to the privileges afforded by the relationship; and the relationship will cease to be effective. This is just as true in the elder-church relationship as in any other. Therefore, the elder who fails to fulfill his obligations loses his privilege of leadership whether he loses his place as an elder or not.

In reality this principle is more applicable to the elder-church relationship than to others that appear similar. Many of the places of leadership among men are also places of authority among men. They are places of official position among men, but in the case of elders the matter is quite different. When Jesus was here, he stressed the fact that among his people there should be equality. Jesus cautioned his disciples, "But be not ye called Rabbi: for one is your teacher, and all ye are brethren. And call no man your father on the earth: for one is your Father, even he who is in heaven. Neither be ye called masters: for one is your master, even the Christ" (Matt. 23:8-10). On a former occasion Jesus had made this teaching more personal. Speaking to ten of the twelve, he said, "Ye know that the rulers of the Gentiles lord it over them, and their great ones exercise authority over them. Not so shall it be among you: but whosoever would become great among you shall be your minister; and whosoever would be first among you shall be your servant" (Matt. 20:25-27). At the last supper occasion arose for Jesus to repeat this much needed teaching. "And there arose also a contention among them, which of them was accounted to be the greatest. And he said unto them, The kings of the Gentiles have lordship over them; and they that have authority over them are called Benefactors. But ye shall not be so: but he that is greater among you, let him become as the younger; and he that is chief, as he that doth serve" (Luke 22:24-26). From these statements it is clear that Christians are to be brethren. They make it unmistakeably clear that overseers or leaders are not to have lordship over the people with whom they are dealing. He speaks of the great ones among Christian people as being their ministers, or servants (diakonos) of a religious type, and adds those who are first shall be your servants (doulos) of the slave type indicating the idea of equality; and that seeking places of honor is seeking places of service, seeking opportunities to help, not seeking places to be looked up to and to be praised.

Unfortunately in the past some teachers have failed to recognize the difference between leadership in Christianity and leadership in world affairs. We note that in Jesus' statement he referred to leadership in world affairs and contrasted it with leadership in Christianity. Preachers have used examples of leadership among men to stress the authority or ruling power of the elders. The place of the elder has been compared with the office of the sheriff, indicating that by virtue of his being in that position he was the one who had the right to exercise certain authority over the congregation. In the effort to do this elders have not been called "masters" but the meaning has been ascribed to the word elders and they have been made a ruling class among the brethren. There is no such teaching in the Bible, and neither can such illustration be sustained by Bible teaching, so far as I have been able to find.

When one is inducted into a civil office, he is authorized to perform acts which he could not do otherwise and which if done by one not empowered by the office would be a violation of the law. In marked contrast to this one who has been appointed an elder is not empowered to do one thing that he could not have done before his appointment. In fact, if he has been one of the leaders of the congregation in which there were no appointed elders prior to his appointment, he would already have been doing or trying to do to the best of his ability the things that he will continue to do as an elder. His appointment makes no change in what he should do, neither does it in any functional way change his relationship to the brethren. It especially identifies him as such a leader and tends to heighten his sense of responsibility. His real power as an elder is not derived from his appointment to the place or "office" of an elder but must be acquired through the power of the word of God in his life. His appointment is a recognition of this power. He must live it and teach it effectively to do the work of an elder. As we shall see later, his power is in his ability to teach and to be an example. If any person who has been appointed as an elder finds it necessary to "pull his rank" in an effort to secure the respect of his brethren, he should be "pulled," because such not only shows his lack of qualification but his lack of understanding. It is true that Christians ought to respect the elders, and the Christians will respect all who deserve respect, but this respect cannot be maintained by constantly reminding them of this as a legal demand.

Some people have labored long and arduously to show that it is in order to speak of an elder as an officer of the church or the place filled by an elder as an "office." These are not Biblical terms; their use is nowhere justified by the words used in the original text of the New Testament.

However, in view of the loose way in which we use words, this does not mean that these terms may never, in any sense, be used to speak of an elder or the place he fills, for anyone who accepts such an appointment has been recognized as a spiritual leader and has been given a place of special service in the assembly or church. In this sense the word "office" may be used but never to indicate that by virtue of his appointment he has been given a special power to exercise authority jointly with the other elders over the church. It is true that he is called a bishop or overseer, but this does not necessarily mean a place of domination; rather he is to be a leader among his brethren.

It is very unfortunate that people have allowed their concepts of human relationships to cause them to read into some of the words used in our New Testament translation that which gives them the wrong idea of the place of an elder. There is no scripture of which I know that assigns to the elder anything that could be called authority that is in any wise comparable to the authority of that person who occupies the civil offices or holds a place in civil government. There are several statements that have been somewhat misinterpreted due to the wording used in some of the translations. We shall notice these rapidly, but carefully.

"But we beseech you, brethren, to know them that labor among you, and are over (take the lead) you in the Lord, and admonish you; and to esteem them exceeding highly in love for their work's sake" (I Thess. 5:12-13). "Or he that exhorteth, to his exhorting: he that giveth, let him do it with liberality; he that ruleth (takes the lead), with diligence; he that showeth mercy, with cheerfulness" (Rom. 12:8). "Let the elders that rule (take the lead) well be counted worthy of double honor, especially those who labor in the word and in teaching" (I Tim. 5:17). In these quotations the expressions "are over you," "ruleth," and "rule" have been construed as representing the powers of control similar to that exercised by one who holds a civil office and have been used as evidence of the authority of the elders. The literal translations shown in the parentheses following the expression in the quotations leave no doubt that such an application is unjustifiable. The word employed in the original text means "take the lead" and, therefore, carries no necessary implication of right to enforce compliance or power of control by virtue of position or office, but rather suggests the guiding influence of Christian work and teaching. Since the word "rule" in its common usage with us implies control, it is natural that an interpretation which depends upon that word alone would include the power of control and doubly natural if one is seeking to establish such an idea or to support such a preconceived conviction.

The word "rule" as it is used in our English translations does not always translate the same Greek word and, consequently, does not or should not always convey the same meaning. For example in I Tim. 5:17, quoted above, it is employed to translate "proestotes" which means "who take the lead" while in the fourteenth verse of the same chapter it is used as part of the translation of "oikodespotein" and refers to power of control. Without any acquaintance with this Greek word, when told that the first part of the word means house or household and the latter part "despotein" means rule, it is easily observable in comparison with our words "despot" or "despotic" that authority is included. We should be careful, however, not to interchange the meanings in these two verses as some people seem inclined to do. Paul wrote "I desire therefore that the younger widows marry, bear children, rule the household" (I Tim. 5:14) and "Let the elders that rule well be counted worthy of double honor" (I Tim. 5:17). His meaning is that these mothers "be masters and lords" over their children and that the elders "take the lead well" in the church, not that the elders be "masters and lords well" over the church, and mothers "take the lead" over their children. This reversal will cause confusion in both cases. Surely, there are times when small children, who are under their mother's care, must be coerced or forcibly restrained, and it is the mother's responsibility to do so, but no such use of authority has been delegated to the elders. They are never to be "masters or lords."

With what has been said about the mother's rule of the household in mind, let us examine a comparison made by Paul in his description of one worthy of being appointed an elder or bishop. "One that ruleth well his own house, having his children in subjection with all gravity; (but if a man knoweth not how to rule his own house, how shall he take care of the church of God?)" (I Tim. 3:4-5). Here the word "ruleth" in verse four and "rule" in verse five are not translating words that mean "be master or lord over" but different forms of the word that means "to care for." The use of this word in speaking of a bishop's accomplishment in his family and describing his work in the church, for which such accomplishment qualifies him, to "take care of the church of God" certainly does not suggest that he is to rule as master or lord. And just as certainly the warning that immediately followed strongly implied a very different meaning for the word "rule" as used. Paul warned, "Not a novice, lest being puffed up he fall into the condemnation of the devil" (I Tim. 3:6). If this warning is not against the danger of a novice who has been made a bishop thinking he is master and lord over his brethren and seeking to rule as such, what could the danger be? What else could cause a person in such a place to be puffed up? And with one in such a place what action as a result of being puffed up would more surely cause one to fall into the condemnation of the devil than seeking to lord it over God's people? Is it not strange, indeed, that the church leaders are seeking to magnify the authority of the elders, the one thing against which Paul warned in the case of the novices? Is it not possible that even those who are not novices might become puffed up over the matter and act so as to bring condemnation upon themselves?

The other quotations where the word "rule" is used in the New Testament that are cited in support of the authority of the elders are all from the thirteenth chapter of Hebrews. They are the following: "Remember them that had the rule over you (your leaders), men that spake unto you the word of God; and considering the issue of their life, imitate their faith" (Heb. 13:7). "Obey them that have the rule over you (your leaders), and submit to them: for they watch in behalf of your souls, as they that shall give account; that they may do this with joy, and not with grief: for this were unprofitable for you" (Heb. 13:17). "Salute all them that have the rule over you (your leaders), and all the saints" (Heb. 13:24).

You will observe that the word "elders" is not used in either statement. It is doubtful that the reference in the first quotation is to elders. In the first place, the only identification of those whom these Christians were urged to remember is given in this expression, "Men that spake unto you the word of God," meaning teachers. And further the expression "had the rule over you" implies that they were not with them at the time of this writing as elders naturally or normally would have been. The same expression "rule over you" in the other two quotations is from the same Greek word and has the same literal translation, "your leaders." Elders may have been included in the designation, but there is no reason to believe that they were the only people to whom the writer was referring. It is likely that two phrases "watch in behalf of your souls" and "give an account" (Heb. 13:17) have led some to think the reference was to the elders because elders are also called "bishops" or "overseers." But were not all of the early leaders and teachers concerned about the souls of the saints and did they not all watch for their safety? If not, what did Paul mean when he wrote, "My little children, of whom I am again in travail until Christ be formed in you" (Gal. 4:19) and "Besides those things that are without, there is that which presseth upon me daily, anxiety for all the churches" (II Cor. 11:28). Why would those who had labored and suffered so much not be concerned about their converts? And surely the serious responsibility of teachers is made clear in James' warning, "Be not many of you teachers, my brethren, knowing that we shall receive heavier judgment? (Jas. 3:1).

Another expression in the same verse "submit to them" has probably encouraged the application to elders also because of the preconceived, erroneous idea that elders are local church rulers rather than leaders. In doing this, Paul's statement to the Corinthians has evidently been overlooked, "Now I beseech you, brethren (ye know the house of Stephanas, that it is the firstfruits of Achaia, and that they have set themselves to minister unto the saints), that ye also be in subjection unto such, and to everyone that helpeth in the work and laboreth" (I Cor. 16:15-16). Surely this statement leaves no doubt that "submit to" or "be in subjection to" was used with reference to other leaders as well as to elders. It might be well also in this connection to recall the fact that special relationships within the church were all for a common purpose. "And he gave some to be apostles; and some, prophets; and some, evangelists; and some, pastors and teachers; for the perfecting of the saints, unto the work of ministering, unto the building up of the body of Christ" (Eph. 4:11-12). They are for strengthening love, the bond of perfectness, for building Christians as living stones into a spiritual house to be a holy priesthood, for perfecting unity in the fear of God; not to set up authority for forceful control. Christians are to work together in love, seeking the good of all and the glory of God, giving honor to whom honor is due, and, therefore, respecting all worthy leadership.

Although these words "rule over you" cannot be applied to elders only, there is no reason to think that elders were not included in "your leaders" and certainly there is no doubt that Christians are taught to obey the elders, for this is demanded by the very nature of the relationship. But just as certainly the fact that elders are called overseers does not enthrone them with special powers of control. Peter pled, "Likewise, ye younger, be subject unto the elder. Yea, all of you gird yourselves with humility, to serve one another" (I Pet. 5:5).

Some people have assumed that the expression "Obey them that have the rule over you" applies to elders only and construing "rule" to mean authority have inferred from this that if Christians are to obey, then elders have the right to demand obedience. The assumption and the inference are both false. The inspired writer did not use the word "obey" but the word "peithesthe," a passive form of the verb "peitho." The basic meaning of peitho is to "persuade." Paul used it in describing his work, "Knowing therefore the fear of the Lord we persuade men." This was also the word used by King Agrippa when he said, "With but little persuasion thou wouldest fain make me a Christian" (Acts 26:28). The passive form of this word means "to be persuaded" and was used by the author of the Hebrew letter in saying "We are persuaded better things of you" (Heb. 6:9). A passive form of this word is also used by Luke in speaking of the people who followed Judas of Galilee. Their experience is translated "All, as many as obeyed him, were scattered abroad" (Acts 5:37). The more exact translation would be "All, as many as were persuaded by him, were scattered abroad." This does not imply that they did not obey him implicitly, but it does show that they were led to obey him through persuasion and not through compulsion. This use of the word "obey" is virtually parallel to the one being considered in Heb. 13:17. Our translation is, "Obey them that have the rule over you." The more exact translation would be, "Be persuaded by your leaders." This in no wise suggests that any less care or effort should be expended by Christians in following the guidance of the elders, but it does definitely indicate that following the guidance of the elders is to be the result of persuasion (influence of teaching and example) and not the product of compulsion, not the mere demand of the law. Thus it is surely evident that the quotation, "Obey them that have the rule over you" (Heb. 13:17) should never be used to justify the "authority" of the elders; and this is the only place in the whole Bible where the word "obey" is used with reference to the elders of the church and here it is used to refer to other leaders as well as elders.

Now that we have seen that the original language referring to elders that is translated "rule" means "take the lead" or "leaders" and that the only place in the Bible where the word "obey" is used with reference to elders, it is used to translate a word that means "be persuaded by," it is evident that any support of the authority of elders that is in any wise comparable to that of civil officers from this source is completely lacking.

QUESTIONS ON LESSON 9

1. What seems to imply a close relationship in the work of pastors and teachers?
2. State the varied use of the word "teachers."
3. What word should have been used in place of pastors? Why?
4. If we are to understand the place and work of elders, we must not overlook what fact?
5. How may the true picture of a relationship be distorted and what causes it to be easily done in the case of the elders' relationships?
6. Name two other similar relationships.
7. What is sure to be the result when an elder fails to fulfill his obligations?
8. Give Jesus' teaching that shows the place of an elder to be different from many of the places of leadership among men.
9. What practice have some preachers followed in their effort to stress the authority or ruling power of the elders?
10. Contrast the change in becoming an elder with the change in being inducted into a civil office.
11. When an elder has to "pull his rank" what does it show?
12. In what sense may the word "office" be used to speak of the place of an elder? And in what sense should it never be used thus?
13. Give three statements from the Bible which have been used unjustifiably in support of the "authority" of the elders.
14. Instead of showing authority, what do these statements really show?
15. Illustrate from the Bible teaching different meanings that are conveyed by the word "rule" as it is used in our English translation.

16. What is the difference in the rule of the household by one who is qualified to be an elder and that of the young widow?
17. What is the real danger of appointing a novice as an elder?
18. Give three statements from the Hebrew letter used by some to support the authority of the elders.
19. Show carefully that there is little reason to believe that any of these statements refer to elders exclusively.
20. Give evidence that the expression "be in subjection to" was used with reference to other leaders as well as to elders.
21. State the meaning of "Obey them that have the rule over you."
22. Show that the quotation, "Obey them that have the rule over you," should never be used to justify the "authority" of the elders.

THE ORGANIZATION OF THE CHURCH

Special Relationships (Continued)

The only real description of the work of the elders to be found in the New Testament is in the first epistle of Peter. "The elders therefore among you I exhort, who am a fellow-elder, and a witness of the sufferings of Christ, who am also a partaker of the glory that shall be revealed: Tend the flock of God which is among you, exercising the oversight, not of constraint, but willingly, according to the will of God; nor yet for filthy lucre, but of a ready mind; neither as lording it over the charge allotted to you, but making yourselves ensamples to the flock. And when the chief Shepherd shall be manifested, ye shall receive the crown of glory that fadeth not away" (I Pet. 5:1-4). It is clear from this picture that the work of an elder is similar to that of a shepherd. Peter exhorted "Tend or shepherd the flock of God." Thus from the figure of the shepherd, we can learn of the nature of the work of the elder.

To be sure the picture suggested in the word "shepherd" is that which applied in the days of the apostles and in the country in which they lived, not the word "shepherd" as it might be used by us today. We have heard stories from those who have visited in the East of that unusual relationship that exists between the shepherd and his sheep, between the sheep and their shepherd. In this figure we have a most beautiful picture of the harmony and cooperation between the leader and those being led. The picture is one that reveals utmost fidelity on the part of those being led. We have been told that the sheep know their shepherd, that they follow him, that they will follow none other. We are told that several flocks of sheep might be intermixed, but when the shepherds of the respective flocks of sheep walk off in different directions, that the sheep without a single exception will follow their own shepherd. Why did these sheep so faithfully follow their own shepherd? Because he had dealt with the sheep in such a way that they honor him, they respect him, they put their trust in him. He has watched for their good. He has carried them to abundant pastures. He has supplied them with water. He has helped them over the rough places. He has rescued them from hard situations. He has provided such experiences for them that he has established himself with them as a leader. On the contrary in our country, in our dealing with sheep, we drive them and sometimes set the dog on them. Why? Because no such relationship or leadership has been established between the sheep and any particular individual. We do have an occasional exception to this—the few cases of sheep that have been raised as pets. They will respond to a trusted leadership.

The contrast between these two figures, the true shepherd of the East and the way we deal with sheep in America, sets forth the great lesson that we need very much to learn. This lesson of contrast is very graphic. The more our elder-church relationships resemble the American way of handling the flock, the less effective it will be, the more numerous and greater our church problems will be, and the surer will be our failure for the simple reason that the relationship will deteriorate and become less effective. This is true today in many cases, and elders have ceased to be honored and respected. If elders are not going to seek to effect and to sustain this close relationship as represented by the Eastern shepherd and his sheep, they will never be God-appointed elders. They will never be able to shepherd the flock. They are unqualified. They cannot do the work. Unless they do the work, or make an honest effort to do it, they deserve no honor, but dishonor. They are in the wrong place. They ought to do better or resign. Any elder who finds it necessary to remind people that he is an elder in an effort to secure respect is unworthy to be called an elder.

The further instruction given in the quotation above is in full keeping with the figure. Elders are taught, not to exercise the oversight of constraint, but willingly, because they love God's people, and they want to give at least a portion of their lives in showing that they love them in doing things for them that show that they love them. The people who are called elders who have never put themselves to any trouble, or who have never suffered any special inconvenience to aid Christians, or to show special kindness even to people who are not Christians, are unworthy of their place. They ought to make an honest effort to be the shepherds they are supposed to be, or they ought to cease to claim to be shepherds.

Yes, elders are to exercise the oversight; and hence, they are called overseers or bishops. But, we should not overlook the fact that they should exercise the oversight as shepherds, not as despots. They are to be leaders, not drivers. As leaders they have unlimited power; as drivers they have none. They have been given no powers of discipline or punishment whatsoever. We sometimes hear people speak of church discipline as though it consisted of some sort of system of penalties under the direction of the elders for the purpose of coercing the flock to do that which is right. This is not the case. There is only one thing mentioned anywhere in the New Testament that could in any wise be called punishment, and that is the practice of withdrawing from the disorderly and it is not done by the elders. Withdrawal is by the congregation (I Cor. 5:3-5, II Thess. 3:6, 14-15). Furthermore, withdrawal is not for the purpose of punishment but for recovery. It is incorrectly spoken of as a punishment in the King James and American Revised versions in II Cor. 2:6. However, Paul did not call it a punishment. The word he used means "rebuke" and is not translated punishment at any other place. The text should read, "Sufficient to such a one is this rebuke which was by the many." The withdrawal is the congregational way of telling a Christian that he is in sin and unworthy of his place as a Christian so long as he continues in it.

Peter also pointed out the fact that they should not exercise oversight for filthy lucre. Jesus gave the reason when he was here. A hireling will not give the care that he should to the sheep. "He that is a hireling, and not a shepherd, whose own the sheep are not, beholdeth the wolf coming, and leaveth the sheep, and fleeth, and the wolf snatcheth them, and scattereth them: he fleeth because he is a hireling, and careth not for the sheep" (John 10:12-13).

Peter's final negative instruction is expressed in these words, "Neither as lording it over the charge allotted to you." This expression is in complete keeping with the statements examined earlier made by Jesus concerning the leaders or those who would be great among his people and, also, those statements quoted from the epistles indicating the lack of that sort of authority on the part of elders that anywise resemble the authority exercised by those who occupy civil offices. Peter closed his instruction with the words "making yourselves ensamples to the flock." This phrase indicates wherein the power of an elder or elders lies—their superior ability to understand and to practice the teaching and to be examples to the flock. They should make honest efforts to fulfill such, or they should not expect the flock to follow their leadership. They should not expect to be followed merely because they had been named elders.

This picture of the work of the elder is given reinforcement by the implied comparison of the elder with the chief Shepherd (I Pet. 5:4). As a shepherd, what was the manner of Jesus' dealings with men? Did he seek to enforce his management upon them? Did he demand the right to dictate the details of their lives? Everyone who has a reasonable acquaintance with the story of

Jesus' life knows that the answer to these questions is "No." This was shown by his manner of dealing with people and expressed in his lament over Jerusalem, "O Jerusalem, Jerusalem, that killeth the prophets, and stoneth them that are sent unto her! how often would I have gathered thy children together, even as a hen gathereth her chickens under her wings, and ye would not!" (Matt. 23:37). The source of his power as a shepherd is revealed in his statement, "I am the good shepherd; and I know mine own, and mine own know me, even as the Father knoweth me, and I know the Father; and I lay down my life for the sheep" (John 10:14-15). The power of the elder or shepherd must find its origin in the same source as that of the chief Shepherd. They must know their own and be known to be worthy to be followed.

This cooperative personal type of leadership on the part of elders is illustrated by the handling of the question of circumcision of the Gentiles by the apostles, the elders, and the church in Jerusalem (Acts 15:1-29) that was presented in the preceding lesson. It is clear that all had a part or concurred in the action taken. The record of this case shows that this was not a matter to be discussed by the apostles and the elders to make a private decision separate and apart from the knowledge of the congregation. If that were true, when the elders were endowed with spiritual gifts, and, also, had the apostles with them, how much more true should it be today. The congregation has an interest in the problems of the church, in the issues that are discussed, and in dealing with those matters. Everyone recognizes the fact that it facilitates decisions if they are made by a small number of the people, but it is hard on the church. We need to teach the church. The people of the church need to know the doctrine of the church and also they need to be motivated by the power of the gospel in their hearts, not by the decision of an ecclesiastical body supported by legal doctrine. If they are incapable of understanding, then they should be taught that which would prepare them to understand. Certainly this does not suggest that there are no people who can be delegated to take care of routine matters, but all matters that seriously concern the church and those in which Christians should have a vital interest and are expected to co-operate with and aid in the carrying out should be dealt with along with the church. What I am trying to say is that this way of elders proposing to control the church by decisions made separate and apart from the church, instead of leading the congregation in the light of the gospel to join in the decisions, make themselves a mere ecclesiastical body. This is without support. No such body has any authorization that I know of anywhere in the New Testament. Elders are leaders and must stay close enough to the Christians to lead. In this work men have been given the place of responsibility. Paul declared, "But I permit not a woman to teach, nor to have dominion over a man, but to be in quietness. For Adam was first formed, then Eve" (I Tim. 2:12-13).

The fact that the elders are not constituted an ecclesiastical board to make decisions for the church, but should work with the church, is made evident from the manner of address employed in the epistles. Is it not strange if the elders are to be the "ruling" body of the church that of all the epistles in the New Testament, the only mention of the elders or bishops in the address of any is found in the letter to the saints at Philippi (Phil. 1:1) where a similar mention is made of deacons and where not one word of special instruction is given to either? Not one single epistle is addressed to the elders. If the elders, as such, have authority over the church and are to manage the affairs of the church, direct the work of preachers, and settle church problems, is it not most unusual that not a single epistle was addressed to the elders to tell them how to accomplish their work? Why did Paul not address the Corinthian letter to the elders and tell them how to manage the affairs of the church at Corinth and adjust the problems of the Christians at that place? Why did he not address the Galatian letter to the elders and direct them in handling the problem of circumcision? It is true that the elders were especially singled out one time, when Paul called the elders of the church at Ephesus to come to Miletus. The nature of the instruction given on this occasion is significant. "Take heed unto yourselves, and to all the flock, in which the Holy Spirit hath made you bishops, to feed the church of the Lord which he purchased with his own blood. I know that after my departing grievous wolves shall enter in among you, not sparing the flock; and from among your own selves shall men arise, speaking perverse things, to draw away the disciples after them. Wherefore watch ye, remembering that by the space of three years I ceased not to admonish every one night and day with tears. And now I commend you to God, and to the word of his grace, which is able to build you up, and to give you the inheritance among all them that are sanctified. I coveted no man's silver, or gold, or apparel. Ye yourselves know that these hands ministered unto my necessities, and to them that were with me. In all things I gave you an example, that so laboring ye ought to help the weak, and to remember the words of the Lord Jesus, that he himself said, It is more blessed to give than to receive" (Acts 20:28-35). It related to themselves and to their helpfulness to others not to know how to exercise authority.

Now since the place of the elders in the church of the Bible in the first century, when they were especially endowed with gifts of the Holy Spirit, was the place of leaders and not "rulers," surely today when they have no such gifts, and when all Christians alike have access to the Bible as the word of God to guide them, there is little justification for a ruling class in the church. However, as has always been the case there is great need for men who have come to know God, having been truly begotten by the word of God, who have sanctified in their hearts Christ Jesus as Lord, being filled with his Spirit, and who, through the influence of the love of God in their hearts, have learned to show love for their brethren and for all of God's creatures through humble service—men who have become big enough to forget themselves and live for others. These qualities of leadership are fully evident in the description of those to be selected as elders or bishops given in I Tim. 3:1-7 and Tit. 1:5-9.

There is one other term that is used to name a special relationship or work; that is the word "deacon." It is found in only four verses of the New Testament and three of those were in the same setting (Phil. 1:1, I Tim. 3:8, 10, 12). It is not a translation strictly speaking. It appears to be an Anglicized form of the Greek word that means "one who serves" and in all other places in the New Testament record it is translated "servant" or "minister." On the two occasions where the word "deacon" is used, it is in conjunction with the word bishop or overseer and apparently is expressing a contrasting idea. The Philippian letter was addressed to the saints "with the bishops or overseers and ministers or those who served." In writing to Timothy Paul first described those who should be selected as bishops or overseers and those who should serve. The expression "let them serve as deacons" (I Tim. 3:10) is a distortion. In the original it is simply "let them serve." The word "deacons" seems to have been added because of a preconceived organizational bias.

The word "deacon" has not only virtually been added to the text, but has been used with a much more limited meaning than the word which it is supposed to translate. It has come to be applied to men only and the work or office apparently limited to men, which completely ignores Paul's statement "I commend unto you Phoebe our sister, who is a servant of the church that is at Cenchrea" (Rom. 16:1). The word "servant" in this verse translates the same word deacon is supposed to translate. It is also commonly used to designate one who renders routine services, generally of a temporal nature, within the congregation; but the Bible uses the word that it is supposed to translate more broadly. It is used to speak of Paul and his work in the gospel (Col. 1:23--25, Eph. 3:7), also of Apollos (I Cor. 3:5), of Epaphras (Col. 1:7), of Tychicus (Col. 4:7), and in all of these cases it is translated "minister." In speaking of that which was to be accomplished by the apostles, prophets, evangelists, pastors, and teachers, a form of this same word is used and translated "the work of ministering" (Eph. 4:12).

This restricted use of the word "deacon" seems to have arisen from the fact that a form of the Greek word "diakonos," which is translated "deacon" in Phil. and I Tim. is translated "serve" in the expression "serve tables" that is used in Acts 6:2 with reference to the work that was done by the seven men appointed by the apostles in response to the murmuring of the Grecian Jews because their widows were neglected in the daily ministration. Such an application of this case, however, appears to be without justification for there are two things that have been overlooked. The translation of diakonein is "to serve" with another word being used, that is translated "tables." Also diakonia, another form of the word translated deacon is used in the apostles' statement, "But we will continue stedfastly in prayer, and in the ministry of the word" (Acts 6:4). It is clear that the apostles' meaning here is that it is not fit that they should give so much of their time to serving tables, but that it should be given to prayer and to serving the word. Thus it is clear from these statements that the various forms of the word "diakoneo" mean "service or to serve" without any implication as the type of service rendered.

These things have not been said to imply that it is wrong to have ministers or servants within the local congregation, or that it is unscriptural to speak of them as "deacons," but rather to point up the fact that this is not the Bible meaning of the word that is translated deacon and to remind us that some of the rigidity of our organizational concepts relative to the local congregation is without support in the scriptures.

QUESTIONS ON LESSON 10

1. Where is the only real description of the work of the elders to be found?
2. What figure is used that shows the relationship of the elders to the flock?
3. Contrast the shepherd of the East with the American sheep herder.
4. From this contrast show wherein the success of elders must lie.
5. What other instruction is in keeping with this figure?
6. Show that elders must be leaders, not drivers.
7. Who are to withdraw from the disorderly and why?
8. Why is one who exercises oversight for filthy lucre disqualified for the work?
9. What final negative instruction did Peter give?
10. Wherein lies the true power of an elder?
11. What comparison did Peter imply that re-enforces the picture?
12. Why was Jesus a good shepherd?
13. The handling of what question illustrates this same cooperative personal type of leadership?
14. What sort of church control has no authorization in the New Testament?
15. Give evidence from the address of the epistles that the elders evidently did not constitute such an ecclesiastical board.

16. To what did the instruction given by Paul to the elders at Miletus relate?
17. What changes have there been since the first century that even lessens the justification for a ruling class in the church today?
18. There is great need for what kind of men in the church today?
19. What is the use of the word "deacon" in the New Testament?
20. From what does the restricted use of the word "deacon" today seem to have arisen?
21. Show this application of the case to be without gratification.
22. Calling this to attention has what purpose?

LESSON 11

THE CHURCH AT WORK

Since there is considerable disagreement among religious people over the work of the church and how it is to be accomplished and especially since this disagreement has given rise to strife and division in some cases, it shall be the purpose of this study to present a picture of the first century church at work in the hope of providing a better understanding of the matter. Every Bible student recognizes the fact that the picture of necessity must be incomplete since the Bible does not provide us with a full record of the activities of the early church. Although this is the case, it is also recognized by those whose love for God impels them to employ the utmost care in doing what he would have them to do, that the practice of those who were guided by the personal efforts and teaching of inspired men are not only safe examples to follow, but that they also represent divine instruction. In view of these things, every reasonable care should be exercised in securing an accurate picture of the first century church activities.

On the first Pentecost after the resurrection of Christ after Peter had told the people to repent and be baptized "and exhorted them, saying, Save yourselves from this crooked generation" (Acts 2:40), we are told "They then that received his word were baptized: and there were

added unto them in that day about three thousand souls"
(Acts 2:41). This was the beginning of the church. These
people who accepted the gospel were called out of their
sinful ways of living to follow the way of holiness. They
were redeemed, purified, sanctified, and reconciled to
God. They made up the ekklesia, the assembly, the
church. Therefore the activities in which they engaged,
and the work which they accomplished, were the activities and the work of the church.

Beginning in the very next verse, we have the description of some of these activities. "And they continued
stedfastly in the apostles' teaching and fellowship, in the
breaking of bread and the prayers. And fear came upon
every soul: and many wonders and signs were done
through the apostles. And all that believed were together,
and had all things common; and they sold their posses-
sions and goods, and parted them to all, according as any
man had need. And day by day, continuing stedfastly
with one accord in the temple, and breaking bread at
home, they took their food with gladness and singleness
of heart, praising God, and having favor with all the
people" (Acts 2:42-47). Here we have brief mention of
miracles by the apostles, faithfulness in living and worship by the disciples, and their generosity in helping those
among them who were in need. This personal interest
and helpfulness is further expressed in these words. "And
the multitudes of them that believed were of one heart
and soul: and not one of them said that aught of the
things which he possessed was his own; but they had all
things common. For neither was there among them any

that lacked: for as many as were possessors of lands or houses sold them, and brought the prices of the things that were sold, and laid them at the apostles' feet: and distribution was made unto each, according as any one had need" (Acts 4:32, 34, 35). Among others, we are told that Barnabas "having a field, sold it, and brought the money and laid it at the apostles' feet" (Acts 4:37). These statements show that the distribution of these funds were entrusted to the apostles, which suggests personal helpfulness rather than personal selfseeking.

It is also evident from the case of Ananias that the gifts to provide for those who were in need were not commanded but voluntary. They gave because they loved one another and wanted to give. "While it remained, did it not remain thine own? and after it was sold, was it not in thy power? How is it that thou hast conceived this thing in thy heart? Thou hast not lied unto men, but unto God" (Acts 5:4).

The most basic and the most important work of the church seems to have had its beginning as a natural activity among Christians. It is the work of helping one another. We are told "And all that believed were together, and had all things common" (Acts 2:44). "And the multitude of them that believed were of one heart and soul" (Acts 4:32). It appears that their conversion was after the true pattern described by Peter. "Seeing ye have purified your souls in your obedience to the truth unto unfeigned love of the brethren, love one another from the heart fervently: having been begotten again, not of corruptible seed, but of incorruptible, through the word of God which liveth and abideth" (I Pet. 1:22-23). These early Christians, having been begotten again, had no need for John's warning. "But whoso hath the world's goods and beholdeth his brother in need, and shutteth up his compassion from him, how doth the love of God abide in him" (I John 3:17). It would be a grave mistake, however, and a violent distortion of the picture if we allowed the material help that was provided by these early Christians, for those among them who were in need, to be thought of as the only or the most important work of the church among them. This, no doubt, was only one of many expressions of that love which they had one for another. It is true that there is no specific mention of acts of long-suffering, forbearance, forgiveness, or encouragement to the weak; but all such were surely included in the term "fellowship" and in the expression "and the multitude of them that believed were of one heart and soul." Surely those who so readily supplied the physical needs of their brethren were not forgetful of their spiritual needs.

Unfortunately, most of these acts of personal helpfulness have come to be thought of as the work of individual Christians in contradiction to the work of the church, with the exception of material aid and what some people call matters of church discipline. An unbiased examination of the picture of the church at work as given in the New Testament, THE BIBLE PICTURE, however, fails completely to provide any basis for any such division or distinction between the work of the church done by individual Christians and that which is to be accomplished by the church as a body or a group of Christians working together. Due to the very nature of the case, there are some works of the church which appear to make more demand upon the church as a group in order to be successful than that made by other works of the church, but there are no grounds whatsoever to support the theory that there are works of the church that are to be accomplished by individual Christians working singlehandedly that are not to be encouraged, aided, and supported in every way that is feasible by other Christians individually or by Christians as a group or by the church as a whole. Any work that can be done by a Christian, as a Christian work, can be done by Christians working together, or by the church, either by the local congregation or several congregations. The works of the church are the works of Christians, and the works of Christians are the works of the church. All that are Christians, They That Are Christ's, those who have truly accepted him as Lord, are seeking to glorify his name among men by aiding in every way they can, both individually and collectively, the accomplishment of the Christian mission to be the light of the world. This real mission of the church, or of the people who make up the church, to be the light of the world can be accomplished only through the influence of Christian living. Jesus exhorted "Even so let your light shine before men; that they may see your good works, and glorify your Father who is in heaven" (Matt. 5:16).

From this it is evident that one of the most important works, or the most important work, of the church is the building up of itself through the edification of its members. This is also abundantly set forth by statements in the epistles which were addressed directly to the people who make up the church. Paul exhorted the Christians at Rome, "So then let us follow after things which make for peace, and things whereby we may edify one another" (Rom. 14:19). "Now we that are strong ought to bear the infirmities of the weak, and not to please ourselves. Let each one of us please his neighbor for that which is good, unto edifying" (Rom. 15:1-2). To the Christians at Corinth Paul declared "Now I would have you all speak with tongues, but rather that ye should prophesy: and greater is he that prophesieth than he that speaketh with tongues, except he interpret, that the church may receive edifying" (I Cor. 14:5). He also exhorted "So also ye, since ye are zealous of spiritual gifts, seek that ye may abound unto the edifying of the church" (I Cor. 14:12) and "Let all things be done unto edifying" (I Cor. 14:26). He urged the Christians at Thessalonica "Wherefore exhort one another, and build each other up, even as also ye do" (I Thess. 5:11), and to those at Ephesus "Let no corrupt speech proceed out of your mouth, but such as is good for edifying as the need may be, that it may give grace to them that hear" (Eph. 4:29). Paul made it clear that the work of edification was most important by declaring "But all things, beloved, are for your edifying" (II Cor. 12:19), and that the power, or the authority, given unto him was for that purpose. "For this cause I write these things while absent, that I may not when present deal sharply, according to the authority which the Lord gave me for building up, and not for casting down" (II Cor. 13:10). Paul also made it clear to the Christians at Ephesus that the special gifts or arrangements within the church were for this very purpose. "And he gave some to be apostles; and some, prophets; and some, evangelists; and some, pastors and teachers; for the perfecting of the saints, unto the work of ministering, unto the building up of the body of Christ: till we all attain unto the unity of the faith, and of the knowledge of the Son of God, unto a fullgrown man, unto the measure of the stature of the fulness of Christ: that we may be no longer children, tossed to and fro and carried about with every wind of doctrine, by the sleight of men, in craftiness, after the wiles of error; but speaking truth in love, may grow up in all things unto him, who is the head, even Christ; from whom all the body fitly framed and knit together through that which every joint supplieth, according to the working in due measure of each several part, maketh the increase of the body unto the building up of itself in love" (Eph. 4:11-16). Also the only appeal to Christians to assemble or to not forsake their assembling together, to be found in the whole New Testament record, is made in the interest of this work. "And let us consider one another to provoke unto love and good works; not forsaking our own assembling together, as the custom of some is, but exhorting one another; and so much the more, as ye see the day drawing nigh" (Heb. 10:24-25).

Is it not strange that this work of the church which has been so strongly emphasized in the scriptures has been so sadly neglected? Is it not surprising, yes, even shocking, that the Christian leadership of today has shown so much concern for those who have not accepted the gospel and so little concern for the edification of those who have accepted the gospel and have continued to do so through the years, apparently ignoring the perpetual warning being sounded by the stark picture of "spiritual mortality" that is ever present among us? Why have those who have occupied places that belong to adult Christians so sadly neglected the babes that have been born into the family of God? Why have those who claim to be spiritual among us overlooked Paul's instruction "Brethren, even of a man be overtaken in any trespass, ye who are spiritual, restore such a one in a spirit of gentleness; looking to thyself, lest thou also be tempted. Bear ye one another's burdens, and so fulfill the law of Christ" (Gal. 6:1-2)? Why have we made so much effort to get the children of the devil to put on the mantle of religion and so little effort to make them worthy children of God? Why do our church leaders so frequently leave this important work of the church to chance, or consider it merely a private matter of the individual, while they give their major attention to financial campaigns or campaigns for the increase of membership? Why do the elders of most congregations concern themselves principly with the routine arrangement, the externals, such as details of worship, construction of church buildings, and the allocation of funds received through the weekly contribution and have given so little attention to the spiritual needs of the flock? Why have the major portion of their efforts often been expended in managerial activities of the church to the virtually total neglect of the personal spiritual problems of weak, struggling individuals or the un-Christlike attitudes that pervade certain segments of the congregation that have destroyed its unity, handicapped its progress, and stifled its spiritual influence? How could they so fully ignore this statement made by Paul to the elders of the church at Ephesus? "In all things I gave you an example, that so laboring ye ought to help the weak, and to remember the words of the Lord Jesus, that he himself said, It is more blessed to give than to receive" (Acts 20:35). How can they so completely forget the personal concern of the true shepherd which Jesus suggested in his parable of the lost sheep who left the ninety and nine to rescue the one that was lost? Or, how can they so completely overlook the admonition of James, "My brethren, if any among you err from the truth, and one convert him; let him know, that he who converteth a sinner from the error of his way shall save a soul from death, and shall cover a multitude of sins" (James 5:19-20)?

This, however, should not be the concern of the elders only but of the whole church. How long are we going to be content to allow a few acts of religious ritual to be naively substituted for Christian living? How long are we going to stand by and witness the infantile and juvenile behavior of a large percentage of those who call themselves Christians and make no effort to build them up in the most Holy faith? How long are we going to continue to neglect our own family? How long are we going to be more concerned about quantity than about quality? How long are we going to continue to coax or to drag the unconverted unto the church and let them remain in their unconverted state? How long will we measure orthodoxy by the extent to which people conform to the outward acts of the first century church, as we conceive of them, completely forgetful of the fact that one must have the Spirit of Christ to be his (Rom. 8:9) and only those who are led by the Spirit of God are the sons of God (Rom. 8:14)? How did the Christians of the first century accomplish the work of helping one another in their love for God and their spiritual needs unto edifying? Were they not truly their brother's keepers?

At this place, we need to give further attention only to their manner of handling material aid. It is reasonably clear that this aid was administered both individually and collectively. John's admonition "But whoso hath the world's goods, and beholdeth his brother in need, and shutteth up his compassion from him, how doth the love of God abide in him" (I John 3:17) suggests the former and this statement from the record of their early work leaves no doubt about the latter "For neither was there among them any that lacked: for as many as were possessors of lands or houses sold them, and brought the prices of the things that were sold, and laid them at the apostles' feet: and distribution was made unto each, according as any one had need" (Acts 4:34-35).

This last statement not only shows that there was a united or group effort to provide what was needed but also strongly implies that it was administered by the apostles. It appears that the apostles continued to minister to the needs for food for a period of some four or five years. However, when the number of disciples had increased so much that the task was too great for the apostles and, as a result, some of the Grecian widows were neglected which gave rise to a complaint from the Grecian Jews, the apostles arranged another way of handling the matter. "And the twelve called the multitude of the disciples unto them, and said, It is not fit that we should forsake the word of God, and serve tables. Look you out therefore, brethren, from among you seven men of good report, full of the Spirit and of wisdom, whom we may appoint over this business" (Acts 6:2-3). We are told, "And the saying pleased the whole multitude: and they chose Stephen, a man full of faith and of the Holy Spirit, and Philip, and Prochorus, and Nicanor, and Timon, and Parmenas, and Nicolaus a proselyte of Antioch; whom they set before the apostles: and when they had prayed, they laid their hands upon them" (Acts 6:5-6). It should be noted here that the disciples were told the kind of men to select, that the disciples selected them, and that the apostles appointed them to the work.

It is easily recognized that the work of the church that we have considered in this lesson thus far has been only that which was directed toward helping the people of the local church: it has been Christians helping fellow Christians. There is one other special case within this field of work for which we do not have an example, but of which Paul gave instructions: "Honor widows that are widows indeed. But if any widow hath children or grand-children, let them learn first to show piety towards their own family, and to requite their parents: for this is acceptable in the sight of God" (I Tim. 5:3-4). He later added, "If any woman that believeth hath widows, let her relieve them, and let not the church be burdened; that it may relieve them that are widows indeed" (I Tim. 5:16). From these statements it is evident that "honoring" included supporting and, further, if she had children or grandchildren, they should support her. He gave this warning: "But if any provideth not for his own, and specially his own household, he hath denied the faith, and is worse than an unbeliever" (I Tim. 5:8). However, Paul gave no instruction on how the widow was to be provided for, either by the church or by relatives.

QUESTIONS ON LESSON 11

1. Over what is there much disagreement among religious people today?
2. What is the purpose of this study?
3. Why must this picture be incomplete?
4. How do those who love God consider the practice of those who were guided by his teaching in the first century?
5. State briefly how the church began and who began the work of the church.
6. Describe the early activity or work of the church.
7. What shows that it was a personal helpfulness, rather than personal self-seeking?
8. Whose example shows that gifts were made voluntarily?
9. What was the most basic and the most important work of the church in its beginning?
10. What would be a grave mistake and a violent distortion of this picture?
11. What is evidently included in the word "fellowship"?
12. Unfortunately how have most of these acts of personal helpfulness come to be thought of?

13. What does an unbiased examination of the Bible picture of the church fail completely to provide?
14. Show that the work of the church is the work of Christians and that the work of Christians is the work of the church?
15. Show by scripture quotations what is probably the most important work of the church.
16. The New Testament appeal to Christians not to forsake the assembly was made in the interest of what work?
17. What is surprising, or even shocking, about the concern of Christian leadership today?
18. What have adult Christians sadly neglected?
19. What instruction from the apostle Paul do the spiritual among us today seem to have overlooked?
20. In what way have we apparently misplaced our effort relative to Christians?
21. To what have our church leaders given their major attention rather than to edification of the church?
22. The major portion of the efforts of elders are often spent in managerial activities to the neglect of what?
23. What statements from Paul and James have they apparently overlooked or ignored?
24. Whom should this work of edification concern other than the elders?
25. What are we allowing to become substituted for Christian living?
26. State some other questions that suggest our neglect of edification.
27. Give Bible evidence that material aid was administered both individually and collectively.
28. How was the group effort to apply material needs administered at first?
29. What change was made in the arrangement and why?
30. Only what works of the church have we considered in this lesson?
31. What instruction did Paul give in regard to helping widows indeed and of what did he give no instruction in this case?

THE CHURCH AT WORK
(Continued)

In the preceding lesson we have learned of the work of Christians in providing for members of the local congregation both financially and spiritually. We learn also from the New Testament record that helpfulness, including financial aid, was also extended to Christians of other congregations. Paul spoke of the love which the Colossians had "toward all the saints" (Col. 1:4), to the Ephesians "the love which ye showed toward all the saints" (Eph. 1:15), and speaking of the love of the Thessalonians, he said, "For indeed ye do it toward all the brethren that are in all Macedonia" (I Thess. 4:10). When Agabus, the prophet, made known at Antioch that there was to be a great famine over all the world, we are told, "And the disciples, every man according to his ability, determined to send relief unto the brethren that dwelt in Judea: which also they did, sending it to the elders by the hand of Barnabas and Saul" (Acts 11:29-30). In Paul's epistles we have the record of another occasion when help was given to the poor brethren in Judea. This time it was provided by the Christians of Macedonia, Achaia, and Galatia. "But now, I say, I go unto Jerusalem, ministering unto the saints. For it hath been the good pleasure of Macedonia and Achaia to make a certain contribution for the poor among the saints that are at Jerusalem" (Rom. 15:25-26). "Now concerning the collection for the saints, as I gave order to the churches of Galatia, so do ye" (I Cor. 16:1). The first is a case where Christians of one congregation sent help to Christians in another section of the country. The second is a case where the Christians of several congregations of different lands join in the work of supplying the needs of their brethren of another land, the land of Judea.

Here we not only have the example of the Christians of a congregation, or of several congregations, joining in the work of supplying the needs of Christians elsewhere, but we also have an example of how they did it. In the first case the Christians at Antioch were moved by a prospective emergency to send help to the brethren in Judea. Every man determined to send relief and sent according to his ability. It was sent to the elders. It was sent by Barnabas and Saul. In the second case the Christians of Macedonia and Achaia and probably those of Galatia were moved by the appeals of Paul (I Cor. 16:1-2, II Cor. 8:9) and of Titus (II Cor. 8:6). The contribution was "for the poor among the saints that are at Jerusalem" (Rom. 15:26) and was apparently a gift of appreciation from the Gentiles to the Jews. "Yea, it hath been their good pleasure; and their debtors they are. For if the Gentiles have been made partakers of their spiritual things, they owe it to them also to minister unto them in carnal things" (Rom. 15:27). However, Paul made it clear to the Corinthians that as Christian brethren they were simply sharing with those who were in need and should the situation reverse itself, they should expect help from the Christians in Jerusalem. "For I say not this that others may be eased and ye distressed; but by equality: your abundance being a supply at this present time for their want, that their abundance also may become a supply for your want; that there may be equality:" (II Cor. 8:13-14). The amount of aid sent must have been substantial, since more than a year was spent in gathering it. "And herein I give my judgment: for this is expedient for you, who were the first to make a beginning a year ago, not only to do, but also to will," (II Cor. 8:10) and the churches of Macedonia had given liberally (II Cor. 8:1-5). Paul proposed to the Corinthians that they select those of their number to carry their bounty to Jerusalem or to accompany Paul in doing so. We are also told of a brother who was appointed or chosen by the churches to travel with Paul and others "in the matter of this grace" (II Cor. 8:18-19).

It has been generally inferred that Paul and those that traveled with him delivered this contribution to the elders of the church at Jerusalem and they dispensed it through the local church organization to the poor among them. This does not appear to be a necessary inference, though it appears likely that they worked through or with the leadership of the church at Jerusalem in accomplishing their mission. Paul twice refers to the contribution in the words "which is ministered by us" (II Cor. 8:19-20). If your thinking is controlled by the overdrawn, unfounded concept of local antonomy with an exaggerated emphasis upon local organization and dictatorial power of the elders, you can but conclude that these funds for the relief of the poor among the brethren were delivered into the hands of the elders. But when you consider what only is said and all that is said, such a conclusion is not too fully justified. If the elders were the authoritative rulers and managers of the local congregation, is it not a little bit strange that besides Paul's effort with the people at Corinth in procuring these funds that Titus had been used, not only to begin but to complete this work (II Cor. 8:6), with never a word said in either of Paul's letters to the Corinthians about the elders' part in the matter? There is not the slightest hint that the appeal was made to the congregation through the elders. It certainly would hardly be reasonable to suggest that the congregation had no elders and little more reason to attribute to them the complete power of local control when such an extensive effort was made by the people who were not members of the congregation, with no mention whatsoever of the elders or their part in the matter. And if the elders of the church at Corinth did not have any special hand in raising the money to be sent to Jerusalem, why should we assume that the elders of the congregation at Jerusalem were given full control of its distribution?

Whether these funds were received by the elders at Jerusalem and distributed to the poor by them or not, it matters little. We do know that the help sent earlier from Antioch was received by the elders and evidently used as the occasion demanded. The important thing, however, is the fact that in each case, Christians, whether members of the same congregation or different congregations, were ministering to the needs of Christians and made use of such arrangements as would serve their purpose. This was not a matter of a church or of churches helping a church. Saints were ministering to the saints as Paul declared, "I go unto Jerusalem ministering unto the saints" (Rom. 15:25). Also in explaining the matter to the Christians at Corinth, Paul wrote, "For I say not this that others may be eased and ye distressed; but by equality: your abundance being a supply at this present time for their want, that their abundance also may become a supply for your want; that there may be equality:" (II Cor. 8:13-14). He did not urge the church at Corinth to help the church at Jerusalem with the encouragement that in case of need the church at Jerusalem would help the church at Corinth. It is clear that each of these cases was a cooperative effort of individual Christians, whether in the same congregation or different congregations, to minister to the needs of Christians in Jerusalem. The decisions to help the brethren who were in need in Jerusalem in both of these cases were made by the individual Christians and it was up to them individually whether or not they would give and how much. There is no indication of an organizational or elders' decision in the matter. This does not imply that the elders as leaders among their brethren did not have their influence in the work, but rather to stress the fact that it was a cooperational effort among Christians in the hope that we more fully understand that the work of the church is the work of Christians, that the church, whether we are speaking locally or universally, is a body of Christians, and nothing more, and that there is no limitation upon the work of the church that does not apply to the work of an individual Christian. What an individual can do as a Christian work may be done by any number of Christians whether or not they worship in the same congregation or in several congregations. The idea that a Christian may do a Christian work that several Christians or that an assembly of Christians, a church, may not do is without scriptural foundation, or the idea that a Christian as an individual may employ a method or means in accomplishing a Christian work that would be wrong if used by a church is likewise unfounded. It is certainly true that Christians are privileged to give to Christians in their home congregation, or in any other congregation anywhere, without it being given through the church treasury. This doctrine that elders must direct all the giving of members of a congregation is without foundation. Surely Christians will share in the efforts of their local congregation.

Certainly the special instruction that Paul gave in regard to a highly selected class of widows who were more than sixty years of age should not be taken to mean that they were the only ones to be aided by the church, for James' statement includes much more. "Pure religion and undefiled before our God and Father is this, to visit the fatherless and widows in their affliction, and to keep oneself unspotted from the world" (Jam. 1:27). This statement not only designates widows without age limitation, but also children without age limitation. It should be observed further that there is no indication that such help should be restricted to church members or church families. It is unlikely that the Christians of the first century were able in most localities of doing more than taking care of their own, but Paul's instruction to the Galatians leaves no doubt that they were to manifest the Spirit of Christ insofar as their means permitted. "So then, as we have opportunity, let us work that which is good toward all men, and especially toward them that are of the household of faith" (Gal. 6:10). One who would oppose the effort of Christian people to provide help for the widows, orphans, and other unfortunates among the non-church people are not only without knowledge of God's teaching, but are also without his Spirit and, consequently, are none of his (Rom. 8:9). There is little to be gained by the effort of church people who preach the love of God to the world but who refuse to show love by aiding those who are in distress due to lack of goods and care. Surely we cannot ignore the fact that this was part of the instruction given even from the time the gospel of the kingdom began to be preached by John. "And the multitudes asked him, saying, What then must we do? And he answered and said unto them, He that hath two coats, let him impart to him that hath none; and he that hath food, let him do likewise" (Luke 3:10-11).

Another work in which the church, the assembly, the Christians of the first century, engaged was preaching the gospel. This has been recognized as a basic activity of the church by all who accept the Bible teaching, but many discussions have arisen over the details of its accomplishment. These discussions have grown out of considering preaching the gospel to be the work of the church, as a body controlled by it as an organization, rather than being the work of Christians, both individually and collectively. Such thinking is without Biblical foundation. An examination of the New Testament record makes it clear that the preaching of the gospel was accomplished by Christians working individually and collectively as was true of other work of the church.

Upon receiving the Holy Spirit the twelve apostles began preaching the gospel in Jerusalem (Acts 3:4-6). Stephen also preached in Jerusalem (Acts 6:8-10). The disciples that were scattered abroad by persecution "went about preaching the word" (Acts 8:4). Of them Philip preached in Samaria (Acts 8:5) and other places (Acts 8:26-40). Some went to Phoenicia, Cyprus, and Antioch preaching to Jews only (Acts 11:19). But there were some of them, men of Cyprus and Cyrene, that preached to the Greeks in Antioch (Acts 11:20). We are told that when the apostles in Jerusalem heard that Samaria had received the word, Peter and John were sent to impart the Holy Spirit unto them, and when the church in Jerusalem heard that a great number of the Greeks in Antioch had turned to the Lord, "They sent forth Barnabas as far as Antioch" (Acts 11:21-22). "They," used to refer to the church, shows this to be the work of Christians collectively, not of the church as an organization.

Saul preached in Damascus (and probably Arabia) before receiving any instruction from the other apostles (Acts 9:19-25, Gal. 1:12) and before he was even recognized as a Christian by the church (Acts 9:26). Saul was brought to Antioch by Barnabas (Acts 11:25-26). The other prophets and teachers at Antioch, directed by the Holy Spirit, sent Barnabas and Saul on the first missionary journey (Acts 13:1-3). There is no mention of the church or the elders having any part in the matter and no indication that they were under the supervision of either. Paul proposed the second missionary journey and when he and Barnabas failed to agree on taking John Mark they parted asunder (Acts 15:37-41). There is not the least implication in the record of this separation that Paul in any way proposed to assert his authority as an apostle and the outcome of the matter certainly shows that Barnabas considered himself at liberty to follow his own personal decision. There is no indication of any supervision by church or elders.

Apollos came to Ephesus preaching the baptism of John, but he was set right by Priscilla and Acquila (Acts 18:25-26). "And when he was minded to pass over into Achaia, the brethren encouraged him, and wrote to the disciples to receive him: and when he was come, he helped them much that had believed through grace" (Acts 18:27). It is apparent from this record that Apollos was not sent by any church when he came to Ephesus, neither was he under the supervision of any elders or church when he went to Achaia. The brethren at Ephesus only commended him.

This brief record of preaching the gospel as it is given in the New Testament makes it evident that it was neither controlled nor supervised by the church, by the local congregation, nor by the elders. This idea that it is mandatory that preachers work under the direction of a congregation, or that elders of a congregation must authorize the beginning of a new congregation by its members or supervise a new congregation that is begun, is without foundation. Certainly there should be united effort and harmony among brethren of any locality and Christian leadership should be respected and should be helpful to a new work in every way, but no one has any special lordship over the work.

Information relative to the financial support of preaching to be found in the New Testament record is very limited. It is clear, however, that preachers sometimes supported themselves: "Neither did we eat bread for nought at any man's hand, but in labor and travail, working night and day, that we might not burden any of you" (II Thess. 3:8). "Ye yourselves know that these hands ministered unto my necessities, and to them that were with me" (Acts 20:34). They received support from individuals: "Receive him (speaking of Epaphroditus) therefore in the Lord with all joy; and hold such in honor: because for the work of Christ he came nigh unto death, hazarding his life to supply that which was lacking in your service toward me" (Phil. 2:29-30) and "Beloved, (to Gaius) thou doest a faithful work in whatsoever thou doest toward them that are brethren and strangers withal; who bare witness to thy love before the church: whom thou wilt do well to set forward on their journey worthily of God" (III John 5-6). They also received support from Christians collectively or churches: "Or did I commit a sin in abasing myself that ye might be exalted, because

I preached to you the gospel of God for nought? I robbed other churches, taking wages of them that I might minister unto you" (II Cor. 11:7-8). It is also evident that more than one church or body of Christians contributed to the support of the same preacher (see II Cor. 11:7-8) and that some continued the support over an extended period of time: "For your fellowship in furtherance of the gospel from the first day until now" (Phil. 1:5) "And ye yourselves also know, ye Philippians, that in the beginning of the gospel, when I departed from Macedonia, no church had fellowship with me in the matter of giving and receiving but ye only" (Phil. 4:15). It is also obvious that the support was sent by brethren: "And when I was present with you and was in want, I was not a burden on any man; for the brethren, when they came from Macedonia, supplied the measure of my want; and in everything I kept myself from being burdensome unto you, and so will I keep myself" (II Cor. 11:9). "But I counted it necessary to send to you Epaphroditus, my brother and fellow-worker and fellow-soldier, and your messenger and minister to my need" (Phil. 2:25).

There is not one word of information in regard to how the support was raised or how it was handled by those to whom it was sent. We know only that it was sent by brethren. This means that we have no record of instruction to the Christians of the first century on how to provide funds for the spread of the gospel or how to handle funds received for that purpose; neither do we have any example of how these things were done. Therefore, anyone who would presume to claim scriptural support for his idea about how these things should be accomplished to the exclusion of all others is a bigot. God grant us the wisdom to avoid any such presumption on untaught matters and the Christian love to work together as brethren doing all things in the name of Christ to the glory of God.

QUESTIONS ON LESSON 12

1. What work of the church did we consider in the preceding lesson?
2. What was extended to Christians of other congregations?
3. What congregations are mentioned in speaking of love for others?
4. Relate the case where Christians of one congregation sent help to Christians of another section of the country.
5. Relate the case where Christians of several congregations joined in the work of supplying the needs of their brethren of another land.
6. In the case of Christians of one congregation sending to Christians of another section of the country, what are we told about the handling of the matter?
7. In the case of Christians of several congregations joining and sending help to Christians of other lands, what churches joined in the matter?
8. Show that this was apparently an effort of the Gentiles to show appreciation to the Jews.
9. What does Paul make clear to the Corinthians relative to this matter?
10. What explanation did he give to the Corinthians for his asking them to do this and what reciprocation might they expect?
11. What are we told of arrangements for carrying this money to Jerusalem?
12. What conclusion relative to the handling of these funds in Jerusalem is not too fully justified? Give evidence.
13. In these cases it is not a matter of a church or churches helping a church, but what is the correct description?

14. Of what is there no indication in the matter, but what does this not imply?
15. What ideas about Christian works, the work of the church, does this show to be without scriptural foundation?
16. What does James' statement show in regard to helping widows and children?
17. Give Paul's statement to the Galatians that indicates that the help should be extended to non-church people.
18. Show the inconsistency of objecting to the aid of non-church people.
19. What other work of the church has given rise to discussions over the details of its accomplishment?
20. The discussions have grown out of considering the preaching of the gospel to be the work of what?
21. Give a brief review of the early preaching.
22. Review the work of Paul's preaching as it related to the other apostles of the church.
23. Tell of Apollos' preaching and its relationship to the church.
24. What does this record of the preaching as given in the New Testament show relative to control and supervision?
25. From what sources were the preachers of the first century financially supported?
26. What record do we have of continuous or repeated support by one congregation?
27. How was the support gotten to the preacher?
28. On what matters relative to the support of preaching in the first century do we have neither instruction nor example?

THE CHURCH AT WORK (Continued)

Unfortunately there are sincere, honest, conscientious people who have accepted the Bible teaching that God's people should care for the needy, but have erroneously come to the conclusion that the most substantial arrangements that have been made for doing so are unscriptural; i.e., the orphan home and home for the aged. Some hold that the homes themselves are unscriptural, while others pronounce them unscriptural because of the methods employed in supporting and operating them. Those who hold that homes are wrong in themselves have come to this erroneous conclusion from the following reasoning.

Major premise: It is unscriptural to use any method, means, or arrangement in caring for the unfortunate today that was not used by Christians in the first century. Minor premise: Christians of the first century did not use "homes" to care for the unfortunate. Conclusion: Therefore, it is unscriptural for Christians to use or support "homes" to care for the unfortunate today. Is this conclusion sound? If so both the major and minor premise must be true.

Is this major premise true? What evidence is there to support it? You may have heard some man say that it is true, but there is not one word of support for it in the New Testament. It is true that Christians were admonished to be examples and to follow examples, but such instructions always have reference to what to do and never applied to the detailed manner in which it was to be done. On the other hand, when we take into consideration the manner in which the gospel teaching was revealed, it is evident that this major premise cannot be true. The epistles of the New Testament reveal to us the major portion of the teaching directed to Christians. We should not overlook the fact that they are not only addressed to the Christians in the first century and, consequently, the instruction given is expressed in terms of the conditions, customs, and experiences of the people of that day, but the messages of the epistles were revealed in vital proximity to the problems with which they had to deal, to guide them in their lives of service as children of God. Surely we should love God and man and show it as the Christians of the first century did by ministering to men's needs, especially those of the household of faith, in a way that they will be led to glorify God; but there is no reason to believe that we are to accomplish these things by the methods and techniques of the first century. It is grossly unreasonable to assume that the work of the church today in this twentieth century civilization, with its vast changes in human relationships and economic conditions that have given rise to problems of human welfare that were unknown to people of the first century, can be achieved successfully by procedures that were practicable in the solution of the problems of that day. Or, speaking from the other side of the picture, it is unthinkable and preposterous that the people of the first century should have been given detailed instructions on how to deal with problems of which they had no acquaintance and with which they would have no experience. Then how could they provide the example we are to follow in the solution of them? It is therefore unrealistic and without foundation in the scriptures to insist that Christians (the church) today must in meticulous detail restrict their efforts in accomplishing the work of the church, including caring for the unfortunate, to those activities for which the Christians of the first century set the example. Surely this is enough to leave no doubt that the major premise is untenable.

Now let us take a look at the minor premise: "Christians of the first century did not use 'homes' to care for the unfortunate." It may be possible that this statement is correct, but there is not one word of positive support for it in the New Testament. Apparently, since there is no specific mention of orphan homes or homes for the aged in the New Testament, people have assumed that they did not exist. Then thinking of the first century in terms of the customs of the twentieth century, they conclude that orphans were "adopted" or taken care of in the homes of others. This conclusion may be correct, but, so far as the New Testament is concerned, there is not one word of positive support for it. There was not one word of instruction given to Christians of that day to do such, neither is there a single case on record where they did. The only specific instruction given in the New Testament relative to caring for the aged is found in Paul's first letter to Timothy (I Tim. 5:1-16). Here Paul makes it plain that children should provide for their widowed mother or grandmother; or, if there were no children and the widow fulfilled the qualifications given, she should be provided for by the church. However, not one word was said as to how the matter was to be handled, either by children or church. Neither are we told how the matter was handled. So where is the example that is to be followed, either in the case of children or of aged people, and what grounds are there for helping an unfortunate man?

Since the major premise is false, and the minor premise is without positive support, upon what ground can we give credence to the conclusion? Furthermore, if it is unscriptural for Christians to own and operate orphan homes or homes for the aged today because they did not have such in New Testament days, how can we justify their owning and using church buildings, educational buildings, preacher's homes, Sunday School buses, and many other things which the Christians of the first century never used? Why should this reasoning be applied to "homes" and be ignored in other matters?

Those who hold "homes" to be unscriptural because of the methods employed in supporting and operating them attempt to support their charge in various ways, all of which are based on erroneous concepts of the church. So long as people think of Christians as separate and apart from the church, they will continue to wrangle over what Christians can do and what the church can do; and so long as people hold to the concept of exaggerated local autonomy in church organization, contentions over the technicalities of control or management in the work of the church will continue. But when the Bible concept of the church and of church organization as presented in these lessons is accepted, these wranglings and contentions will be without foundation and will naturally cease. These erroneous concepts of the church or of church organization or government have not only given rise to the charge that orphan homes and homes for the aged are unscriptural, but also have made it possible for the promoters of the charge to divide congregations, to steal church buildings, to ignore basic teachings of Christianity, and to disregard principles of social ethics. It is astonishing how religious zeal for some particular idea can blind people who have generally been considered honest and sincere, and lead them to follow and to justify practices that violate the inherent principles of their religion if they contribute to the success of their efforts. The efforts of these people are directed toward imposing their false doctrine upon congregations of Christians, and whatever success they may have attained can be attributed to the fact that the church of Christ people generally have accepted or countenanced the "rule" of the elders in the local congregation.

Taking advantage of this doctrinal error their scheme of operation seems to have been after this fashion. A preacher whose zeal and pride in personal accomplishment far outweigh his spiritual understanding of the word of God is led to accept the teaching that it is unscriptural for a congregation to give money to help support an orphan home. He arranges to preach for a congregation that holds no such idea and employs him without knowing that he does. In order to get the arrangement, he hides his convictions on this matter, leading the people to think that he believes as they do, in some cases even denying that he believes otherwise. (In some cases the congregation knows the preacher's conviction but employs him with the understanding that he will not preach the doctrine. This agreement is complied with in the pulpit, but in private the weight of the preacher's conviction is genuinely felt. The results, however, are much less effective.) He preaches for the congregation one, two, or even three years energetically pressing the Bible teaching on other subjects, thus winning the confidence of the people and by his personal attentions winning the favor of the people. At the same time, he carefully avoids saying anything in public that would reveal his conviction relative to orphan homes, but in private he takes advantage of every reasonable opportunity to indoctrinate many of the confiding members of the congregation, including the elders, if possible. When his private efforts have advanced to the point that he considers it advisable, he gradually takes the issue to the pulpit. If he has not succeeded in winning a majority of the elders, he will likely be asked to resign but may succeed in carrying a number of the members of the congregation away with him, or cause a split in the congregation and start a new one. If he succeeds in winning the elders, however, the situation becomes much worse. They announce that the congregation will no longer give to the support of orphan homes because it is unscriptural. Sometimes the members of the congregation, generally with little interest in helping the needy, acquiesce to the dictum of the elders and continue to be fed on the false doctrine; but more frequently a large percentage of the congregation is conscientiously opposed to the change and is unwilling to be party to the propagation of error by continuing to be part of the congregation. Thus, many members who have been a part of the congregation for a long time (in some cases from its very beginning), have contributed liberally to its spiritual development, and have struggled to help pay for the building or buildings which it occupies, are driven out from their rightful place to seek another place to worship because of their honest convictions. In fact, they are mercilessly robbed of that which is rightfully their own.

Is a preacher worthy of being trusted who secures arrangements to preach for a congregation under false pretense, who takes advantage of the situation by sneakingly peddling his false doctrine in private while deliberately giving or allowing through his public teaching the impression that he does not foster such ideas, and who not only deliberately sows discord among brethren but also is the chief promoter of action which forcibly takes away the property rights of many of those who cannot conscientiously accept the erroneous stand forced upon the congregation? In this he plays a role very similar to that of the hitchhiker who accepts the hospitality of the car owner and rides as far as it is convenient for the car owner to go, draws his gun and forces the rightful owner to get out of the car, then drives on.

Are elders worthy to be trusted who are so ignorant of

the word of God; who are so unstable in their convictions and so gullible that they can be turned away by the teaching of one man from a practice that not only they have endorsed and followed for years but one that has been followed by a brotherhood; and who issue the dictum without making an unbiased re-study of the matter that the congregation will no longer give to the support of orphan homes, knowing that they are ignoring the long standing conviction of a large part of the congregation, that they are driving a wedge that will split the congregation and that they are taking away the privileges and the property rights of a large number of the brethren by forcing them out of the congregation? They have surely overlooked or ignored Paul's charge to the elders of the church at Ephesus to feed ALL the flock. "Take heed unto yourselves, and to all the flock, in which the Holy Spirit hath made you bishops, to feed the church of the Lord which he purchased with his own blood" (Acts 20:28).

You may wonder how the preachers, the elders, and their followers in this campaign against congregational support of orphan homes can be party to such unchristian and unethical practices and then add insult to injury in an effort to justify the whole dastardly performance by charging those who oppose them with institutionalizing the church. In reality it is the natural result of a combination of two basic influences, zeal and ignorance. In Bible terms, "They have a zeal for God, but not according to knowledge" (Rom. 10:2). It is strikingly coincidental that the charge against those who practice the congregational support of orphan homes does name the most potent factor in the development of this ugly situation, although it is falsely identified and misapplied. The use of orphan homes and other similar means in accomplishing Christian work can by no reasonable stretch of the imagination be designated as "institutionalizing the church," but the misunderstanding of these arrangements that has given rise to the charge that they are unscriptural and also the unchristian practices that have accompanied it, have been the result of "institutionalizing the church." What has been thought of as the church, the local church, was institutionalized years ago by the accusers and the accused conjointly. To "institutionalize" means to make a thing an institution; that is, to make it an organization with certain vested powers of control. In the local congregation these powers were attributed to the elders. The people of the church generally subscribed to the arrangement theoretically. Those who have pressed this contention over the orphan homes etc., have simply put the theory into application. Accept the institutional concept of the local congregation and you have laid a foundation which will logically support just what has been happening. The acceptance of the concept of the local congregation as an organization in which the elders are vested with dictatorial powers inescapably poses the question of control.

Several years ago when the church people began to awaken to some sense of obligation beyond that of having preaching in the local congregation the most outstanding example of this matter of control was the contention that all work should be done through the church, and that it was unscriptural for an individual to contribute to a Christian work directly or personally. In recent years, however, since the work being attempted by the church has increased so much that ways and means to accomplish it have become matters of concern, not only has the right of the individual Christian to give to a Christian directly been generally accepted as being scriptural, but there are also many people who insist that there are Christian works that can be done by individual Christians which cannot be done by the church; that Christians can give individually to the support of orphan homes, but it is unscriptural for a congregation to do so. The question of control is responsible for the contention that an orphan home should be under the direct control of the elders of a congregation and for all other contentions that are a part of this situation.

From this discussion it should be clear that not only the contentions and the divisions that have arisen over the orphan home question, but also the unchristian practices that have accompanied them, have been a logical outgrowth of the erroneous concept of the church. As long as elders are thought of as rulers with the power of arbitrary decisions, we have a local situation which is very similar to the total situation in the Catholic church. Those who grant the pope the place that he proposes to occupy accept his decree as having divine endorsement. Likewise those who accept elders as rulers of the congregation seem to regard their decision as having Biblical endorsement and consequently feel justified in complying with it without giving consideration to the inconvenience and injustice it brings to their brethren. If we will quit consuming the most of our time in wrangling over the detailed acts of Christianity and learn and teach the basic Bible concepts and principles that should govern our behavior, we would accomplish much more in the cause of our Lord. Every honest, sincere person who has the Spirit of Christ and understands that elders are to be shepherds and not dictators, with a personal responsibility for the welfare of every member of the flock (Acts 20:28), as a leader not as a driver, will find the methods that have been employed to impose the false doctrine relative to orphan homes upon Christian people repulsive and intolerable. No honest, sincere elder who has learned that he is to be a shepherd of God's people, who loves the brethren as every Christian does who loves God (I John 5:1, 4:20), and who has shared with his brethren the conviction that congregational help to orphan homes is scriptural and good, can selfishly ignore the right of his brethren who still hold the conviction to continue to share in the joint effort to accomplish the work.

You may ask, "What will, or what can, such elders do under the circumstances?" When this new teaching is introduced by the local preacher, or by some visiting preacher in a meeting, the elders will proceed to evaluate it through individual and collective Bible study with the help of Bible students who oppose such teaching as well as those who favor it. If they fail to come to an agreement on the matter, they will continue the study until they do, or will leave the matter unchanged. If they come to an agreement that the change is demanded by the Bible teaching, they will make every reasonable effort to teach the congregation. If they succeed, the change should be made. If they fail they will remember that elders are leaders, not drivers, that they have no right to enforce their convictions upon the brethren, and that sins are individual and not congregational. Those who do not agree in the matter and want to continue their group support should be permitted to do so. If such an elder becomes discontent and is unwilling to continue patiently his effort to lead the congregation, he will resign his place of leadership or withdraw from the congregation to worship elsewhere, but he will not be party to forcing other members to leave. He will not stoop to such unchristian practices.

This erroneous concept of the church and church organization has not only laid many congregations open to abuse by those who are at present teaching error relative to orphan homes etc., but it was also largely responsible for the havoc wrought in the church by those who introduced the society and instrumental music, and it will continue down through the years to make the church an easy prey for those who rebel against the present order of things or seek to impose new devisive doctrines. Why not correct the error that is inviting error and encouraging the spread of error by learning the Bible concept of the church and church organization?

In the New Testament description of the church at work, it is clear that not only was financial aid extended to Christians of other congregations, to the people who needed it who were not Christians, but the spiritual help was also given to Christians of other localities and the gospel was preached to those who were not Christians. All of this work was accomplished by Christians working individually or collectively and not by churches as organizations.

QUESTIONS ON LESSON 13

1. On what two bases have some people pronounced orphan homes and homes for the aged unscriptural?
2. Give the reasoning from which many have concluded that homes are wrong in themselves.
3. Consideration of what makes it evident that the major premise cannot be true?
4. The New Testament teaching directed to Christians was addressed to whom, expressed in what terms, and given for what purpose?
5. What must Christians today do that the Christians of the first century did?
6. Why is there no reason to believe that this must be accomplished today by the same methods or techniques employed in the first century?
7. Why is it unthinkable and preposterous that the people of the first century should have been given detailed instructions on how to handle the problems of the twentieth century?
8. What is unrealistic and without foundation in the scriptures relative to the work of Christians today?
9. How much positive support is there to be found in the New Testament for the idea that Christians of the first century did not use homes to care for the unfortunate?
10. In the only specific instruction given in the New Testament relative to caring for the aged what instruction is completely lacking?
11. What has been shown to be wrong with the major premise and with the minor premise?

12. If we can make use only of means and methods employed by the Christians of the first century in accomplishing their work what practices among us are unscriptural?

13. The support employed by those who hold "homes" to be unscriptural because of the methods employed in operating and supporting them is based in what erroneous concepts?

14. How long will these contentions over the technicalities of control or management in the work of the church continue?

15. When will these wranglings cease?

16. What other activities that have been practiced among us have been made possible by these false concepts of the church?

17. To what can their success in these matters be attributed?

18. Briefly outline the scheme that is often followed in the effort to spread the erroneous doctrine about "homes."

19. Depict the ugly place of the preacher in such a scheme.

20. What illustration is used to point out the role which he plays?

21. Describe the part played by the elders in this scheme.

22. What charge to elders have they surely overlooked or ignored?

23. How do the supporters of this erroneous doctrine add insult to injury?

24. Instead of the use of orphan homes, etc. being the "institutionalizing of the church," how has the church been institutionalized?

25. What only have those who have pressed this contention over the orphan homes, etc. done?

26. Several years ago wherein lay the control of the work that should be done by the church and what change has been accepted in recent years?

27. What other contention over the orphan home has been a result of this question of control?

28. According to this discussion what have been outgrowths of the erroneous concepts of the church?

29. What influence do elders, when accepted as rulers, have that is similar to that of the pope?

30. What changes in our activities would lead to the accomplishment of much more in the cause of our Lord?

31. Who will find the methods used to impose the false doctrine relative to orphan homes repulsive and intolerable?

32. Who cannot selfishly ignore the right of his brethren to share jointly in this work?
33. What can elders do who have decided an established practice is wrong?
34. What other false teaching wrought havoc after the same fashion because of the erroneous concept of the church?

THE ORGANIZATION OF THE CHURCH

Human and Divine

Since our study of the Bible teaching relative to the church and its organization has been somewhat analytical in character and has been somewhat extended through the method of comparison with erroneous concepts, it appears advisable that we give further emphasis to the divine plan of organization of the church by contrasting it with the human plans. We shall not attempt to contrast it with the separate plans individually for they are legion. All of the human forms of church government may be very well classified into two groups on the basis of their respective characteristic departures from the truth.

The majority of the churches or denominations have adopted for their respective peoples some form of universal human organization. Each of these religious peoples have vested the power of control of their entire church or total population either in one man or in a body of men that exercises its authority over the individual members or through local organizations or through regional and local organizations. These various religious peoples not only vary widely in the details of their respective organizations, but also in the powers attributed to the individual or the body at its head. In some cases these powers may be only nominal or routine, in others the unrestricted power of interpreting the scriptures and dictating the practices of its membership, while still others are allowed the power of decree through which they may set aside certain Bible teachings or may impose human demands presumably with divine sanction. All of these have departed from the church organization of the first century as it is revealed in the Bible in that they have interposed a human control between God and man attributing to the church as they represent it powers and rights that tend to exalt the human and to depreciate the divine.

There are other religious people who have virtually overlooked the divine, universal organization of the church and in their opposition to the human plans of universal church organizations, they have overdrawn the authorities and powers of the local congregation. They have pled for the autonomy of the local congregation and have declared control through any type of human universal organization to be unscriptural. The latter is correct, but the former is only partly correct. The idea of local autonomy is applicable only in a negative sense. It can only be taken to indicate that the local congregation is not subject to the control of any universal human organization, but it cannot mean that the local organization of the congregation exercises a power of control over its membership in any sense comparable to that of the human universal organization.

In the church of the first century there was no such thing as congregational autonomy, neither is there any such thing as congregational autonomy in the church of the Bible today. This doctrine of local or congregational autonomy is the outgrowth of the ruler concept of elders. This concept has already been shown to be without scriptural foundation. No man, or set of men, has ever been given the power of rule over a congregation, or over any member of a congregation, of God's people. Christ is Lord and ruler and there is none other. The word "autonomy" means power of self government. Strictly speaking, the word has no place in Christianity and even if it is to be used loosely, it is more suitably applied to the individual. If there is such a thing as autonomy, it is individual autonomy. The individual Christian is personally responsible for what he does and therefore holds the right to make his own decisions. This is especially true today as everyone has access to the word of God and is responsible for making his decisions in keeping with it. This in no wise prevents unity of action or cooperative effort, but it does require that such be the result of unity of thinking. Elders are leaders, and leadership is made effective through harmonious thinking.

The divine organization of the church as revealed in the New Testament is simply this: Christ is Lord and ruler over the church or assembly of God's people. He is Lord and ruler of each individual Christian and each Christian is subject to him directly and personally. The relationship of Christians to each other in the church is that of children in the same family or of the members in the human body subject to the one head. No child in the family or member in the body has power or control over any other, but there should be mutual consideration (Eph. 5:21). The more mature, the more spiritual, should take the lead and should be respected as leaders in the cooperative effort of Christians (I Cor. 16: 15-16, I Thess. 5:12-13). This cooperative effort has been made more effective by the appointment of elders, bishops, or shepherds to lead the flock of which they are a part. This leadership is primarily functional in the local congregation (Titus 1:5, Acts 14:23), but its influence should contribute to the edification and work of the universal church (Eph. 4:11-16). An elder's leadership is coextensive with his Christian influence and his obligations parallel his opportunities for helpfulness to every child of God whether he is a member of the congregation where the elder attends or not. The establishing or formal placing of one's membership with a congregation is not requisite to being under the leadership of its elders; this should be the natural result of Christian association. If we consider elders as leaders not dictators our forms and technicalities become unnecessary.

May God hasten the day when we open our hearts to his divine message and learn to rely fully upon its power and be content with its organization, the effectiveness of which is the natural product of the vital Christian relationships.

Printed in the United States
117201LV00001B/376/A

The HOUND
of DISTRIBUTISM

Edited by Richard Aleman

CONTRIBUTING WRITERS:
Dale Ahlquist, Dr. William E. Fahey, G.K.Chesterton,
Russell Sparkes, Thomas Storck, Joseph Pearce, Dr. Peter Chojnowski,
David W. Cooney, Mark & Louise Zwick, John Médaille,
Phillip Blond, Philippe Maxence, Donald P. Goodman III, Bill Powell,
Hon. Dr. Race Mathews, Ryan Grant, Richard Aleman

ACS
BOOKS

Printed in the United States of America

Cover and Interior design by Ted Schluenderfritz

LCCN: 2011945191

ISBN: 978-0-974495-3-9

Dedicated to the memory of
Richard J. Gill, who passed
away on October 31st, 2011.

Requiescat in Pace.

Domini canes *or "The Hounds of the Lord" is a name given to The Order of Preachers, commonly known as the Dominican Order. According to tradition, while pregnant with the great saint, St. Dominic's mother had a vision of a black dog with torch in mouth setting fire to the world with the Gospel. In art, St. Dominic is typically depicted with a white or black canine by his side. As the symbol of the historic Guild of St. Joseph and St. Dominic, the Distributist fraternity of craftworkers in Ditchling, England, the hound has also grown to be associated with Distributism.*

TABLE OF CONTENTS

v

WHAT'S WRONG WITH THE WORLD
(and How to Fix It)

BY DALE AHLQUIST

"That Keyword, which unlocks the doors of all politics and all economy, is Family." —G.K.CHESTERTON

MOST NORMAL, CAREFREE PEOPLE WOULD RATHER AVOID ARGUING about politics and religion. They fall in love and get married and, in the normal course of events, have children. Then they begin thinking about two things: the world in which they are raising their child, and the soul of their child. In other words, they start thinking about politics and religion.

Unfortunately, most people with families don't have the time and money to become political activists. Most of the people who do have the time and the money to be political activists don't have families; the laws these people lobby for with great success represent *special* interest groups, but they do not represent the interests of that *general* interest group, the family. As a result, most laws are very much anti-family.

Liberals are always defending the rights of various oppressed minorities. Many people are oppressed and need to be defended. Unfortunately, liberals tend to defend rights that are not rights at all. They are wrongs, such as abortion and same-sex "marriage."

Conservatives are always defending free trade, but there is nothing free about it. It is very expensive and thus reserved for the realm of the very rich. Conservatives are always defending less government and lower taxes. And indeed, government is too big and taxes are too high. But the rich pay too many taxes only because they make too much money. Poor people don't pay enough taxes because they don't make enough money. G.K.Chesterton says, "It is a bad economic sign in the State that masses of our fellow-citizens are too poor to be taxed." [1]

In general, the Left represents big government and the Right represents big business. The Left represents socialism and the Right represents capitalism. The two are the same thing because both are against the widespread distribution of private property. Chesterton says, "Socialism and Capitalism are today fundamentally the same. They both aim at control of a servile nation by a bureaucratic class, centralized; which of course, means a centralized financial control."

The liberal few and the conservative few want to control property and capital. Both use each other and even depend on each other. Big government has its hands on big money. Big money has its hands on big government. Hilaire Belloc described this as the *Servile State*, and Chesterton says, "The Servile State uses Socialists and Anti-Socialists alike as its tools."

There is something desperately wrong with the world when something so basic, so traditional, so universal, and so *normal* as the family has to be defended. The family is the strength of any strong society. It is what passes the culture from one generation to the next. It is what lasts in any lasting society. It is what thrives in any thriving society.

Chesterton calls the family a tiny kingdom that creates and loves its own citizens. The family will do a better job of protecting, nurturing, educating, and helping people than any outside official agency or any hired servant. Everything about the *Servile State* undermines the family. Big government tries to replace the authority and functions of the family. Big business breaks up the family by pulling both the father and the mother out of the home and reducing them to wage slaves.

"It has come to pass that workingmen have been surrendered, all isolated and helpless, to the hard-heartedness of employers and the

---

[1] *The Collected Works of G.K.Chesterton*, Volume 33.

greed of unchecked competition... A small number of very rich men have been able to lay upon the teeming masses of the laboring poor a yoke little better than that of slavery itself." [2]

These are the words of Pope Leo XIII in his 1891 Encyclical *Rerum Novarum,* which is the basis of Catholic social teaching and is also the basis for Distributism. In order for the family to have its proper authority in a society, local government must be more influential than state or federal government. Local government means neighbors who are accountable to each other.

"When politics were more local," says Chesterton, "they were more truthful." The state should fulfill no more than its minor role in our lives. This is the principle known as *subsidiarity* that speaks of what the higher orders owe the lower orders. The most important decisions must be left to individuals, to families, to local communities. The central government's only responsibility should be to provide those services, which cannot be provided otherwise—and that should be a short list.

Government should not provide for needs, including humanitarian and educational needs that traditionally were served by religion. Religion provided these things because religion has a higher purpose. When the state provides them, there is no higher purpose and the things become ends in themselves. State support of the arts leads to art for art's sake. State support of health care leads to health for health's sake. State support of education leads to the vanity and dead end of knowledge for knowledge's sake. A large, purely secular state will be empty at its core and will collapse on itself; it simply cannot be sustained, certainly not when the only thing left to sustain it is sheer coercion. The state that is supposed to defend our freedom slowly destroys our freedom, which is why Chesterton says, "We do not get good laws to restrain bad people. We get good people to restrain bad laws."

The word *liberal* has to do with freedom. The word *conservative* has to do with keeping tradition. Freedom and tradition are good things.

---

[2] Leo XIII, *Rerum Novarum* §3.

But freedom means responsibility, not irresponsibility. And conservative does not mean leaving something alone; it means we have to work hard just to keep things the same. If we want a white post, we have to keep painting it white.

Nevertheless, it is useful to remind liberals and conservatives about the meanings of the words they use to describe themselves. It is not *liberal* to have compulsory education, compulsory insurance, and compulsory temperance. It is not *conservative* when small businesses are not conserved, when local shops owned by our neighbors are not conserved, when small farms are not conserved.

While liberals and the conservatives bicker about who has the better system, the real problem is that we are living under both systems right now. Socialism and capitalism are not at war with each other—they are in cahoots with each other. They have formed that unholy alliance, the *Servile State*—big government propped up by big business, and big business propped up by big government.

We see examples of the *Servile State* everywhere: the military-industrial complex; the state and federal highway system that supports the automobile industry; a news industry that has a mutually parasitic relationship with the government; a huge bureaucracy that is supported by the regulation of industry; an industry that is supported by huge government contracts, and government bailouts of banks and insurance companies.

We have an economy that is largely based on exchange rather than on production. Our main industries are Health and Education, which are also big branches of government (which is why we are moving toward national health insurance to match a national education system—to prop up another huge industry that cannot support itself).

Farming has become industrialized and so is subsidized. In every town there once was a public square, a free, open area, not only for buying and selling, but also for talking and yelling and arguing. Now we have shopping malls, which are private places for buying and selling, where people are herded along and kept in line, and these giant commercial spaces are underwritten by the state through tax increment financing.

4

The vast majority of the population are either wage slaves or bureaucrats. A clerk sitting at a desk does not know the difference, whether he is working for a large corporation or a large state agency.

Both liberals and conservatives have gotten it wrong. One side emphasizes freedom without responsibility (or rights without responsibility). The other emphasizes the responsibility without the freedom. Which side does which? It depends on whether you're talking about sex or money. Liberals want sex without responsibility and conservatives want money without responsibility. The liberals' liberalization of sex and the conservatives' conservation of money are both gigantic moral problems that damage our society because they both undermine the family.

Catholic social teaching is about protecting the family; all the social encyclicals reinforce this. But the most important Catholic document defending the family in the modern world arrived in 1968, *Humanae Vitae*. Pope Paul VI saw the dangers of contraception at the time, but the destruction today is even more pervasive than he foretold. A contraceptive mentality is raping the earth. It is the contraceptive mentality that is responsible for the the "myopic nature of modern economics." More wealth actually brings more misery, engendering fruitless, self-serving desires that can never be fulfilled. An economy based on the philosophy that "bigger is better" can never be satisfied, because there can never be *enough*; there can only be *more*.

The contraceptive mentality also leads to the notion of lending, that is, of building endless debt and never paying for anything. Take the pleasure and run. But a consumer-driven society that is buying but never paying is headed for collapse. This is the same mode of insanity described by Chesterton when he talks about the modern world that "exalts lust but forbids fertility." It cannot be sustained.

Yet, anyone who talks about restraint is vilified, whether it is restraint in "free trade" or "free love." The truth is that neither trade nor love is free. Both require responsibility and discipline; both require limits. It is the idea of limits that the modern world finds so repugnant. Freedom is mistakenly understood as the throwing off of restraint. But true freedom exists within the rules. Freedom, which is self-government, means self-control. The essence of Distributism is self-government, self-control, and self-sufficiency. The foundation of Distributism is ownership. The heart of Distributism is the family. The state and the marketplace must serve the family; not the other way around. We must make government and commerce more local and more accountable.

Where do we begin? By hating the world enough to change it, and loving it enough to think it worth changing.

Dale Ahlquist is the president of the American Chesterton Society. He is the creator and host of the Eternal Word Television Network series, G.K.Chesterton: The Apostle of Common Sense. *Dale is the author of three books including* Common Sense 101: Lessons From G.K.Chesterton, *the publisher of* Gilbert Magazine, *and co-founder of Chesterton Academy, a new high school in Minneapolis.*

Towards a Description of Distributism

BY DR. WILLIAM E. FAHEY

"Half our time is taken up with explaining to the Communist that we are not defending Capitalism; and explaining to the Capitalist that we are not defending Communism." —G.K.CHESTERTON

LECTOR   *This looks like a play.*

SCRIPTOR   Perhaps, but it does not have the formal discipline of parts. A scholar might say that it is a "dialogic propaedeutic."

LECTOR   *Is that painful?*

SCRIPTOR   Always.

LECTOR   *But what does it mean, "dialogic pro-pae-deu-tic"?*

SCRIPTOR   An initial conversation, not unlike a play.

LECTOR   *What is the point of that? After all, this is a book on economics is it not? If I want a play, I will go elsewhere. I want to understand economics and politics—hard things about the real world. And that means prose.*

SCRIPTOR   I would prefer to chat first, about ideas.

LECTOR   *Are these ideas related to the world, the real world?*

SCRIPTOR   Oh yes, they spring to life in it, they can move it or at least give it some meaning. You'll find them interesting, Lector.

LECTOR *Why all the Latin—"scriptor-lector"—nonsense?*

SCRIPTOR Because it is traditional, and if you want to proceed in this book, you need to learn how to participate in tradition.

LECTOR *It doesn't seem very informed by real concerns. I want my prose. At the very least, I want to learn something about economics and all the bally-who about "Distributism." That is a very ugly word, but it seems to be used more and more these days. I don't like it. It is foreign.*

SCRIPTOR I like your instincts. It is an ugly word. I am willing to try to help you learn, but on several conditions.

LECTOR *Which are?*

SCRIPTOR First, we proceed with the dialogic propaedeutic. I find it more inviting; it gives you a stake and a place. You'll have some ownership in this little introduction.

LECTOR *Fine, I want a part in things. But aren't you the one directing the whole affair? I mean, how is it really mine if I am not writing my own part? I am just a slave to your directions. I'm just reading another fellow's words.*

SCRIPTOR Fair enough, but I wouldn't go all that far with always being an absolutely free creator of your own destiny. You'll find yourself in a garden staring at a tree with fruit good to eat and a delight to the eyes, and the next thing you know you'll be sprawling in the dust. Why read anything written by others? Why not just create your own essays? Doesn't learning require a bit of direction and more often than not, quite a bit?

LECTOR *Yes, I see. But why the "dialogic" stuff?*

SCRIPTOR Because… it allows you to enact things in your imagination. That's not a good place to end, but it's a fair place to start. For a short space, I will offer you as much experience on the matter and in such a way that you can turn it all over in your mind and make your own judgment. That seems to respect your freedom and creativity considerably. We chat, and then you act. Fair?

LECTOR *We'll see. What were those other conditions?*

SCRIPTOR Second, I bring in authorities to speak as I see fit without notation.

LECTOR *Wait a minute. That seems dodgy.*

SCRIPTOR Not in the least. I will be upfront on who is speaking directly; after all, I want you to rub up against some seasoned minds, not just my own thoughts. What's more, I solemnly promise to quote accurately and allude appropriately, but I don't want to hide behind the barricade of footnotes or an enlarged apparatus criticus.

LECTOR *Apparatus criticus... I believe that is what did in my great uncle.*

SCRIPTOR Was he German?

LECTOR *I believe so.*

SCRIPTOR Yes, well, in any case, dense notes rarely denote pleasant reading. I will respect your judgment and leave you the initiative to go read more on your own. In fact, I would quite like it if you did.

LECTOR *All right, but let's not move too fast and don't throw too many authors at me. Just give me some basics. From the looks of it, these other authors in this book seem to cover a lot of ground.*

SCRIPTOR Good. Then, I shall rely on perhaps three authorities. That is a good number. Now, why is it that you are interested in the matter of Distributism? How did you hear of it?

LECTOR *I read a bit about it and the people I read are talking about it. It is in blogs and magazines. There are whole books on it now, but I don't know where to start. No one really agrees on what it is. It doesn't quite seem to be anything modern.*

SCRIPTOR How true. Let's just start with the word itself.

LECTOR *Begin. Tell me, what does it mean—Distributism: it has an "-ism" at the end: as in "socialism," or "communism." I don't like it.*

SCRIPTOR Surely, the "-ism" itself is not the issue: after all, there is "liberalism," and "conservatism" (or so they say); there is "polytheism" and "monotheism;" "cosmopolitanism" and "patriotism;" "Catholicism," "gingerism," and a thousand more.

LECTOR *What's that last one?*

SCRIPTOR It pertains to redheads. Best left alone. The suffix "-ism" typically refers to a practice or condition, or ideas that lead to actions or conditions, or sometimes it is just a group of ideas that describes a way of thinking about things.

LECTOR *So, "Distributism" is a group of ideas that lead to distributing something or at least a word that names the ideas about distributing something? What thing? And who gets to distribute and why?*

SCRIPTOR Well, I haven't finished with the word itself, but if you must know, let's just look at a famous definition of Distributism by Mr. Hilaire Belloc:

"A state of society in which the families composing it are, in a determining number, owners of the land and the means of production as well as themselves the agents of production (that is, the people who by their human energy produce wealth with the means of production)…"

That comes from his book…

LECTOR *I am lost. There is too much I don't understand in that statement.*

SCRIPTOR As I was trying to say, that comes from Mr. Belloc's book, *Economics for Helen*, which was written for his young niece. Along with his *Servile State* and An Essay on the Restoration of Property, it presents Belloc's major views on politics and economics.

LECTOR *It seems hopelessly dated. I mean "owners of land," and "means of production"… what are we all supposed to be peasant farmers and brewers?*

SCRIPTOR No. Belloc is a very apt writer. He requires apt readers. Note his expression "determining number."

LECTOR *Yes, I was confused on that. What's it mean?*

SCRIPTOR It means that society is very good if there are enough of those who own land independently and brew their own beer that the larger society takes inspiration from them and agrees that such a life is jolly, noble, and worth living.

LECTOR *Well, I must admit, I would like to own land myself. And I do like beer.*

SCRIPTOR Then, my friend, you are practically a distributist already. Of course, by "brewing beer" I mean making things for yourself and others, in general; it needn't be beer.

LECTOR *Could it be cheese?*

SCRIPTOR Most assuredly. The world needs more cheese, especially artisan goat cheese.

LECTOR *But we can't make everything ourselves. What about free exchange and markets and the benefits that come from the division of labor and specialization, and all that.*

SCRIPTOR Good questions, but you're losing your focus. Distributists do not deny that great goods can come from craftsmanship and specialized work and exchange.

LECTOR *Wait, wait. I have heard that distributists want everyone to live in a primitive, self-sufficient state. No credit cards, no coffee shops, no modern medicine, everyone wears straw hats, etc.*

SCRIPTOR Etc. Well, let's put aside what constitutes the good of society for the moment and just address a misconception. First, though you may say "distributists" and I may say "distributists," we must be clear—there is a lot of diversity under that rubric. Some are more in favor of new technology, some less, but that doesn't address the essence of Distributism. Belloc was clear on the issue you really are driving at—economic exchange and the blessings of surplus wealth:

"Men cannot fulfill themselves save through a diversity of interests and ideas ... Each, in a society, will concentrate upon what he has the best opportunity for producing and, by exchanging his surplus of it for that which another has the best opportunity of producing, will increase the wealth of all."

On the business of the simple life and living like figures of the past... well, to be honest, the distributists did not agree; nor did they need to.

LECTOR *Yes, but what about creativity and the very personal nature of value inherit in wealth? Again, I have heard that distributists only want a static society and have no real understanding of creativity.*

SCRIPTOR If only the critics would read the old books by distributists, they would find both specific answers, but also a grand degree of creativity. Let these two statements by Belloc satisfy you:

"Wealth is made up, not of things, but of economic values attaching to things."

"Man is perpetually changing the things around him from a condition in which they are less useful to him into a condition where they are more useful to him. Whenever a man does that he is said to be creating, and adding to, Human Wealth."

LECTOR *So, they do like creativity and exchange and... wealth.*

SCRIPTOR In fact, they revel in it, in a way, but it is not the center of life, it isn't even the center of Distributism. They wish to encourage a certain amount of spiritedness with respect to property and responsibilities in community life.

LECTOR *Stop right there. Do these distributists or do they not believe in private property? If they do, why do they attach the discussion to community life. And why do they seem to hate big businesses, by the way?*

SCRIPTOR Private property is a fundamental doctrine of Distributism, my friend. Yet distributists are rather traditional in believing all "private" affairs are embedded in a larger social reality. But to speak to what seems to be your concern: Distributists are only against big things which seem to diminish the freedom and creativity of little things. To the extent that a big brewery swallows up smaller ones and over time destroys men's sense of the goodness of that thing called beer, it will be opposed. This is not because the Distributist is against the freedom of the big business, it is because he thinks the freedom of the little business should take priority.

LECTOR *Just because it is little. That is idiotic. Sometimes big things get the job done.*

SCRIPTOR Indeed, and distributists have always encouraged a sense of scale; and certain sectors of economic life, they contended, need to be large and co-ordinated—transportation systems, for example. Yet, as many businesses as possible should be localized, or decentralized, because most information and consumption and accountability is kept close to home.

LECTOR *What do you mean?*

SCRIPTOR Well, first a negative point—consider most cases of financial ne-glect or mismanagement, or for that matter what is now called "environmental disasters." Are these typically little affairs or big? Are they generated through large or small institutions? Do they effect small regions or large?

LECTOR *Big in every case, but individuals are still responsible—big or small. What's the point? Big business means a big problem when the business fails.*

SCRIPTOR Exactly. Little business, little problems. Information is exchanged and change happens—even in our mercurial world—most effectively over time in a little world. When we have a problem with a little business we can fix it or kill it quickly through complaints. But when a big business (mind you, a big business that does not in any absolute sense need to be big—like our brewery), when a big business is not interested in responding or unable to respond to local variation or concern, it can ride it out because of its bigness. In fact, a big business can usually change local perceptions and actions over time for the worse.

LECTOR *Give me an example, one that helps me see why this is a problem.*

SCRIPTOR Beer. Once brewed everywhere it was then destroyed as a household affair or a local affair and breweries—with some ham-fisted government intervention—became big and without variety, but with great economies of scale that allowed those big breweries to kill the little ones…

LECTOR *Wait a minute. There are plenty of little breweries now and anyone can buy a beer kit. The market responded to a need and restored little breweries and lots of diversity. Why are you against the market?*

SCRIPTOR I never said I was against the market. I am for the market. The market is a very good place to buy bacon, and sweaters, and beer. Distributists are not against the market, nor exchange. And your noticing the restoration of little breweries only underscores my point, and a great victory of the distributist spirit: the restoration of small enterprises, happily done through the market… but only after the right ideas took hold. The market, in this instance, brought us right back to the more natural level of production and distribution that a distributist champions. It was collusion between government and business that created the industrial beer giants during Prohibition. The distributists, by the way, hated the idea of Prohibition.

LECTOR *I am against Prohibition, too. But tell me more about "the right ideas" part of what you were saying. This is interesting and real. Oh, by the way, I should say, I do, now and again, on a hot day, like to have one of those big beer company beers.*

SCRIPTOR My friend, so do I. As I said, what a distributist is against is really secondary, so long as what he is for is vibrant and shapes the society. A good society—for the distributist—would be one with many, many little breweries. If in that world there were also a few very large breweries, then may God bless them. The key is that society be shot through with a central idea and that idea be sustained in real enterprises. Belloc said in another of his books—An Essay on the Restoration of Property—that he was trying to awaken a "mood" or an "attitude of mind," what I might call desire.

LECTOR *Desire? That's sounds rather racy for politics and economics. Tell me more, please.*

SCRIPTOR The desire is the desire to wish for a worthy life and to work for it by establishing a certain degree of freedom from political or economic coercion. That freedom traditionally came from living in a society where "the determining number" of families owned things like land and the means of production, so that their creativity bore fruit and sustained a good life.

LECTOR *And what's the "mood" for?*

SCRIPTOR I like how you end with "for". That's good thinking, if bad syntax. Perhaps you've read some Aristotle. The mood is a mood for doing things yourself, for living and for making and for being free to live and make and support your family. It's a mood or disposition against feeling that you can't do those things or that they must be done for you by a company or a government. It's the very desire to live for some good purpose and…

LECTOR *Hold on, you're getting ahead of me. There's another one of those expressions that confuses me—"the determining number". You place it in quotes…*

SCRIPTOR Quotation marks.

LECTOR *You place it in quotation marks; therefore, it must mean something; that whole passage must mean something, because you're quoting an authority. What does it mean?*

SCRIPTOR The quotation marks give the expression a defined place in the sentence. The three words, we could say, give the sentence a tone—which you naturally detected. Not every word contributed the same way to the tone. Those words within the quotation, by the means of the boundaries of those quotations, really are the determining number of words that change the very nature of the whole sentence. So, do you see now? "Determining number" is not necessarily a majority. It depends on the context and the strength of the determining body. But a determining number clearly is enough to establish the tone and, in fact, helps enormously to define everything else around it.

LECTOR *In a sentence or a society.*

SCRIPTOR Exactly. Now, as I was saying. Distributism has a first part: "distribute" which is based on two old Latin roots that essentially mean "to arrange with distinct care." Applied to the realm of politics, Distributism is the arrangement of property and anything else that helps generate sustaining wealth for families. This wealth—whether it be derived from land, property, or other means by which wealth is produced—comes from things held independently by families.

LECTOR *Why do you keep saying families? Don't you mean individuals?*

SCRIPTOR Oh no, good reader (id est, lector bonus), I do not. It is very true that the right to own is private, that it is a right that belongs to individual men.

LECTOR *And women!*

SCRIPTOR I concede the point to you, lector and to thee, fair lectrix. The right to private property by its nature belongs to an individual, but individuals live in society; and distributists are emphatic that property is to support that bedrock unit of society, the family. In fact, the great grandfather of Distributism, Pope Leo XIII, said that "a person must possess this right so much the more clearly in proportion as his position multiplies his duties," by which he meant the duties of sustaining families and sustaining society.

LECTOR *Wait a minute, Distributism has as its founder a Roman Pope?*

SCRIPTOR Is there another kind?

LECTOR *You know what I mean: Distributism is the creation of the Catholic Church? I thought it was a group of Englishmen?*

SCRIPTOR A group of Englishmen spent a fair amount of time giving the idea a fresh articulation, but they derived it from older sources, the most vigorous of which was the Catholic Church. She taught that things should be distributed to each according to their need and…

LECTOR *"…from each according to his ability." I've heard that; that's Marx. So, Distributism is a form of communism!*

SCRIPTOR No, no, no. Didn't we cover this earlier? The quotation that I had in mind was from the Rule of St. Benedict, which in turn lifted the words from the Acts of the Apostles, which, if I remember my first year at University is not a Marxist tract.

LECTOR *Well, answer my question then: what is being distributed?*

SCRIPTOR The goal would be to encourage a society in which there was a sentiment in favor of ownership and, therefore, customs, conventions, and structures that encouraged the distribution of property and means of production.

LECTOR *"Structures," you say. That sounds like it involves government. Politics means coercion.*

SCRIPTOR Now you sound like a Marxist; certainly you are a rather close cousin if you think that politics is just coercion. Distributists, with Aristotle and most sensible men in the western tradition, believe that there is a place for government and enforceable policies enacted by local and larger forms of government.

LECTOR *"Enforceable policies?" I don't like the sound of that... what do you mean?*

SCRIPTOR Well, meditate for a moment on government with unenforceable policies. Not much of a government. So, first choice: do you or do you not have government that can act for the sake of others? Choose carefully. On one side is the western political tradition, on the other side are fallen angels and orangutans.

LECTOR *Fair enough: I am for government as long as it is good. But surely, Distributism does not envision a limited government. If you want to see the redistribution of property, then you are placing arbitrary limits on one man's property, so that's going to require a big state apparatus...*

SCRIPTOR You mean distribution of property, not redistribution.

LECTOR *What's the difference?*

SCRIPTOR The difference between a distributist and a redistributionist is like the difference between a monogamist and polygamist. Both the monogamist and the polygamist like marriage on the surface. The monogamist wants to see a society that encourages one man with one woman for their mutual benefit and the benefit of their children. In short, for happiness. The polygamist wants a harem, either all at once or sequentially over time. In short, for pleasure. A harem usually leads to some having many and others having few spouses, correct?

LECTOR *Yes.*

SCRIPTOR Well, the distributist wants to see the conditions for ownership in place and stable. That is what law and custom establish in a distributist society. The redistributionist wants to play a constant game of recalibration and special interest stock-piling. I will concede that most governments by the power of taxation redistribute some wealth or property, but the distributist, in fact, wants to avoid that tinkering as much as possible.

LECTOR *But surely, if you want policies or even customs in place that prevent the natural accumulation of wealth and property—and the means of production—then you are calling for what seems a radical system of property laws overseen by a interventionist government.*

SCRIPTOR I will come back to your expression "natural accumulation of wealth, etc." in a moment. First, listen to this catena of Mr. Belloc…

LECTOR *What is a catena?*

SCRIPTOR Please, just listen to this beautiful chain of thoughts:

"I propose no general scheme for restoring freedom and property… the restoration of property must be essentially the product of a new mood not a new scheme."

"Restoration of property… could never approach mechanical perfection. We are only attempting to change the general tone of society and restore property as a commonly present, not universal, institution."

"Property being a personal and human institution, normal to man, will always be, and must be, diversified."

Does this, dear reader, sound like a man about to propose the state control of everything financial?

LECTOR *No. But, then again, perhaps it would happen anyway. After all, how does it happen, except with state intervention. Furthermore, I have heard that the distributists are in favor of very, very high taxation to subsidize little businesses.*

SCRIPTOR You would be very hard pressed in a work by a distributist or a biography of a distributist to find anything but serious opposition to socialism, communism, or statism in any guise. Just the opposite. In fact, Belloc, when he was a member of parliament earned fame for his opposition to the introduction of socialism. He has dozens of books against communism. All of the distributists fought to protect the family against the over-reaching of the state. The natural acquisition of property is rooted first and foremost in this: sustaining a family.

LECTOR *And taxation? Is what they say true?*

SCRIPTOR A misunderstanding perpetuated by either simpletons or the wicked. Here, listen to Belloc in a book that his critics claim argued for high taxation and the greatest system of confiscation known to man:

"That high taxation is the enemy of well distributed property is apparent in two ways. First, it is apparent in the fact that it can be levied effectively only in proportion as well distributed property has disappeared. Second, its effect in operation is to destroy the process whereby well distributed property is accumulated..."

LECTOR *How then do Belloc's critics argue that he wanted high taxation?*

SCRIPTOR Perhaps they fear an alternative group of ideas to those that comfort them. I do not know; these men do not like to discuss the matter in public debate and they do not like it when you ground your ideas in printed words. In any case, Belloc is clear that income tax in a good society would range from just under 2% to about 10%.

LECTOR *What? We don't even have that in free, democratic, capitalist societies!*

SCRIPTOR No. It makes one wonder about all those adjectives, doesn't it, reader? Belloc predicted that you would not have low taxation in the society that calls itself "free, democratic, and capitalist" but doesn't it actually attend to the wide-spread distribution of property and ownership.

"We may lay it down, then, as a general principle that high taxation can be levied with more success in proportion as property is ill-distributed: high taxation is incompatible with a wide and equitable distribution of ownership."

LECTOR *So, distributists did not want to have collective ownership and collective redistribution of property?*

SCRIPTOR You are beginning to see it. Belloc once said, "… the innumerable acts of choice and expression which make up human life can never work through a system of delegation. Ownership by delegation is a contradiction in terms."

LECTOR *So, you could have Distributism in our country, under our system?*

SCRIPTOR Distributism is a disposition toward politics, economics, and social life. You could have Distributism under many forms of government. The distributists saw the principles emerge in the later Roman Empire, flower in medieval Europe—an age of monarchy and aristocracy—and endure under modern democracies.

LECTOR *You say, "principles." Let's just have a sentence or two that gives me the heart of it all. What is it all about, then?*

SCRIPTOR Well, we have gone on for a while here and I have so much more to say. I will stick with Belloc, since our discussion kept coming back to him. Consider this:

"There is discoverable in man, Free will. His actions are of moral value to him if they are undertaken upon his own initiative, not if they are undertaken under compulsion. Therefore the use of choice is necessary to human dignity. It is only in the possession of economic freedom that [the] multiplicity of his desires and creative faculties can be effective."

LECTOR *So, Distributism is about freedom?*

SCRIPTOR Some distributists have said that is the central tenet. Chesterton reminds us, however, that "the aim of human polity is human happiness."

LECTOR *What is a polity?*

SCRIPTOR My dear reader, you have much to learn. A polity is an organized social unit—a state, a city, a village, an estate, a community. It has various levels of authority and action. The point is this, Distributism is an organized body of ideas that offers to men the vision of a social life that does not require a high degree of governmental intervention, but neither does it try at every turn to overthrow government. It looks to establish stability by good customs and good habits as well as by good government and good laws, all of which encourage local networks of production, exchange, and consumption. The family is central to a distributist vision. The family must remain the center of economic life—not the individual, not the corporation, and not the government. The tone of this society is set by an idea that is somewhere lived and visible and vibrant.

LECTOR *So, the essence is an idea meeting reality. I need to think more about ideas and reality together. They seemed separate worlds to me.*

SCRIPTOR They are for most people. That is at the origin of foul ideology—ideas without reality or matter without spirit. Deadening and foul. Look for the idea of Distributism and test it, reader, test it in reality.

LECTOR *Where can I experience the spirit of it?*

SCRIPTOR You can see it in a Bruegel painting and when the sun hits a bowl of peaches from your own orchard. You can read of it in the novels of Wendell Berry. You can hear it in the music of Ralph Vaughn Williams. You can taste it in Greek cheese that no store sells, but some family in some valley really made to share or exchange with friends and neighbors. You can feel it in the rust and green wool of an old plaid blanket. You can read about it in the history of guilds and credit unions; and you can sense its loss with the disappearance of a good family business. You can smell it when your wife bakes bread. It was once said that the spirit and reality of Distributism is met in the planting of a cucumber seed, the harvesting of a cucumber and slicing of that same cucumber, and the sharing of it. I believe the prophet Jonah slept under such a plant and was refreshed.

I am not sure, reader, where you will find it. I felt it once in Scotland and on a little island off the coast of Ireland. I tasted it in the thousand dishes of rural Turkey and urban Italy. I can smell it in cut burley and perique. I lived with it once by a river in Virginia and I hear its approach through fallen leaves on the old hills of New England. I know that it can be found, but you must desire it first, just where you are. Read on, reader; read on.

Dr. William Edmund Fahey is president of Thomas More College. His contributions include the Preface to Fr. Vincent McNabb's The Church and the Land *and the book* Beyond Capitalism and Socialism. *Dr. Fahey has been published in the* St. Austin Review, Faith & Reason, The University Bookman, Classical World, *and* The Classical Bulletin.

ON A TIRESOME WORD

BY G.K.CHESTERTON

"We do not mind calling capitalism "x" and Distributism "y" so long as nobody falls into the fallacy of supposing that x = y."—G.K.CHESTERTON

IN THE FIRST NUMBER EVER PRINTED OF THIS PAPER, WE REMARKED that the world was suffering from certain words which were dangerously misleading. We noted that one of them is the word "Capitalism." We marked that it would really be much clearer to call the same thing "Proletarianism." For what is wrong with the world just now is not that some men are capitalists, but that most men are proletarians. It is not that some men possess private property, but that most men do not possess private property, or at any rate not the primary forms of private property. But when we suggested the change, nobody seemed particularly disposed to adopt it; and it would lead to confusion worse confounded if one person were to adopt it alone. The object of language is to be understood; sad as things stand, if we were simply to accuse the Duke of Northumberland of "proletarianism" we are by no means certain that we should be understood. Probably most people would connect proletarianism with ideas rather remote from those of the Duke of Northumberland, or even from those of Lord Leverhulme or Henry Ford. Many would probably think proletarianism had something to do with the dictatorship of the proletariat.

Therefore we continue to use the word capitalism; but we know exactly what we mean and what we do not mean by capitalism. It does not matter, comparatively speaking, whether we have got the right word, so long as we are sure we are arguing about the right thing. If both disputants agree on that thing, it does not matter whether they call it capitalism or cannibalism and one person merely means exploiting men, while the other person is still haunted by the notion of eating them. When we say "capitalism" in a current conversational or controversial fashion, we mean something that may be defined thus: "That economic condition in which capital belongs in bulk to a relatively small class called capitalists, and in which the large or determining mass of the citizens, being themselves without capital, are obliged to hire themselves out to these few capitalists for a wage." That is a perfectly definite definition; it is a definition that is really a difference; it is a definition that is really a description of something that really exists. We must have some word for that thing. It is as much the dominant character of the twentieth century as feudalism was the dominant character of the twelfth century. It is not feudalism; it is not yet slavery; it is obviously not collectivism or communism; and it is not Distributism. We therefore call it capitalism because we must call it something. But we entirely agree, and indeed long ago insisted, that it is really a very unlucky and unworkable word by which to call it. For many people seem to be using the word capitalism for anything involving the use of capital. If it comes to that they might use the word socialism for anything like a social evening or a social glass.

But, oddly enough, if we use the word in this literal way, we shall actually find that the sense which is too literal is also too loose and even too large. It is pedantic but it is not narrow; it is not narrow enough. Capitalism covers too much if it covers everything that uses capital. In that sense certainly Distributism is capitalism. But in that sense Bolshevism is capitalism, and anarchist communism is capitalism and the most extreme sorts of revolutionary socialism are all respectably covered by the conventional name of capitalism. Every man outside a madhouse wishes the economic operations of to-day to leave something over the economic operations of to-morrow. And that is all that capital means in its economic sense. Lenin and Trotsky believed in that as much as Lloyd George and Thomas; and probably insisted on it rather more lucidly than Lansbury and Saklatvala. But everybody admits it, clearly or cloudily; and therefore so wide a word would remain rather cloudy than clear. There is not much good in denouncing the millionaire in Park Lane by a term that would include the leveler in Hyde Park; and if we must stick to this strict interpretation of capitalism (in the sense of the valuing of capital) we cannot apply it to anybody because we must apply it to everybody. It is doubtless unfortunate that the form of the word gives rise to these misunderstandings at all. But whenever such a misunderstanding arises, the right thing is to refer back to the real meaning of what we have in mind. Our proposal of the better distribution of capital remains the same, whatever we call it, or whatever we call the present antithesis of it. It is the same whether we state it by saying that there is too much capitalism in the one sense or too little capitalism in the other.

Thus we noted last week that the controversy between Mr. Cole and Mr. Colvin in the *Morning Post* left off exactly where we begin. But it also left off so as to leave us not only the next word but the last word. Given the facts as both controversialists accepted them, and our conclusion is really the only conclusion that is the least conclusive. Both test the matter by the Guilds of the Middle Ages. Mr. Colvin claims that the guildsman used private property and admits that the guild regulated the trade. Mr. Cole admits that the guildsmen used private property and claims that they preserved a wide distribution of that property. Both appeared as contradicting each other in a highly combative manner. And both, of course, are perfectly right. For the control of the trade, which Mr. Colvin admits, largely consisted of preserving the distribution which Mr. Cole admires. And the element, which Mr. Cole calls distribution was the same element which Mr. Colvin calls capitalism. But that striking result, we may say this striking reconciliation, has probably been turned for most people into a wildly misleading logomachy and cross purposes, merely because Mr. Colvin does insist on calling it capitalism. In other words, he had very nearly put everybody right; only by one accidental word he has probably put everybody wrong.

Readers of the *Morning Post* will probably go away with the impression that something has been said for capitalism, in the sense of the existing state of things. Whereas the whole object both of Guild regulation and of Guild distribution was to prevent the possibility of the present state of things. The sort of capitalism that the *Morning Post* largely exists to preserve is precisely the sort of capitalism that the Medieval Guild only existed to prevent. That is a sufficient commentary on the convenience of using the same word for the two things.

For the whole point about trade as modern capitalists understand it, is precisely that there never has been any Guild or anything else to "regulate it"; and in consequence it has not been regulated. Nobody has ever tried, nobody has ever been allowed to try, to insure that its capital shall be "distributed." And if this is what Mr. Cole means by modern capitalism contradicting medieval Guilds, his case against capitalism is complete. If Mr. Cole means that, he is obviously right; and if Mr. Colvin contradicts that, he is obviously wrong. But it is by no means certain that either of them does really contradict the other, except on this purely verbal point of the meaning of the word "capitalism." On the side of practical journalism and popular effect, however, a word can do a great deal of harm. To say to the normal and numerous readers of a newspaper like the *Morning Post*, "There never has been, in historical times, an alternative to capitalism," is probably to produce the impression that there has never been an alternative to the present herding and drifting of harassed wage-slaves, whereas as a fact there have been all sorts of alternatives to it. There has been slavery; there has been feudalism; there have been multitudes of small proprietors; there have been Guilds like the Medieval Guilds, in which trade was regulated that property might remain distributed. There have also doubtless, as Mr. Colvin said, been periods of a capitalism bearing some resemblance to our own capitalism; especially the Roman Empire, which resembled us in the possession of bankers and financiers, just as it may well be our model in the matter of nightclubs and nasty stories. Modern capitalist society does certainly find some parallel in the Roman Empire, in many details, and especially in those two characteristics that give their title to the great work of Gibbon. But the practical and immediate moral of the Cole and the Colvin controversy is that a discussion so important, conducted by men so intelligent, is in serious danger of being brought

ON A TIRESOME WORD ■ BY G.K. CHESTERTON

to a deadlock, and doing no good but a great deal of harm, unless we can make up our minds what the chief terms of the problem are to mean. We ourselves are perfectly indifferent to the term as compared to the meaning. We do not care whether we call one thing or the other by this mere printed word beginning with a "C"; so long as it is applied to one thing and not the other. We do not mind using a term as arbitrary as a mathematical sign, if it is as exact as a mathematical sign. We do not mind calling capitalism "x" and Distributism "y" so long as nobody falls into the fallacy of supposing that x = y. We do not mind saying "cat" for capitalism and "dog" for distribution, so long as people understand that the things are different enough to fight like cat and dog. We quite agree that capitalism might cover a condition in which small men traded with their own capital. But in that case we must find some other name for the present commercial system of this country and this epoch, in which small men are paid a small salary to work with somebody else's capital. And those who use it thus must remember that nothing they say in defence of any such capitalism is a particle of use as part of the defence of any existing capitalist. If they define it thus they may defend it thus. But they are not an inch nearer to defending any of the actual things that are now on the defensive. We shall not gain the solid advantages that come from really protecting the real profiteer; we shall comfort no heartbroken millionaire, we shall dry the tears of no sensitive usurer or rackrenter, we shall do no sort of real practical good for ourselves, by proving that a poor carpenter of the fourteenth century owned his own hammer or traded with his own capital.

Essay taken from *G.K.'s Weekly*, Vol. II No.35, 14 November 1925

CHESTERTON
AS ECONOMIST

BY RUSSELL SPARKES

"When most men are wage-earners, it is more and more difficult for most men to be customers. For the capitalist is always trying to cut down what his servant demands, and in doing so is cutting down what his customer can spend." —G.K.CHESTERTON

WHEN PEOPLE THINK OF G.K.CHESTERTON TODAY THEY remember his literary achievements: the essays, the Father Brown stories, the wealth of aphorisms that are still widely quoted. However, I suspect that if you had asked the man himself what part of his work he was most proud of, he would have said something that is almost totally forgotten: his advocacy of an economic and political philosophy called Distributism.

Distributism's main tenet was that property should be as widely distributed as possible, and business should be local. There was advocacy of the economy being centered upon the production of goods, and suspicion of the role of high finance. Advocated principally by G.K. Chesterton and Hilaire Belloc from 1910 onwards, its key texts were Chesterton's *The Outline of Sanity* published in 1926, and Belloc's *Essay on the Restoration of Property* of 1936.

In the depressed economic conditions of the 1920s Distributism became a political movement as well as an economic program, which was led and inspired by Chesterton through a little magazine that he edited and whose heavy losses he funded. He didn't like the title, but it was called *G.K.'s Weekly*. As the eminent Chesterton scholar Father Ian Boyd notes:

"If there was a classical period of Distributism, it occurred during the years 1926 and 1936 when he (GKC) was at once president of the Distributist League, and the editor of *G.K.'s Weekly* which was its political organ. During this last decade of his life, he and his associates produced a considerable body of literature in which they attempted to supply Distributist answers to the political and economic questions of the day." [1]

When Chesterton died in 1936 his magazine died with him. Without him Distributism lost its inspirational force; it lingered on for a few years but was essentially finished when war came in 1939. However, indifference to Distributism ignores the fact that it became a political movement of national significance from the late 1920s onwards, with Chesterton as its Chairman.

As a movement it began shortly before the First World War, when in books like Belloc's *The Servile State* (1912) and Chesterton's *What's Wrong with the World* (1910) the two authors observed closely the actual way the economic system worked in practice, including its political interconnections, and the way it impacted on the politically weak ordinary person. Indeed, their warnings of an "unholy alliance" between monopoly capital and the "progressive" advocates of greater state intervention seems uncannily prescient. Chesterton's *What's Wrong with the World* analyzes the curious alliance and effective similarity of outlook between Gudge, the capitalist, and Hudge, the would-be reformer:

"A horrible suspicion that has sometimes haunted me: the suspicion that Hudge and Gudge are secretly in partnership... Gudge the plutocrat wants an anarchic industrialism; Hudge the idealist provides him with lyric praises of anarchy. Gudge wants women workers because they are cheaper; Hudge calls the woman's work 'freedom to live her own life.'" [2]

---

[1] Ian Boyd, *New Blackfriars* 55, 1974.

[2] G.K.Chesterton, *What's Wrong With the World* (London: Cassell, 1910).

THE INSPIRATION OF DISTRIBUTISM

It is important to describe the theoretical background and intellectual origins of Distributism in order to counter some of the ill-informed criticisms made against it both by contemporaries, but also recently revived by critics worried by the renewed interest in it. Probably the greatest and most persistent attack on Distributism was the notion propagated by its enemies that it was an otherworldly invention by Chesterton and Belloc as part of their romantic attachment to the Middle Ages, and alleged desire to return there. This was often caricatured as policy of giving everybody "three acres and a cow," which was in fact a policy slogan of Joseph Chamberlain in the 1880s.

There is little truth in this argument, for, Chesterton did not reject modern technology, but he did fundamentally disagree with the *economic system* on which modern society is based. *G.K.'s Weekly* called this "plutocracy," or rule by the rich. Admittedly, those free market apologists who identify capitalism with "enterprise" have attacked Distributism on this point, often with some kind of innuendo that it is a kind of closet socialism. Chesterton rebutted such attacks with his usual zest in *The Outline of Sanity*:

> "A pickpocket is obviously a champion of private enterprise. But it would be perhaps be an exaggeration to say that a pickpocket is a champion of private property." [3]

The original inspiration behind Distributism was both Chesterton and Belloc's keen interest in English political, social, and economic history. Chesterton was also struck by a vein of social commentary found in literary men like Dickens as well as the campaigns of William Cobbett, that doughty fighter for the poor of England. Chesterton describes Dickens' hatred of the way the free-market economists of the Nineteenth Century, the so-called Manchester School, advocated starvation and misery for the poor as a necessary evil:

---

[3] G.K.Chesterton, *The Outline of Sanity* (first published 1926), reprinted Ignatius Press, 1992.

"He didn't like the *mean* side of the Manchester philosophy: the preaching of an impossible thrift and an intolerable temperance… Thus, for instance, he hated that Little Bethel (a workhouse) to which Kit's mother went: he hated it simply as Kit hated it. (This system) was a monstrous mushroom that grows in the moonshine and dies in the dawn. Dickens knew no more of religious history than Kit; he simply smelt the fungus, and it stank." [4]

Distributism was also inspired by the recent practical success of Land Reform in Ireland; Belloc and Chesterton were impressed by the peaceful and successful redistribution of land in Ireland which had been carried out following the 1903 Wyndham Act. They both knew its author, the Conservative Minister George Wyndham, who became a great friend of Belloc. Researching Cobbett's works was another inspiration for Chesterton's Distributist thinking. (Indeed, when he cut the price of *G.K.'s Weekly* from 6 to 2 pence to advance the work of the Distributist League, Chesterton's leading article proudly described his paper as "two-penny trash." This was the nickname of Cobbett's own paper a hundred years before. As Chesterton lamented in his 1925 biography of *Cobbett*,

"It is obvious that the process which Cobbett condemned has gone far beyond anything that he described… If ownership be the test, it has been a process and a period of people losing things and not gaining them. It has been a process of people going into service, in the language of servants, into service if not into servitude. It has been a process of people losing even the little booth at the fair, that was thought to be so poor a substitute for the little farm in the fields… Cobbett was sorry that the small capitalists were being ruined; in the long run he may be right." [5]

Indeed, Chesterton repeatedly warned that the overwhelming economic trend of the last two centuries has been for the concentration

---

[4] G.K.Chesterton, *The Victorian Age in Literature* (London: Home University Press, 1910).

[5] G.K.Chesterton, *William Cobbett* (London: Hodder & Stoughton, 1925).

CHESTERTON AS ECONOMIST ■ BY RUSSELL SPARKES

of wealth and the destruction of small businesses in both England and America. This process started in agriculture, moved on to small industry, and has now spread to distribution. Since the Second World War, such growing concentration has been most visible in retailing and other distribution sectors. The high streets of the 1960s had their small greengrocers, dairies, and bakeries, as well as small grocers shops. Over the last thirty years the majority of these small shops have disappeared. They have been replaced by names like Tesco, Sainsbury, and Wal-Mart.

Another factor that contributed to Distributist thinking was the 1891 Papal encyclical *Rerum Novarum*, criticizing current economic and social arrangements, and demanding better treatment for working people. The Latin words *Rerum Novarum* translate into English as "Of the New Order of Things," but its official subtitle *On the Condition of Labour*, makes its import clear:

> "By degrees it has come to pass that Working Men have been given over, isolated and defenceless, to the callousness of employers and the greed of unrestrained competition. The evil has been increased by rapacious usury… And to this must be added the custom of working by contract, and the concentration of so many branches of trade in the hands of a few individuals, so that a small number of very rich men have been able to lay upon the masses of the poor a yoke little better than slavery itself." [6]

Both Chesterton and Belloc were inspired by the nineteenth century work of Edward Cardinal Manning, a powerful influence on *Rerum Novarum,* in improving the lot of the poor. Chesterton gives a wonderful word-portrait of seeing the Cardinal as a young man in his *Autobiography,*[7] while Belloc took spiritual advice from him as a youth.[8] As early as 1878 Manning had campaigned for recognition to be given

---

[6] *Rerum Novarum, On the Condition of Labour,* 15 March 1891, §3. Official translation, the Vatican Polyglot Press, included in *The Social Teachings of the Church,* ed. Anne Freemantle (Mentor-Orbis Books, 1963).

[7] G.K.Chesterton, *Autobiography* (London: Hutchinson, 1936).

[8] Hilaire Belloc, *The Cruise of the Nona* (London: Constable, 1926).

to associations of working men, and pointing out the work of mutual support carried out by the medieval guilds. Manning also urged consideration for the family, pointing out how families of 14 or 15 people were huddled together in one room, usually in appalling sanitary conditions. In any case, it is clear that *Rerum Novarum* explicitly sets out ideas later classed as Distributist:

> "We have seen that this great labour question cannot be solved except by assuming as a principle that private ownership must be held sacred and inviolable. The law, therefore, should favour ownership, and its policy should be to induce as many people as possible to become owners."[9]

Hence the received wisdom on Distributism—that its main proponents were well-meaning idealists ignorant of the real world of politics and economics—is quite wrong. Hilaire Belloc was a Member of Parliament from 1906-1910 before he resigned his seat in disgust. Chesterton was a well-known and widely respected journalist whose views helped shape popular opinion, and as such someone who was courted by the leading politicians and thinkers of his day.

THE DISTRIBUTIST PROGRAM

In 1934 the Distributist League, with Chesterton as its President, published its program:

- The restraint of unjust competition.
- The redistribution of property.
- The creation of conditions favouring small ownership.
- Extended ownership of industries that necessitated large-scale production.
- Laws to protect distributed property.
- A return to the land.
- The encouragement of Distributist principles by the individual.

In *The Outline of Sanity* Chesterton advocated boycotts as one means of effecting the change to a Distributist system:

---

[9] *Rerum Novarum*, op cit.

"If we chose to make a vow, if we chose to make a league, for dealing only with little local shops and never with large centralised shops, the campaign could be every bit as practical as the Land League in Ireland. It would probably be nearly as successful. It will be said, of course, that people will go to the best shop. I deny it, for Irish boy-cotters did not take the best offer." [10]

Other proposals in the book are:

- The taxation of contracts so as to discourage the sale of small property to big proprietors and encourage the break-up of big property among small proprietors.
- Something like the Napoleonic testamentary law and the destruction of primogeniture.
- The establishment of free law for the poor, so that small property could always be defended against great.
- The deliberate protection of certain experiments in small property, if necessary by tariffs and even local tariffs.
- Subsidies to foster the starting of such experiments.
- A league of voluntary dedication.

Two things are striking about Chesterton's list. First, how practical it is—nothing about "cows and acres" here. Instead, there is a pragmatic assessment of a modern economic and political system. Also, note the second point about inheritance—it is exactly the same as that made by Thomas Jefferson at the birth of the United States of America. If we think that great extremes of wealth and poverty are a bad thing—and Distributists do, then we must have means to prevent great fortunes accumulating across the generations. The Middle Ages were sufficiently worried about this to have a law, *mortmain,* preventing perpetual trusts. It is also worth noting that after the Second World War most of Continental Europe passed laws prohibiting the excessive development of supermarkets. Whether the generally Christian Democratic governments knew of Distributism is unclear, but they certainly saw the survival of the small shopkeeper as a bulwark against the revival of Fascism.

---

[10] *The Outline of Sanity,* op cit.

Of course nothing similar occurred in the United Kingdom, only the opposite. For example, retail price maintenance, whereby manufacturers could insist that all shops charged the same price for their products, was abolished by government decree in 1963. The economic theory was that this would lead to cheaper prices. In practice it enabled well-capitalised companies to cut prices *temporarily*, until small food shops were driven out of business. The result in most areas was a local monopoly of one large superstore and *permanently high prices*. The same phenomenon can be seen in the book trade since the recent collapse of the agreement not to discount books. Bestsellers are sold like baked beans in supermarkets and small bookshops close everywhere.

Chesterton also advocated that small shops should be allowed to open on certain holidays when large shops should be forced to shut. This is what happened, in effect, in the United Kingdom owing to the Sunday Trading laws. Small food shops were allowed to open, while larger shops had to remain closed. In the late 1980s the retail chains found this too restrictive, and started to break the law by opening on Sunday. Rather than enforce the law, the Conservative government decided to change it as the "law was coming into disrepute," and the Sunday Trading Act of 1991 did so—one more nail in the coffin of the small trader.

CHESTERTON AS ECONOMIST

In 1927, Chesterton was invited to lecture at the London School of Economics.

> "What impressed (me) most in the debate, entertaining and energetic as it was, was that the prevailing process of thought seemed to be not so much a pedantic or academic detachment as an almost childish literalism. Some of the brightest debaters seem to be like the schoolboy who cannot even imagine a triangle without turning it into a three-cornered tart." [11]

---

[11] G.K.Chesterton, "The Simple Realist," from *G.K.'s Weekly*, 22 October 1927.

Chesterton's comment about simple-minded literalism seems justified. In 1936, Keynes revolutionalised economics by inventing macroeconomics in his *The General Theory of Employment, Interest, and Money*. Keynes' great discovery was that the focus of previous economists on the individual firm meant that they had ignored the fact that the economy was an organic whole; what to an individual firm was a cut in costs (wages) was to the worker a cut in income. Chesterton made exactly the same point in 1926, *before* the Great Depression began in 1929—but then he was not blinkered by having absorbed the doctrines of economics:

> "Capitalism is contradictory as soon as it is complete; because it is dealing with the mass of men in two different ways at once. When most men are wage-earners, it is more and more difficult for most men to be customers. For the capitalist is always trying to cut down what his servant demands, and in doing so is cutting down what his customer can spend. As soon as his business is in any difficulties, as at present in the coal business, he tries to reduce what he has to spend on wages, and in doing so reduces what others have to spend on coal. He is wanting the same man to be rich and poor at the same time." [12]

One last point about classical economics is how it has often mirrored the wishes of the rich and powerful, contradicting its earlier teaching to do so. (For example, economists urged governments to use fiscal policy to control the economy in the Keynesian 1950s and 1960s, and they forbade governments to use fiscal policy to control the economy in the monetarist 1980s.) As Chesterton wrote in 1927:

> "But what is interesting to note is the way in which the sophistry of political economy changes and adapts itself to the needs of the luxurious at any particular moment. Whatever the politician may want to do, there is always a political economist beside him to say that

---

[12] G.K.Chesterton, *The Outline of Sanity*, op cit.

it must be done, and whenever the rich want to be luxurious, it is always opportunely discovered that luxury is a form of economy." [13]

He also pointed out that Adam Smith's insistence on the need to specialize and trade, rather than to produce locally, led economics to neglect transport costs, the uncertainty involved in trade, and broader environmental considerations. The priest, Father Vincent McNabb, used the language of economics to question Smith's assumptions:

"I have often said that the most efficient social and economic unit is one wherein the area of production tends to be co-terminous with the area of consumption; i.e. that things will be produced where they are to be consumed." [14]

Reflecting on the Great Depression of the 1930s, with mass unemployment because of "overcapacity," with widespread hunger while governments bought up and burnt food, Chesterton wrote:

"No pope or priest ever asked (a man) to believe that thousands died of starvation in the desert because they were loaded with loaves and fishes. No creed or dogma ever declared that there was too little food because there was too much fish. But that is the precise, practical and prosaic definition of the present situation in the modern science of economics... *Credo quia impossibile.*" [15]

Of course, Distributism was also a philosophy. Chesterton and Belloc recoiled from the idea that the best humanity could achieve was a balance of grasping selfishness. In one of his later editorials of *G.K.'s Weekly*, Chesterton wrote:

"When I began it, I merely thought it reasonable that there should be one weekly paper to represent a reasonable alternative to conventional Socialism and academic Socialism. But I now realise... that we

---

[13] G.K.Chesterton, "Very Political Economy," from *G.K.'s Weekly*, 5 August 1927.

[14] Fr. Vincent McNabb, *Old Principles and the New Order* (London: Sheed and Ward, 1942).

[15] G.K.Chesterton, "Reflections on a Rotten Apple," published in *The Well and the Shallows* (London: Sheed and Ward, 1935).

have taken on something much bigger than modern Capitalism or Communism combined. I realise that we are trying to fight the whole world; to turn the tide of the whole time we live in; to resist everything that seems irresistible… For the thing we oppose is something of which capitalism and collectivism are only economic by products… It is so vast and vague that its offensiveness is largely atmospheric; it is perhaps easier to defy than to define. But it might be approximately adumbrated thus; it is that spirit which refuses Recognition or Respect."[16]

A NEW DAWN FOR DISTRIBUTISM?

Whilst Distributism became more or less moribund soon after Chesterton's death in 1936, there are signs that its ideas are being taken up again. Within the last twelve months three books have been published which look critically at the unquestioning application of "free market economics," and turn to Distributism for answers. One of these books was American,[17] one was by the British conservative thinker Phillip Blond.[18] However, what was most surprising given the radical "leftwing" viewpoint of *The New Economics* is the book's statement that the origins of the "new economics" derive from Catholic Social Teaching as publicised by Chesterton and Belloc as Distributism.

"The one 20th century movement that embedded elements of what is now the new economics was Distributism… (this) knitted together the old Catholic social doctrine of Pope Leo XIII that was so close to Belloc's heart, inspired originally by Ruskin via Cardinal Manning… At its heart was the redistribution of land and property so that everyone had some on the grounds that small enterprises, smallholdings and small units were the only basis for dignity, independence and liberty."[19]

---

[16] G.K.Chesterton, "Spiritual over Political," *GK's Weekly*, 7 December 1929.

[17] John C. Médaille, *Towards a Truly Free Market: a Distributist Perspective on the Role of Government, Taxes, Health Care, Deficits, and More* (Wilmington, Delaware: ISI Books, 2010).

[18] Phillip Blond, *Red Tory: How the Left and Right Have Broken Britain and How We Can Fix It* (London: Faber & Faber, 2010).

[19] D. Boyle and A. Simms, *The New Economics: A Bigger Picture* (London: Earthscan, 2009).

Russell Sparkes is Chief Investment Officer of the Central Finance Board of the Methodist Church. He was Chairman of the Chesterton Institute, promoting the thought of G.K. Chesterton, particularly its economic philosophy based upon Catholic social teaching. His writings include G.K.Chesterton, Prophet of Orthodoxy *and* Sound of Heaven: A Treasury of Catholic Verse. *He is currently working on a study of the medieval guilds and their modern relevance.*

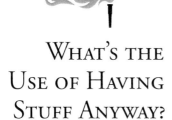

WHAT'S THE USE OF HAVING STUFF ANYWAY?

BY THOMAS STORCK

"One would think, to hear people talk, that the Rothchilds and the Rockefellers were on the side of property. But obviously they are the enemies of property; because they are enemies of their own limitations. They do not want their own land; but other people's... It is the negation of property that the Duke of Sutherland should have all the farms in one estate; just as it would be the negation of marriage if he had all our wives in one harem."[1] —G.K.CHESTERTON

I F WE LOOK AT THE ANIMAL CALLED MAN WE MIGHT NOTICE CERTAIN things that we do not observe in the case of the other animals. We share a lot of characteristics with those other animals. We all need nourishment and shelter, we all reproduce to continue our kind, and some of them, such as ants or bees, even live in complex aggregations and build rather remarkable dwellings. But there is one big difference. Bees and ants do what they do to create conditions for their survival: food, shelter, continuation of the species. We do that too, of course. But much of our activity is devoted to other ends. Ants work and sleep, we work and sleep but we do all sorts of other things that make our lives really *human*. God created us in such a way that we need food, water, shelter and clothing just to survive. But to live in a human way, to fulfill our natural needs for family and social life we need other objects, things for recreation, for education, things of beauty. Without all these our lives would be lacking, even if we had enough simply to survive. For although human beings are animals, we are *rational* animals, and as such we transcend the merely material level at which other animals live.

---

[1] G.K.Chesterton, *What's Wrong With the World* (San Francisco: Ignatius, 1994), p. 42.

Now the way God created us requires that in order to obtain the things we need both for mere survival and for truly human life we generally must do work. Even in those climates warm enough so that food and shelter are there for the taking, if their inhabitants want to make musical instruments or anything else to enhance their lives, they have to exert at least a little effort of their own.

The kind of activity we engage in both merely to survive and to live more fully is what we call economic activity. By approaching it as we just did, we've already come to see what its purpose is, what it's for. Economic activity exists to provide what we need both for survival and for living our lives in a more human way. It is for the sake of human life and therefore subordinate to human life. Economic activity fulfills its purpose only when it helps us both to survive and to live as rational animals whose ultimate purpose is to live forever with God in heaven.

Some might think that this is pretty obvious. What else would economic activity be for? But I think that if we consider carefully what this purpose implies, we'll be able to say a lot about the rightness or wrongness of our own economy. We might begin by asking whether our economy does a good job of fulfilling this purpose, that is, does it provide well for what we need both to survive and to enhance life in a human way? That might seem like a silly question. Of course it does. Don't we have all kinds of cheap goods and abundant food too? Well, I'm afraid that if we look more closely we might find that this judgment is not quite accurate.

In the first place, all those external goods necessary for survival and for human living are needed not for themselves, but for their use. For example, we don't need shoes to stick in our closets, but to wear. There is a rational relation between these external goods and human need. We can use only so many of them and at some point we simply don't need any more. Even storing them becomes a problem. We have only so much closet space or bookcases. How does the U.S. economy stack up with regard to this? Does it produce pretty much what we need or does it produce a lot of junk, junk which we have to throw away just to make room for new junk? And does the commercial spirit that our economy fuels make us satisfied with what we need for the twin purposes of the economy that we've been talking about, or does it make us ever less satisfied although we might have much more than we need, even if shopping has become recreational and consumer spending constitutes around ¾ of the total economy?

One of the reasons the economy is stuck in the recession, so we are told, is that people are not buying enough. In some cases this means that people aren't getting what they truly and reasonably need. But I'm afraid that in other cases it means that people aren't buying the latest gadgets or new clothes or a new car—things that probably serve neither our survival nor a reasonable standard of life. For surely we have a wrong idea of human good if we think that it consists in having more and more stuff, rather than in having enough so that we can enjoy time with our families and friends, read some good books, and worship God.

External things, then, are for human survival and life. They are subordinate to that. If someone invented a machine that turned out ten pairs of shoes every minute, soon the world would have enough shoes and we'd have to prevent this person from making more shoes until some had worn out. Otherwise we'd be smothered in shoes. It's irrational to make or buy more than we can reasonably use or reasonably store for later use. At some point the acquisition of more stuff no longer serves its purpose. And similarly it is irrational to expend effort, to do work, in order to produce more than we can reasonably use or store for the future. But our economy promotes a spirit of acquisition so that we are not satisfied with what we need, but want to buy more. We have advertising to promote such dissatisfaction, to make people feel the need to buy some product, and even if it doesn't convince someone to buy the very product that's advertised, it tends to generate an acquisitive spirit so that we always want new stuff.

Does any of this have implications for the question of an economic system? The following words from G.K.Chesterton's friend, Hilaire Belloc, might make this point more clear.

"But wealth obtained indirectly as profit out of other men's work, or by process of exchange, becomes a thing abstracted from the process of production. As the interest of a man in things diminishes, his interest in abstract wealth—money—increases. The man who makes a table or grows a crop makes the success of the crop or the table a test of excellence.

The intermediary who buys and sells the crop or the table is not concerned with the goodness of table or crop, but with the profit he makes between their purchase and sale. In a productive society the superiority of the things produced is the measure of success: in a commercial society the amount of wealth accumulated by the dealer is the measure of success." [2]

The chief reason our economy requires that people buy more and more without reference to any reasonable need, and thus uses advertising to create that habit of buying, is its separation of ownership from work. Those who own the means of production generally do not do the actual work of making things. And so, "As the interest of a man in *things* diminishes, his interest in abstract wealth—money—increases." When producers see their role as simply providing the necessary goods that human society needs, production has a natural limit. There is no need to persuade people to buy something, because they already know their needs. And the producers themselves will tend to limit their own desire for wealth to what they and their families need in order to survive and to live in a truly human manner. When our economic activity becomes an end in itself, and we produce and sell and buy only for the sake of gain and getting more stuff, then the economy has turned against its real purpose. It has turned on itself and turned on those it is supposed to serve. Even if someone can claim that he himself is largely immune to the blandishments of the commercial society, can anyone honestly say that most people are immune? And if the economy has that effect on the average person, then is that a healthy way of conducting our economic affairs?

If we want a "productive society," as Belloc termed it, then the surest way of achieving that is an economy in which, as much as is feasible, ownership and work are not separated anymore. In such a

---

[2] *An Essay on the Nature of Contemporary England* (London: Sheed and Ward, 1937), p. 67.

case producers would be related to their products as more than sales-men. They would take pride in a product well made. The commercial spirit—the endless desire to buy and sell, the evaluation of everything by how much of a profit it will make—would no longer be fostered by our economic system. Producers of course would expect to provide for their needs by means of their work, but they would feel less of a desire to simply accumulate more and more without any relation to the reasonable needs of their families.

Although greed, the inordinate desire for material goods, is one of the sad results of original sin, our kind of economy artificially nourishes that greed. No economic arrangements or rearrangements can create perfection, but they can remove some of the incentives to sin and can guide human activity toward better and higher goals than simply amass-ing goods. In fact they can help to create a different rhythm of life, a kind of life and society that values both things and human talents for more than their ability to produce wealth.

Only if we pay attention to the purpose of a thing can we judge whether that thing is doing its job or not. And if we look at the purpose of an economy, then I think it is clear that ours does a poor job. But a distributist economy, an economy characterized by the widespread ownership of productive property, offers a way of subordinating human economic activity to its purpose again. And if the human race is to escape from any of its many present difficulties, then surely that is a good place to begin.

Thomas Storck is the author of Foundations of a Catholic Political Order, The Catholic Milieu, *and* Christendom and the West. *His work has appeared in various publications including* Homiletic and Pastoral Review *and the book,* Beyond Capitalism and Socialism. *Mr. Storck is a former contributing editor of* New Oxford Review *and* Caelum et Terra, *and he serves on the editorial board of* The Chesterton Review.

SMALL IS BEAUTIFUL VERSUS BIG IS BEST

BY JOSEPH PEARCE

"That which is large enough for the rich to covet is large enough for the poor to defend." —G.K.CHESTERTON

THE PHRASE, "SMALL IS BEAUTIFUL," WAS COINED, OR AT LEAST popularized, by the economist E.F. Schumacher who chose it for the title of his international bestseller, a groundbreaking work, published in 1973, that exploded like a beneficent bomb, demolishing, or at least throwing into serious question, many of the presumptions of *laissez-faire* economics. The sub-title of Schumacher's book, "A Study of Economics as if People Mattered," reflects Schumacher's insistence that the question of scale in economic life should not—and, indeed, morally speaking, cannot—be separated from the overriding dignity of the human person. The tendency of modern economics to genuflect before Mammon in the name of quasi-mysterious market forces, and to disregard the dignity of the human person, is ultimately not an economic question at all. It is a moral question. As such, we should not be surprised that the whole issue has concerned the Catholic Church for more than a century.

Perhaps Schumacher's lasting legacy is to illustrate that "subsidiarity," the essence of the Church's social teaching as expounded in social encyclicals by popes such as Leo XIII, Pius XI and John Paul II, and as defined in *The Catechism of the Catholic Church*, has worldwide popular appeal and, more significantly, that it is a practical and viable alternative to *laissez-faire* concepts of economics.

Schumacher warned of impending calamity if rampant consumerism and economic expansionism were not checked by human and environmental considerations. Like a latter-day prophet he asserted that humanity was lurching blindly in the wrong direction, that the pursuit of wealth could not ultimately lead to happiness or fulfillment, that the pillaging of finite resources and the pollution of the planet constituted a threat to global ecological and economic stability, and that a renewal of moral and spiritual perception was essential if disaster was to be avoided. His greatest achievement was the fusion of ancient wisdom and modern economics in a language that encapsulated contemporary doubts and fears about the industrialized world. He confronted the presumptions of modernity with the dynamism of tradition. He stressed that the wisdom of the ages, the perennial truth that has guided humanity throughout its history, serves as a constant reminder to each new generation of the dangers of self-gratification. The lessons of the past, if heeded, should always empower the present.

In practical terms Schumacher counteracted the idolatry of gigantism with the beauty of smallness. People, he argued, could only feel at home in human-scale environments. If structures—economic, political or social—became too large they became impersonal and unresponsive to human needs and aspirations. Under these conditions individuals felt functionally futile, dispossessed, voiceless, powerless, excluded and alienated. He applied similar criteria with regard to technolatry, the idolization of technology as being intrinsically good. He felt that modern technology often pursued size, speed, novelty and violence in defiance of all laws of natural harmony. The machine was becoming the master and not the servant of man, severing him from his natural environment and encasing him in an increasingly artificial world. Since Schumacher's time this process has accelerated. Reality is being systematically replaced by virtual reality, the real for the sub-real. How can humanity address the urgent problems confronting the real world when it is being simultaneously stimulated and stupefied by electronic fantasies? As techno-man plugs himself into the latest electronic illusions he simultaneously disconnects himself from the real world and its very real problems.

The harsh reality, unheeded by those hooked on fantasy, is that the ecological "bottom line"—conservation of limited resources—is not compatible with the economic "bottom line"—consumer-driven expansionism without limit. The fact is that the globalist's dream is the realist's nightmare. As Schumacher observed: "Modern man does not experience himself as a part of nature but as an outside force destined to dominate and conquer it. He even tells of a battle with nature, forgetting that, if he won the battle, he would find himself on the losing side." We were given authority over our environment as stewards of the goodness it has to offer, not as locusts devouring what we have no intention of replenishing. The moral is easy enough to discern for those who have ears to hear. It is this: that, ultimately, small is beautiful because the earth itself is not only beautiful, *but* small.

Isn't this a little alarmist? Wasn't Schumacher overstating the case? Certainly many conventional economists would have us believe so. When it comes to explaining, or explaining away, the possible problems confronting a blind faith in *laissez-faire* economics, these apologists for continual economic expansion are the proverbial eternal optimists. This touching optimism is attributable to what might be called the Micawber Factor, in honor of Dickens's endearingly feckless character who believed that "something will turn up." Few, however, would suggest that Mr Micawber's willfully extravagant and futile short-sightedness offers a model of sound economic living. On the contrary, isn't it merely *prudent* to be conservative in our approach to conserving resources which might be in short supply; and, similarly, isn't it prudent to assume that pollution might be a contributor to global warming until irrefutable evidence is provided to the contrary? Aren't those so-called "conservatives" who urge that we throw caution to the wind being somewhat less than conservative in the practice of their beliefs? In truth what might be termed the Theoretical Virtues of economic orthodoxy—faith in the hidden hand of market forces, hope that "something will turn up" and love of economic growth—are all inimical to conservatism, truly conceived.

What then is conservatism, truly conceived, and how does it diverge from *laissez-faire* economics? On a purely political level—and conservatism, truly conceived, can never subsist solely on the purely political level—it might be said that Edmund Burke is the original conservative. Burke analyzed the anarchy of the French Revolution and wrote a devastating critique of the destructive forces unleashed by that debacle. "Liberty," he wrote, "must be limited in order to be possessed." This is the paradox at the heart of human life—and, therefore, at the heart of economics—which is ignored by *laissez-faire* libertarians. In reality, these libertarians are economic anarchists who say that nothing must restrict the liberty of market forces. In exactly the same way that political anarchists believe that a perfect world would be ushered in by the removal of all government and all law, these economic anarchists believe that a better world will be ushered in by the removal of all efforts to limit the liberty of the "hidden hand" of the free market. Yet why should we believe that this mysterious "hidden hand" is always and infallibly beneficial? On what authority should we have such faith in this mystery? What did Christ have to say on the subject? Did He command us to genuflect before the Almighty Market? Not exactly. His great Commandment is that we love the Lord our God with all our heart and that we love our neighbor as ourselves. This is not an option, it is a Commandment. What happens if and when there is a conflict between this Commandment and the worship of the free market? In such cases, which should prevail? What if the free market should dictate that sex and drugs and rock n' roll are the most profitable sectors of the economy? Prostitution and pedophilia are both highly profitable areas and, no doubt, would be even more so if the hidden hand of the market were not thwarted by the prudishness of Christian morality enshrined in law to protect women and children. Clearly, in such circumstances, prudishness is simply prudence and the freedom of the market merely madness.

And this brings us to the crux of the matter: the godlessness of modern economic life. The absence of what might be termed a "soul" in economics, its unremitting materialism, has many damaging ramifications. It leads to the assumption that all humanity's problems can be solved by the attainment of universal material prosperity. The road to riches is the road to happiness. This dominant modern belief is particularly alluring because it suggests that the faster you get one desirable thing the more surely do you attain another. It has the added attraction of being devoid of any ethical constraints, such as the need for self-sacrifice. On the contrary, the more we try to selfishly enrich ourselves the happier we shall be. The materialist mantra is "Get Rich, Be Happy." Once this golden rule is accepted the only problem confronting humanity is an economic and technological one: how do we make everybody richer so that everybody can be happier?

Gandhi spoke disparagingly about "dreaming of systems so perfect that no one will need to be good." Yet the golden rule just cited doesn't mention being good, for that is irrelevant. On the contrary, if goodness is an obstacle to happiness it is to be shunned. The name of the game is self-gratification, not self-sacrifice. And this raises an interesting question. At what point will people decide that they are rich enough to be happy? Indeed, what exactly is "enough"? Conventional economics, obsessed with perpetual growth, has no concept of "enough." The key word is not "enough" but "more." And although there are poor societies that have too little, there are no rich societies saying that they have enough, still less that they have too much.

This prompts another question: Can a society be called "happy," however materially affluent, if it always wants more? Clearly the answer is "no." It is not satisfied, a word whose root in Latin, *satis*, means "enough." It can be seen, therefore, that the "Get Rich, Be Happy" mantra is a futile hymn to a false god. It is neither satisfying in practice nor satisfactory in principle. In fact, a more appropriate hymn for the restlessly rich countries of the world would be the Rolling Stones anthem, "I Can't Get No Satisfaction." A message, which is not only negative, but double-negative!

Ultimately, conventional economists are making the perennially fatal mistake of ignoring the metaphysical truths that underpin physical facts. They forget that greed is a metaphysical reality and is, therefore, in a physical sense, unlimited. Greed is larger than the world and may, if unchecked, outstrip the world's ability to meet its demands. As Gandhi said, "Earth provides enough for every man's need, but not every man's greed." Or, as Alexander Solzhenitsyn put it, "Man has set for himself the goal of conquering the world but in the process loses his soul." And

Solzhenitsyn's words are, of course, a variation on the words of Jesus Christ: "For what is a man profited, if he shall gain the whole world, and lose his own soul?" Such is the folly of economic man that he is not even leaving himself a choice. He is set to lose his soul *and* the world, poisoning the one with greed and the other with the pillage and pollution it causes.

The solution is to replace the soulless economics which knows the price of everything and the value of nothing with an economics with soul; an economics as if people mattered. As Pope Pius XII put it: "The wound of our individualistic and materialistic society will not be healed, the deep chasm will not be bridged, by no matter what system, if the system itself is materialistic in principle and mechanical in practice."

Burdened by materialism and mechanism, humanity has enslaved itself to the rule of the Giants. In economics, global corporations rule the roost, assisted by international financial institutions such as the IMF and the World Bank. Small businesses struggle to survive in a system weighted unfairly in the direction of the Giants. In politics, power continues to be centralized into larger and larger entities which are further and further removed from the needs and aspirations of ordinary people and families. In the United States, the Federal Government and the Supreme Court erode the power of the individual states; in Europe, the essentially undemocratic European Union continues to swallow up smaller sovereign states with its voraciously secular appetite. Everywhere, the small and the beautiful are being threatened by the big and the ugly. Small business is threatened by big business; small government by big government.

The fact is that size matters. "To the size of states there is a limit as there is to other things, plants, animals, implements; for none of these retain their natural power when they are too large or two small, but they either wholly lose their nature or are spoilt." Thus wrote Aristotle and, as Schumacher commented, "it's hard to equal the language of the ancients" when dealing with these fundamental problems of life. Then, echoing Aristotle's ancient wisdom, Schumacher reiterated his belief that "the question of the proper scale of things [was] the most neglected subject in modern society." This, of course, is at the centre of the Catholic Church's teaching on subsidiarity; a teaching which is rooted in the belief that power should be devolved upwards from the family, not imposed downward by large impersonal centralized power.

Perhaps the whole matter was summed up succinctly by another great Catholic thinker who, inspired by the social teaching of the Church, fought for the principle of "small-is-beautiful" as opposed to "big-is-best." It was G.K.Chesterton who put the whole matter in the proverbial nutshell as indeed only he could do. "That which is large enough for the rich to covet," he wrote, "is large enough for the poor to defend." Let this be a rallying cry for all true conservatives.

Joseph Pearce is the author of numerous acclaimed biographies of major Catholic literary figures. He is editor-in-chief of Ave Maria University Communications and Sapientia Press, as well as co-editor of The Saint Austin Review, *and author of the highly acclaimed book,* Small is Still Beautiful, *which successfully exports E.F. Schumacher's economics into the 21st century.*

USURY
From Brotherhood to Universal Otherhood

BY DR. PETER CHOJNOWSKI

"It is absolutely necessary to the capitalist to distinguish more delicately between two kinds of usury; the kind he finds useful and the kind he does not find useful." —G.K.CHESTERTON

I T WAS ONLY AFTER BECOMING A FAMILY MAN, THAT I FIRST BEGAN to have my doubts concerning the viability and equity of the present American economic system, which became the model by which all other national economic systems were judged. For a number of years, the economic "task" before us, seemed to me to be what the American Establishment Conservatives (i.e., Classical Liberals) said that it was, to remove the governmental regulation and excess taxation which hinders the free flow of capital and goods so as to contribute to the expansion of the economy and, hence, to the financial betterment of all of those willing to work. What this particular ideological scheme overlooks is exactly what each man who finds himself being riveted to the dynamics of social and economic life through marriage and fatherhood cannot overlook, the fact that to provide a family with the basic goods which it needs to cultivate a normal human life one must go into debt or, rather, further into debt, depending on the circumstances of a man's life before marriage. To get the phone call from the bank conveying the news that one has been approved for a new mortgage, therefore owing anonymous financial institutions hundred of thousands of dollars for decades, has, sadly enough, become one of those fulfilling moments of imperfect happiness which mark our trek to maturity. The evidence is really undeniable. To provide oneself and one's own with the basic goods of life, one must owe money to another. Since the wages of the average father of a family are not adequate to cover the basics of life (e.g., a house, car, vocational or academic training, land), he finds that he must borrow that money he and his family need to avoid destitution. First, he must be judged "worthy" of such a loan by those with the money to lend. For this, he must have already proved himself to be a "good investment" capable of yielding a return, in amounts far above the principal. In our economic system, one must be a debtor in order to be considered a full-fledged member of the economic "household"; *oeconomia*, of course, being the Greek word for "household management."

These steps on the path of modern "masculinity," the school loan, the house loan, the car loan, the credit card, the gold card, all of which produce the appearance but not the reality of ownership and property, finally lead to a point in which there is a realization that soon such "acquisitions" must cease lest one cease treading economic water and, instead, sink because of the inability to pay back the interest on the money borrowed. Since completely paying off such a debt, while, at the same time, paying for a family's current expenses, is normally not an option, the average father of a household has to count on the "generosity" of those financial institutions which offer a lower interest rate than that which he is currently paying. Shopping for a "better" interest rate, and not the acquisition of real property, Is, probably, one of the most common of all economic acts.

INTEREST IN HISTORY

My encounter with the economic generosity of the contemporary money-lender incited my interest in the whole question of the taking of loans, both within the contemporary capitalist context and in the historical context of Christendom. For someone used to the utilitarian and instrumentalist approach to economics, a historical encounter with the traditional absolute prohibition on the taking of interest on a loan of money (*mutuum*) was morally and intellectually fetching. When the history of this prohibition is analyzed closely, we find that its fate follows closely the fate of Christendom itself. The historical periods in which the two major ruptures in Christendom occurred, the Protestant Reformation and the French Revolution with its Napoleonic aftermath, were precisely the periods of time in which we see the fatal weakening, if not the abolition of, the traditional prohibition against the taking of interest (i.e., usury). Certainly, the enemies of Christendom saw this both moral and legal prohibition as a brick in the citadel of Catholic civilization. To remove it was to contribute to the crumbling of the edifice.

If something is the object of scorn and attack by the enemies of the Social Kingship of Our Lord Jesus Christ, we who wish to restore a sane and Christian society ought to study both its historical reality and its theoretical justification as such a justification was given by the Fathers of the Church, the Scholastic doctors—especially St. Thomas Aquinas, the Ecumenical Councils, and the encyclicals of the Roman Pontiffs. In this way, we might recover, at least intellectually, one more of those bricks with which to begin the restoration of all things. To understand the collapse of the prohibition of usury is to understand the historical movement from Christendom's brotherhood to the modern "universal otherhood."

When looking at the authoritative writings on the question of usury, we find that all trace this prohibition to the one that was promulgated to the Israelites by which they were forbidden to take interest on a loan made to a fellow Jew. The taking of any money above that of the principal loaned was considered to be a violation of the bond of brotherhood, which united men who were of the same blood and of the same faith. To do otherwise, was to exploit a brother for profit, it was to violate *commutative justice* by which each is required to render to another exactly what is owed him. The Old Testament texts that relate this prohibition are numerous. They are, however, all based upon the prohibition stated in *Deuteronomy* 23, 19-20: "Thou shalt not lend to thy brother money to usury, nor corn, nor any other thing: But to the stranger. To thy brother thou shalt lend that which he wanteth without usury: that the Lord thy God may bless thee in all thy works in the land, which thou shalt go in to possess."

Deuteronomy's general prohibition was preceded by a prohibition in *Exodus* 22, 25 which emphasized the exploitative character of the charging of interest on money loaned. Here we read: "If thou lend money to any of my people that is poor, that dwelt with thee, thou shalt not be hard upon them as an extortioner, nor oppress them with usuries." This prohibition, against the economic exploitation of a "brother" was applied to the Catholic Church by the Fathers of both the East and the West. In this regard, Clement of Alexandria declares that the Law, as exhibited in the Deuteronomic prohibition, treats as a "brother" not only one who was born of the same parents, but also, whoever is of the same tribe, or the same faith, and who participates in the same *logos* (i.e., intellectual and spiritual understanding).[1]

Seeing that Our Lord Jesus Christ's universal call to salvation overcame the tribal emphasis of the ancient Israelites, St. Jerome insists that the prohibition against the taking of usury was likewise universalized by both the prophets, as precursors of Our Lord, and by the New Testament doctrine. According to St. Jerome, there was no scriptural warrant for the taking of usury from anyone.[2] The derision which usury incites in the Eastern Fathers is manifest in the writings of St. Basil the Great as he plays on the Greek word *tokos*, which can mean either childbirth or interest (usury). Here, St. Basil locates one of the main principles, along with that of universal brotherhood, which guide the Catholic tradition's analysis of usury, the inherent sterility of money. With a tone that cannot be called anything but sardonic, St. Basil states that the taking of interest on what ought, by its very nature, be a gratuitous offering to a needy brother, is fittingly given the name *tokos*, both because of the fecundity of the evil and since it produces anguish and travail in the souls of those who find that they must "give birth" to extra money to repay one's debt to the usurer. Describing the one indebted to the usurer as in a position of slavery, he states "there is interest upon

---

[1] Benjamin Nelson, *The Idea of Usury: From Tribal Brotherhood to Universal Otherhood* (Princeton, New Jersey: Princeton University Press, 1949), p. 3.

[2] St. Jerome, *Comment. in Ezechielem*, vi:18, in Migne, PL, xxv, col. 176. Cf. Nelson, pp. 1-3.

interest, the wicked offspring of wicked parents." [3]

Understanding the Heavenly Father's lordship over His creation to be our chief incentive to generosity and forgiveness, St. Basil contrasts the Divine Goodness, which seeks to share Itself with that which is other than Itself even though It receives no increase because of the relationship, with the exaction of the usurer: "You have the pledge of paradise and a worth token. If you seek further, [you can see that] the entire world is the possession of a fair Debtor who wisely takes care to obtain abundance and wealth. The whole world is gold, and belongs to your debtor; silver, copper, and every other material is subject to his authority." [4] St. Gregory of Nyssa, brother of St. Basil the Great, also makes the comparison between the fecundity of the created natural order and the attempt of usurers to render fruitful what is by its nature stagnant and sterile: "Only animate beings have the distinction between male and female... But from what kind of marriage does the birth [*tokos*] of gold derive? What sort of conception brings it to fruition? I am aware of the pains belonging to such a birth from the prophet's words, 'Behold, he has traveled with unrighteousness, has conceived trouble and has brought forth iniquity'(Ps. 7.14)... Such is the birth which avarice yields, iniquity begets, and hate delivers... The calamity of a loan has no remedy; instead, it becomes worse.'" [5]

THE SCHOLASTICS: CONTRA NATURAM

BASING IT ON THE UNIVERSALLY ACCEPTED SCRIPTURAL AND MAGISTE-rial teaching, the Carolingian Age (i.e., the ninth century), saw the promulgation of a general prohibition of usury among Christians, whether lay or ecclesiastical. [6] Rabanus Maurus (784-856), a scholar and theologian of the period, interprets the word "brother" in the

---

[3] St. Basil the Great, J. 198. 26 - 199.2.

[4] Ibid.

[5] St. Gregory of Nyssa, *Commentary on Ecclesiastes*, J. 344.16 - 345.5.

[6] Cf. Nelson, p. 4.

Deuteronomic prohibition to signify, in the context of Christendom, any Catholic. Trying to place the prohibition against the taking of usury from fellow members of the Mystical Body, under a general spiritual principle, Rabanus states that we ought to freely provide the fruit of the Word to every Catholic brother, inasmuch as he joins us in partaking of the celestial wafer. The "alien" in Deuteronomy, Rabanus explains, refers to infidels and criminals.[7] At the time, the emphasis on usury being a violation of Catholic brotherhood was, unfortunately, taken by the Jews to mean that they could extract usury from Catholics.[8]

It was in the High Middle Ages, however, where we find the concept emerging that this fundamental element of the economic system of Christendom, was not only based upon the Deuteronomic prohibition and the Patristic commentary on that text. Rather, the mentor of St. Thomas, St. Albert the Great, who always respected Nature for its intelligibility and for its intrinsic order, stressed that usury is and always has been a sin by its own nature (*secundum se*), being a violation of the Natural Law, not because its prohibition by positive law (i.e., law which is publicly promulgated, either by God or by human government) made it such. When St. Thomas Aquinas takes up the question of whether usury, which he insists is *always* an evil, is wrong because a law has made it such or because it is contrary to the moral structure of created reality, he is faced with two historical problems. The first problem concerns the ancient Romans and the second the Jews, both those of the Old Covenant and those in his own times. With regard to the Romans, whose *jus gentium* (i.e., law of the peoples) was considered the most perfect purely rational expression of the Natural Law, a problem arises on account of the fact that during the Empire, as opposed to the early Republic, usury was allowed on a *mutuum* (i.e., a loan). In the case of the Jews, the Deuteronomic prohibition only seemed to apply to "brothers" in the faith and not to the Gentiles. Moreover, in St. Thomas'

---

[7] Rabanus Maurus, *Enarratio super Deuteronomium*, lib. iii, cap. 12, in *PL*, cviii, col. 934.

[8] Nelson, p. 5.

own time, there were states that allowed the taking of usury by Jews while forbidding the same practice to Christians. If the taking of usury is *intrinsically wrong*, why did not the positive law of both man and God forbid it in all circumstances as being contrary to the Natural Law?

In this regard, St. Thomas, along with the other medieval scholastics, attributed the Roman allowance to have been nothing other than an opportunistic concession to the hardness of men's hearts. Even this concession, the Scholastics held, was abrogated by the Emperor Justinian's adherence to the Council of Nicea's condemnation of usury.[9] In the case of the Jews, St. Thomas, both in the *Secunda Secundae* and in his work *De regimine Judaeorum* in which he is replying to the inquiry of the Duchess of Brabant, states that this was simply a temporary allowance on the part of God in order to avoid the greater evil of taking usury from other Jews, who were worshippers of the true God. This "concession" needed to be granted because the Israelites were prone to avarice, as is stated in *Isaiah*. According to St. Thomas, "The Jews were forbidden to take usury from their brethren, i.e., from other Jews. By this we are given to understand that to take usury from any man is simply evil, because we ought to treat every man as our neighbor and brother, especially in the state of the Gospel, whereto all are called… They were permitted, however, to take usury from foreigners, not as though it were lawful, but in order to avoid a greater evil, lest, to wit, through avarice, to which they were prone… they should take usury from Jews, who were worshippers of God."[10] In a point to be pondered during our own time, when there are so many laws passed by national governments which directly contradict the Natural Law, St. Thomas is in accord with the entire Scholastic tradition when he states that all civil laws which allow for usury are *intrinsically null and void*.[11] Indeed, the Council of Vienne (1311-1312) decreed (in *Ex gravi*) that sponsors and partisans of such legislation were rendered subject to excommunication.

---

[9] Cf. Nelson, p. 100. Cf. *ST*, II-II, Q. 78, Art. 1, ad 3.

[10] *ST*, II-II, Q. 78, Art. 1, ad 2.

[11] St. Thomas Aquinas, *De regimine Judaeorm* in *Opera omnia*. Cf. Nelson, p. 100.

In what is, actually, a typical expression of his trust in human intelligence to, unaided by supernatural revelation, gain a basic insight into the divinely established natural order, St. Thomas relies heavily on the understanding that Roman Law had concerning the nature of a loan (*mutuum*). Unlike such things as rental or lease agreements, or investments which entitled the investor to a certain return based upon the gain made as a consequence of the investment (i.e., the *census*),[12] the loan was understood as involving a transference of "fungibles" or, simply, "goods." The loaner would, then, be repaid in kind. The original good loaned would not be returned, but rather, something of equal worth or similar type. What St. Thomas specifically took from the Romans, was their understanding that in a loan property rights over the thing loaned were transferred to the borrower. This was even the case for a loan of money, a type of durable capital. Since the lender would never regain dominion over the relevant article, the Scholastic tradition reasoned that because of the passage of ownership to the borrower, any payment above principal, or any usury, would be a receipt or payment for the use of something that the lender does not own. According to St. Thomas, ownership must be transferred because use involves destruction. In regards to money, use involves alienation of the good from the holder, a type of destruction from the borrower's viewpoint.[13]

CHRISTENDOM'S JUSTIFICATION

WHEN WE SEARCH FOR THE THEORETICAL PRINCIPLES, WHICH UNDERLIE these various condemnations of usury, especially the one of St. Thomas, we must remember the most basic principle concerning man and society held by both Aristotle and St. Thomas. Man is by nature, and by natural inclination, a "social animal," a being which cannot fulfill even his most basic needs outside of the context of a community, whether

---

[12] Raymond de Roover, "Some Further Reassessment of the Scholastic Doctrine of Usury" in *Pioneers in Economics, St. Thomas Aquinas*, ed. Mark Blaug (Edward Elgar Publishing Company: Brookfield, Vermont, 1991), pp. 171-172. Cf. John T. Noonan, Jr., *The Scholastic Analysis of Usury* (Cambridge, Mass. : Harvard University Press, 1957), pp. 84-86.

[13] De Roover, pp. 178-179. Cf. *ST*, II-II, Q. 78, Art. 1 and 2.

that community be that of the family or of civil society.[14] In the case of Aristotle, man's naturally social state is mentioned almost every time a social or economic topic is discussed.[15] The most basic reason why man is social is on account of the fact that on his own, or even within the context of the family, he cannot satisfy either the highest or even all of the most basic desires. He certainly would not be able, on his own, to develop his rational faculty, which is the most perfect power man possesses.[16] The multifarious nature of human needs itself is the origin of the specialization of economic and social function, which is a prerequisite for civilized and developed communities. A man can only truly do one thing well. Since all men are in need, and only society can collectively provide for those needs, each man is a recipient of the goods of society and a producer of those goods. Both Aristotle and St. Thomas understand civil society, therefore, to be organic in nature, with the various "organs" (i.e., *corpora* or guilds) of the state providing for one specific need so that the entire organism of the state could live. We can say, then, for St. Thomas, in civic relationships, all men who belong to the same community are regarded as one body, and the whole community as one man.[17] Since all were part of one body, rather than trying to "kill off" one of the organs of that body, by way of competition or by the offering of loans at interest, society ought be so ordered that the whole and each part of the whole are provided for. Usury, by its very nature, is an exploitation of social need in order to gain profit for one part of that organism. The mind of Christendom simply understood usury as the treating of a brother like a stranger. By demanding more than had been given, the usurer violated the basic bonds of commutative justice, according to which, I give to a man exactly what I owe him. Add to this, the fraternal

---

[14] St. Thomas Aquinas, *Summa Contra Gentiles*, Book III, c. 85.

[15] Aristotle, *Nicomachean Ethics*, Book I, c. 7.

[16] Bernard W. Dempsey, "Just Price in a Functional Economy" in *Pioneers in Economics: St. Thomas Aquinas*, ed. Mark Blaug (Brookfield, Vermont: Edward Elgar Publishing Company, 1991), p. 48.

[17] *ST*, I-II, Q. 81, Art. 1.

bond of those who are members not only of the same state, but of the Mystical Body, and we come to see usury as a perversion of the spirit of charity which is expressed in a loan.

REVENGE OF THE MONEY-CHANGERS

SINCE DURING THE PROTESTANT REFORMATION AND THE FRENCH Revolution, the organicity of Christendom was dealt a fatal blow, it should not be surprising that the economic and moral law, the strict prohibition against the taking of interest on a loan, which testified to that organicity should, on account of these events, also be eliminated. Although one could date the demise of the 2,000-year tradition of not taking interest on a loan to co-religionists to the beginnings of the Lutheran rebellion, the first serious intellectual and theological challenge to the long-standing practice came from John Calvin. Due to Calvin's critique of the prohibition found in Deuteronomy, within 30 years of Luther's nailing of his theses to the cathedral doors at Wittenburg, this fundamental and universally recognized economic principle was discarded. What Calvin denied was that the prohibition against usury was a universal moral law, insisting that it was meant to apply only to the ancient Jewish polity. While Calvin claimed that usury was not to be tolerated "in every case, at all times, under all forms, from everybody" (*neque passim, neque semper, neque omnia, neque ab omnibus*), he still denied its absolute prohibition. All subsequent economic theorists, from the 16th to the 19th century, that advocated increasingly liberal usury law turned to Calvin for support.[18] Although lawyers, bankers, and businessmen took advantage of this allowance in the Protestant North, the body of Continental Christendom continued to cleave to the traditional prohibition, enforced both in the legal courts and in the confessional (we can surmise this because of the numerous medieval and post-medieval wills which

---

[18] John Calvin, *Opera quae supersunt omnia*, XL (CR LXVIII), ed. W. Baum, E. Cuntiz, and E. Reuss (Brunswick, 1863-1900), pp. 431-432.

provided for restitution of usury).[19] The prohibition was magisteri-
ally validated in 1745 with the encyclical letter *Vix Pervenit* by Pope
Benedict XIV in which he restates the absolute prohibition and reiter-
ates the point that it is a grave violation of commutative justice. The
death knell for the laws against usury came with the advent and aftermath of the French Revolution. It was the *Code Napoleon*, intended
to institutionalize and codify the Jacobin and Masonic ideology of
the Revolution in all the territories conquered by the French Army,
which legally ended the prohibition against the taking of usury in
Western Europe. It was this *fait accompli* that induced the Catholic
Church to drop the prohibition as an "issue" in 1830, when the
Sacred Penitentiary issued a statement to confessors, telling them
not to disturb penitents who lent money at the legal rate of interest without any title other than the sanction of the civil law. In the
Code of Canon Law promulgated by Pope Benedict XV in 1917, the
validity of the legal title was admitted, although it still upholds the
principle that a loan is *per se* a gratuitous contract. And so it stands.[20]
No less a personage that Sir William Blackstone, jurist and *the* authority on the English Common Law tradition, clearly recognized Calvin's
attack on Deuteronomy to be the point of initiation of modern capitalism. He also, however, positive for the thesis of this article alone,
describes the prohibition of usury to be the work of the "Dark Ages"
and of "monkish superstitions and civil tyranny," when "commerce
was at its lowest ebb." Clearly linking the prohibition with Catholic
Christendom, Blackstone touts the "credit economy" and its "insepa-
rable companion, the doctrine of loans upon interest," by linking its
birth to the "revival of true religion and real liberty" in the Protestant

---

[19] Benjamin Nelson, "The Usurer and the Merchant Prince: Italian Businessmen and the
Ecclesiastical Law of Restitution, 1100-1550 in *Supplement to the Journal of Economic History*,
VII (1947), pp. 104-122.

[20] Dempsey, *Just Price*, p. 82. Cf. Raymond de Roover, "Scholastic Economics: The Survival
and Lasting Influence From the Sixteenth Century to Adam Smith" in *The Quarterly Journal of
Economics*, May, 1955), vol. lxix, no. 2.

Reformation.[21] Christendom and a charitable non-exploitation of the need of a brother go together; even her enemies testify to the fact. For those men, Calvin charted the way for all to be "brothers" by being equally "others."

A PARALLEL ECONOMY

WHY IS ALL THIS HISTORICAL DISCUSSION SIGNIFICANT? ARE WE NOT relegated to operating within a credit-driven, debt-dependent economy? Perhaps on the macroeconomic level, the level of nation-states, we are, for the time being. On the microeconomic level, the level of the household, the family-owned business, the community, perhaps we need not be. What a fundamental objective of economic life is the attainment and maintenance of real property. Here we do not speak about "property" which, because it was mortgaged or purchased on credit, is no more than a leased or rented good. It is not a fixed "realm" or source of goodness which can sustain a family as its permanent possession. In many ways, the medieval serf, who had to work the land but could not be thrown off it and could pass it entire to his sons, was better off than we. By striving to attain real, debt-free, property, we begin to establish the boundary lines of that familial realm, so desired by our ancestors, which can be a foothold of Christendom and natural sanity.

The avoidance of debt, which renders unstable the family's economic situation, both in the present and in the future, can only be realized in the contemporary circumstances with a certain aestheticism within the family itself. It will require that we become a sacrificial people rather than a people driven by a consuming need to satisfy all desires and whims. Desire must immolate itself on the altar of the good. Now that many for religious and ideological reasons have begun to create "parallel" structures in the educational, religious, and social realms, perhaps it is time that we contemplated creating such parallel structures in the economic sphere. What is meant by "parallel structure"

---

[21] Sir William Blackstone, *Commentaries on the Laws of England*, 1st edition, 4 vols., ed. William Draper Lewis (Philadelphia, Pennsylvania, 1902), Book II, chapter 30. Cf. T. P. Laughlin, "The Teachings of the Canonists on Usury" in *Medieval Studies*, I (1939), p. 125.

is a structure that fills the same needs as those filled by the system, but in a way different. These would be operative on the microeconomic level, the level of the family, the family-owned business, and of the various alternative economic communities now forming both in the United States and elsewhere.

In these newly created economic structures and associations, members could strive to implement the economic teachings of the Church by establishing a system of work and familial sustenance, by which members could avoid both interest-bearing debt and competition undercutting the efforts and work of a co-religionist "brother." A new barter system of goods and services, based upon the theological virtue of charity, could allow the brethren to avoid the rapaciousness of the modern usurer.

Dr. Peter Chojnowski has degrees in political science and philosophy from Christendom College, Virginia, and a Ph.D. in Philosophy from Fordham University, New York. He specializes in the philosophy of St. Thomas Aquinas and Catholic Social Thought and has written over 120 articles and reviews on Catholic, philosophical, economic, historical, and Distributist topics in such publications as Faith and Reason, The Angelus, Catholic Family News, *and* The Remnant. *He currently teaches at Gonzaga University.*

Understanding Subsidiarity

BY DAVID W. COONEY

"The moral philosophy behind most modern experiments means one of two things: either the theory that a centralized plan can be so perfect that we need never criticize the action of the centre; or else that some one idea, such as Centralization, can be pushed further and further forever." —G.K.CHESTERTON

WHILE DISTRIBUTISM PRIMARILY FOCUSES ON THE ECONOMIC question, it is founded on a philosophical view that addresses all aspects of society. Indeed, the conflicts between Distributism, capitalism, and socialism ultimately stem from the different philosophies that underlie each of them and the different views each of those philosophies has regarding the nature and structure of society. Each, of course, considers the positions of the others to be false views; therefore each has the responsibility of presenting and defending its view as well as exposing why the opposing views are unacceptable.

When discussing the structures of society, Distributists use the term "subsidiarity," to articulate what has been clearly established in the social patrimony of the Catholic Church. Subsidiarity is characterized by the stipulation that, "a community of a higher order should not interfere in the internal life of a community of a lower order, depriving the latter of its functions," rather, the higher echelons of order "should support it in case of need and help to co-ordinate its activity with the activities of the rest of society," and should be directed "with a view of the common good." This definition, however, while sufficient for explaining the *essence* of subsidiarity fails to explain why people should accept the *idea* of subsidiarity. Neither is this definition of subsidiarity complete, as the *conditions* upon which the lower order may not usurp the higher are left unclear. Finally, we cannot simply offer this definition to societies that have long been trained to accept a different view. The answer to these questions is important because it establishes the intent and purpose of the various levels of society. Once we understand why different levels of society exist, and which levels are the most basic ones on which all others depend, we can build our foundation for determining their proper authority and powers by virtue of their existence.

Capitalism is founded on a view that the most basic unit of society is the individual. Capitalists do not claim their system can operate with a man who lives in isolation. Indeed, the adherents of capitalism would readily admit capitalism cannot function without society; otherwise, to whom would the individual sell? However, can the individual be the most basic level of society? Society is the sum of relationships, therefore the individual cannot be the most basic level of society because the individual cannot, by himself, be considered a relationship and therefore constitute a society. In fact, if humanity were reduced to one person, it would soon cease to exist. Society may be constituted of individuals, but no individual can constitute a society by himself.

Socialism proper is founded on a view that the most basic level of society is the state. Socialists understand that other levels of society must already exist in order for the state to exist, but their view is that, as each higher level is established, that higher level takes primacy over the lower levels, reducing the lower levels to virtually complete subjugation. However, the idea of the most basic level of society is not merely that level which currently exercises the greatest power, but that level which is fundamental to the very idea of society. It is unarguable that other levels of society must already exist before the state can exist. Therefore, even if we were to concede that its establishment grants it complete primacy over the lower levels, the state cannot be the considered as the most basic level of society.

Distributism holds that the most basic level of society is the family. The family is a form of human relationship and is therefore a society in and of itself. It fulfills the need for humanity's continued existence.

The family is also the level of society on which all other levels depend for their existence. Various associations and groups come into existence when members of families work together or have common interests and concerns. They can help address common things that are beyond the ability of a family on its own. Community exists when several families live near each other and have a need for the establishment and enforcement of laws. Higher levels of government come into being when there is a need to address concerns beyond the ability of the community, like the defense of region or state, and so forth. But, the family can exist, even if marginally, without depending on any of other levels. Therefore, the family must be the most basic level of society, with the other levels existing to fulfill the needs of families living in community, that is, as larger orders organized in higher levels of society.

Another important aspect of these views is how each perceives power within society. This can be seen in the various arguments made about the role of government, what it should or should not do and why it should or should not do it. Capitalists frequently complain about government interference in free enterprise and how largesse government should be reduced to almost nothing. Socialists, on the other hand, argue that government should strictly regulate businesses and individuals through legislation and taxes. Both are based on erroneous philosophies and goals.

The capitalist philosophy embraces individuals as the source of power within society. It is derived from the view that the power of government is determined by the consent of the governed. Most capitalists agree that government must have certain powers by its nature. Disagreements within the capitalist camp over the extent of that power abound, but they all agree the power of government is derived from the will of the people. The authority of government extends only as far as the individuals, either collectively or by majority vote, agree.

The philosophy that underscores socialism is that, by virtue of its establishment, the state becomes the source of power within society. All socialists agree that individuals and groups have rights, but these are derived from society as a whole and the state gets to define what those rights are. Even when the majority of the people believe certain things, those who tend to the socialist view look to different levels of the government to establish what rights exist and should be enforced.

This view, like that of the capitalists, represents a very fundamental difference in the ordering of society. To properly respond to this, we must ask ourselves why the state exists. Since, humanity can, albeit imperfectly, live in relationships without the state, why do we establish states? In order for the state to be the most basic level of society, it would seem that it would need to be the first level of society established. As humanity can, albeit imperfectly, live in relationships without the state, the existence of the state is dependent on other levels of society that come into some sort of conflict. Therefore, the most basic level of society cannot be the state.

Distributism measures the authority of each level of society on the needs that level exists to fulfill. When considering which level of society has the authority to address a given need, distributists ask what is the lowest level of society capable of sufficiently addressing that need. When needs can be addressed by lower levels of society, it is an abuse of power for a higher level to usurp that role. Thus, for the state, or even the city, to usurp the family's authority over the education of its children by enforcing what must be taught or by establishing difficulties or restrictions on religious education; for the city to establish zoning laws that force economic burdens, like the need to commute, on its citizens; for the state to establish regulations or economic policies that give advantage to large corporations over small community-based businesses; for the state or federal government to impose its views on how health care should be managed; all constitute examples of a higher level of society unjustly depriving the lower level of its rightful authority. As higher levels exist to meet that which cannot be sufficiently met by the lower, and as systematic problems require systematic solutions, the central authority is to exercise its power when needs of society as a whole cannot be determined or fragmented by the discernment of smaller authorities (the regulation of imports, drugs, or legislation against severe crimes such as abortion or human trafficking). Thus, subsidiarity is conditional and measured by competence, while also an active agent in favor of the lower levels of society.

The important feature of subsidiarity is that authority is neither granted from below (the people) or above (the state), but from outside. The establishment of a given level of society bestows upon it the level of authority appropriate to its nature according to the moral and natural law, which comes from God. This is the essence of subsidiarity. Higher levels of society exist to fulfill those needs and functions that cannot be met by the lower levels. However, a higher level must not usurp the functions of a lower level. The scope of authority decreases as the level of government increases. However, the authority of each level of government is not derived or granted from the lower level; it is inherent to itself by virtue of its existence in accordance with the moral and natural law.

Another important feature of subsidiarity is that it includes the idea of solidarity, that the society as a whole has a responsibility for all of its members. Thus, when we say that higher levels must not usurp the authority of the lower levels, we also say that the higher levels must support lower levels in cases of need and help coordinate activities with a view to the common good. To understand this, we must understand how to distinguish at what level of society a need should truly be met. We must avoid the temptation to think that, just because a problem is widespread, it must naturally be within the jurisdiction of the higher level of society. Take, for example, the problem of tending to the needs of the poor. If only one community had the problem, then we would naturally say that the families, churches, social organizations, and possibly even the community government would have the primary duty of tending to their needs. However, the fact that poor exist throughout the state has been used a justification for the state to take over tending to their needs. This constitutes an unjust usurpation of authority and a disordering of society. Just as we would expect neighboring communities to assist when needed, the role of the state is merely to assist the lower levels as *they* tend to that responsibility. On the other hand, if we look at the case of rioting and looting, this is naturally the responsibility of the local community, and while it would be commendable for citizens to step forward to assist the community authorities in dealing with the situation, it would be wrong for bands of citizens to act as vigilantes.

Both capitalism and socialism contain some good points, but because the philosophies on which they are founded are ultimately based on a false view of the fundamental form of society and how authority within a society is derived, they ultimately fail to provide true justice. Distributism seeks to establish an economic and social order that is based on justice and the Natural Law. Subsidiarity, as the basis for the social order, establishes the greatest protections for family and individual rights. By keeping authority as local as possible, the citizens maintain the most direct control over laws and regulations that impact their everyday lives, and they are more empowered to make necessary changes when power is abused. Because subsidiarity does not neglect the communal responsibility for all citizens, and it also acknowledges when certain issues are properly the responsibility of higher levels of society, a distributist society is still capable of addressing widespread problems without usurping the authority of the lower levels. This view represents a true philosophical shift from those that are prevalent in our societies today.

Originally from Southern California, David W. Cooney lives with his wife and two children in Washington State where he works as a network administrator.

Dorothy Day, Peter Maurin, & Distributism

BY MARK AND LOUISE ZWICK

"They say it is Utopian, and they are right. They say it is idealistic, and they are right. They say it is quixotic, and they are right. It deserves every name that will indicate how completely they have driven justice out of the world." —G.K.CHESTERTON

DOROTHY DAY AND PETER MAURIN, THE FOUNDERS OF THE Catholic Worker movement, believed there had to be a better system than one run by robber barons, in which the majority of workers did not earn enough to support their families and the conditions under which they worked violated the dignity of the person. They advocated instead the economics of Distributism—an economics the Catholic Workers considered worthy of the human person made in the image and likeness of God, an economics which allowed each person the ownership of a piece of land or participation in the ownership of the means of production of an enterprise.

Peter Maurin had investigated alternative economic models in France before he emigrated to Canada and the United States, where he confirmed that it was possible to have just policies towards workers and still run a successful business. He had learned of the story of Leon Harmel, an industrialist, who having been inspired by the high Christian ideals and good labor practices of his father, introduced many constructive changes in the spinning mills owned by his family. Peter knew that Harmel had been assisted in his approach by priests of the Sacred Heart especially dedicated to helping workers, and that he had worked out some solutions to the ever-present problems of old age, sickness, poverty, and hunger, changes that were ahead of their time, including profit-sharing and groups of employees working together on solving problems. Peter later wrote an Easy Essay for *The Catholic Worker* about Harmel and his ideas and practice. In the January 1947 *CW* Dorothy described Harmel's life work as an employer who brought his policies as an employer in harmony with the teachings of the Gospel, and mentioned how he inspired Pope Leo XIII, who wrote the important social encyclical *Rerum Novarum* (On the Condition of Labor) which advocated policies related to Distributism.

Maurin also visited the cooperatives and small enterprises in the South of France, which were developed on the economic ideas of Prince Peter Kropotkin. Interestingly, both Dorothy and Peter had studied Kropotkin's books even before they met. Their ideas on economics were influenced by him. Dorothy Day said on several occasions in her writings (for example, in the February 1974 *CW*) that Peter Maurin came to her with St. Francis in one hand and Kropotkin in the other. In one of the early chapters of *The Long Loneliness*, Dorothy mentioned four of Kropotkin's books of which she was aware before she met Peter: *Fields, Factories and Workshops, Mutual Aid, The Conquest of Bread*, and *Memoirs of a Revolutionist*. These books had come out while Peter was still in France. Dorothy described his economic vision: "Kropotkin looked back to the guilds and cities of the Middle Ages, and thought of the new society as made up of federated associations, co-operating in the same way as the railway companies of Europe or the postal departments of various countries co-operate now."

Kropotkin scathingly criticized the consequences of the idea division of labor championed by Adam Smith. The assembly line separated white collar or business owners from workers to such an extreme that Kropotkin called it a caste system, almost as firmly established as those of old India:

"We have, first, the broad division into producers and consumers... Then, amidst the former, a series of further subdivisions: the manual worker and the intellectual worker, sharply separated from one another to the detriment of both; the agricultural labourers and the workers in the manufacture; and amidst the mass of the latter, numberless subdivisions again—so minute, indeed that the modern ideal of a workman seems to be a man or a woman, or even a girl or a boy, without the knowledge of any handicraft, without any conception whatever of the industry he or she is employed in, who is only capable of making all day long and for a whole life the infinitesimal part of something: who from the age of 13 to that of 60 pushes the coal cart at a given spot of the mine or makes the spring of a penknife, or 'the eighteenth part of a pin.'" [1]

As Kropotkin wrote of the evils of the assembly line and the precarious situation of the employees he called wage slaves, he emphasized the uprooting of the agricultural laborer who, instead of working on the family farm he loved, was forced to become a migrant worker.

Kropotkin, a scientist, had faith in the human person and believed that, at heart, people were open to working together in a spirit of cooperation. His book *Mutual Aid* refuted the Darwinian idea that the nature of humanity allowed only the approach of the "survival of the fittest." Kropotkin gave many examples of cooperation even in the animal kingdom to show that Darwin's basic premise was mistaken.

Peter, convinced of the basic goodness of the human person even though wounded by original sin, and believing in freedom and responsibility for the person, was interested in Kropotkin's alternative to Darwinism and cutthroat competition. Kropotkin's emphasis on the participation of each person in some aspect of manual labor or crafts work related well to the Benedictine tradition on work and prayer so much a part of the Catholic Worker program. Kropotkin's *Fields, Factories and Workshops* introduced Maurin to another idea that appeared in the Worker movement—that the intellectual could find in manual labor, especially in intensive gardening and fine craft work, an enriching dimension to intellectual work.

Kropotkin's economic ideas were similar to those of the English distributists, whose ideas the Catholic Workers followed closely, although as Dorothy said, they would have objected to his ideas on peaceful

----

[1] Peter Kropotkin, *Fields, Factories and Workshops* (New York: Harper & Row, 1974), pp. 1-2.

anarchism. Dorothy and Peter read and recommended to readers of *The Catholic Worker* the writings of G.K.Chesterton, Hilaire Belloc and Fr. Vincent McNabb, O.P., and their advocacy of decentralization and small ownership as the basis for the economic system: These English writers insisted that people should not be treated like cogs in a machine or made to work twelve hours a day in back-breaking work in coal mines or factories while the directors and stockholders of the corporations became fabulously wealthy.

While the distributists criticized monopoly capitalism, they made it quite clear that they did not advocate socialism. Dorothy noted that the people she called robber barons also spoke against socialism and defended private property. Their understanding of the right to private property was quite different, however, than that of distributists or of the Church. The Workers pointed out the difference to their readers, quoting St. Thomas Aquinas on property, that each person should be able to have some. Frequently, when Dorothy quoted Thomas, in the next sentence she emphasized St. Gertrude's maxim: "Property, the more common it is, the more holy it is" (e.g., May 1972 *CW*). Fr. McNabb, often quoted in *The Catholic Worker* said, "The Divine Right of Property means, not that some men shall have all property, but that all men shall have some property."

The Catholic Workers' advocacy of property for everyone was quite different from the Fannie Mae and Freddie Mac approach of insupportable loans. Like other distributists, Peter and Dorothy opposed usury and backbreaking loans.

Dorothy quoted Peter on property and responsibility in an article called "Maurin's Program" in one of the earliest issues of the *CW* in June-July of 1933: "I am not opposed to private property with responsibility. But those who own private property should never forget that it is a trust." When he said this, Peter was following the tradition of the Church on the universal destination of goods, that the right of private property does not mean the right to destroy it or to use it completely selfishly, but that persons are stewards of creation and must make a social usage of the goods which are privately owned. Peter spoke strongly about acceptance of the responsibility ownership entailed.

Dorothy wrote about Distributism and property in the December 1948 *CW* citing Chesterton's sharp response to those who criticized Distributism as being dreamy and utopian. Her account of the "refugees from ruthless industrialism" who came to stay at the Houses of Hospitality or receive food at the Catholic Worker lent authenticity to the critique:

> "One of the saddest things about this whole controversy is that our opponents look upon agrarianism as visionary. Here is what Chesterton said about such a criticism: 'They say it (the peasant society) is Utopian, and they are right. They say it is idealistic, and they are right. They say it is quixotic, and they are right. It deserves every name that will indicate how completely they have driven justice out of the world; every name that measures how remote from them and their sort is the standard of honorable living; every name that will emphasize and repeat the fact that property and liberty are sundered from them and theirs, by an abyss between heaven and hell.'"

This sounds pretty harsh from the gentle Chesterton, but we, who witness the thousands of refugees from our ruthless industrialism, year after year, the homeless, the hungry, the crippled, the maimed, and see the lack of sympathy and understanding, the lack of Christian charity accorded them (to most they represent the loafers and the bums, and our critics shrink in horror to hear them compared to Christ, as our Lord Himself compared them) to us, I say, who daily suffer the ugly reality of industrial capitalism and its fruits—these words of Chesterton ring strong.

Dorothy explained in the July-August 1948 *CW*, however, that while Distributism had an agrarian emphasis, that "does not mean that everyone must be a farmer." In *House of Hospitality*, she wrote: "While we stress the back-to-the-land movement so that the worker may be 'deproletarianized,' we are not going to leave the city to the Communists." However, the farms were an important part of the attempt to live out the principles of Distributism, a voice against the corporate and government policies which have destroyed so many small farms in favor of agribusiness, and some Catholic Worker farms continue today.

Along with the English distributists, the Catholic Workers saw the modern state tied up with monopoly capitalism almost as a religion with strict doctrines, demanding absolute obedience from all its members. Chesterton, following Belloc, spoke of the "Church of the Servile State." Dorothy often referred to the irony of so many people granting unquestioning obedience to what she called Holy Mother the State while criticizing the idea of the leadership of Holy Mother the Church. She saw that what was presented as freedom and democracy could easily become totalitarian, and that what was recommended by press and politicians or mass movements might have little to do with truth, charity and justice.

Criticism of Catholic Worker advocacy of Distributism came from both right and left. Critics dismissed it as impractical. Dorothy responded to those critics in the July-August 1956 *CW*, in an article called "Distributism is not Dead," restating the relevance and importance of this approach to economics: "The very fact that people are always burying [D]istributism is evidence of the fact that it is not dead as a solution. John Stanley buried it last year in the *Commonweal* and *Social Justice* of the Central Verein in St. Louis some months ago buried it. But it is an issue that won't be buried, because [D]istributism is a system conformable to the need of man and his nature."

In the May 1972 *CW,* in an article on "Catholic Worker Positions," Dorothy reaffirmed the Catholic Worker position on worker ownership and decentralization: "We believe in worker-ownership of the means of production and distribution, as distinguished from nationalization. This is to be accomplished by decentralized co-operatives and the elimination of a distinct employer class."

Catholic Workers argued that laws must be changed from those that favor enormous corporations, giving them every break, to those that help the small farmer or entrepreneur.

Chesterton, for example, had specific recommendations for legislation that would help to create a society of owners instead of laws to create monopoly. They included "the taxation of contracts so as to discourage the sale of small property to big proprietors and encourage the break-up of big property among small proprietors, the establishment of free law for the poor, so that small property could always be defended against great, the deliberate protection of certain experiments in small property, if necessary, by tariffs and even local tariffs, and subsidies to foster the starting of such experiments." [2]

Even with support from society, distributists knew that the change from centuries of individualism, robber barons and massive corporations would not come easily. Dorothy and Peter believed that ethics and economics were related to their faith and they wanted to change the social order to reflect a vision of justice and peace. For Dorothy and Peter, ethics in economics was related to their faith. Dorothy often said, "All is grace." In the 1943 *CW*, reflecting on her participation in one of the retreats which had become so much a part of the Catholic Worker, she applied the Retreat teaching to Catholic Worker efforts to change the social order, to build an economics that reflected human dignity:

> "For ten years, here in the Catholic Worker, in Houses of Hospitality and on farming communes, speaking and writing and working, I have been trying to change the social order. Now I realize that I must go further, go deeper, and work to make those means available for people to change themselves, so that they can change the social order."

Mark and Louise Zwick, founders of Houston's Casa Juan Diego, have been putting "the gospel into action" by opening their doors to thousands of immigrant men, women and children in the form of food, clothing, shelter and medical care for over 30 years. The Zwicks are co-authors of The Catholic Worker Movement: Intellectual and Spiritual Origins *as well as the recent* Mercy Without Borders: The Catholic Worker and Immigration.

---

[2] G. K. Chesterton, *The Outline of Sanity* (Norfolk, Virginia: IHS Press, 2001), p. 79.

The Guild Idea, the Guild Possibility

BY G.K.CHESTERTON

"Destroy the Guild and you destroy the natural classification of men" —G.K.CHESTERTON

T HE WORD GUILD IS A WORD THE MODERNS AND NOT THE medievals use in a romantic and irrational way. Anything in the world may be called a Guild nowadays: a society for picking up orange-peel may be the Guild of the Golden Gleaners; or a company of pierrots performing at Margate and Ramsgate may be the Guild of the Ghostly Guitars; or a movement for muzzling cats as well as dogs may be a Guild for Equal Rights for Four-Footed Friends. But whenever *we*, who are accused of this mysterious medievalism, happen to say a word in favour of the Guild idea, nobody seems to imagine for a moment that it is really an idea. Now, as a matter of fact, it is an idea, and in that sense nothing less or more than an idea.

It is an economic and ethical theory for the construction of certain parts of society; and it has nothing in the world to do with the romance or ritual externals or picturesque costume of that society. To say that you believe in Guilds is like saying that you believe in Trusts, or in State Ownership, or in Syndicalism, or in any other definite way of managing certain matters of trade and employment and exchange. In my opinion, the Middle Ages were fortunate in having begun to develop industry in this way. But the Middle Ages were extremely unfortunate in many other ways; and not least in being ultimately unable to develop it. But if anybody says that I merely behold, as in a dream, ideal craftsmen in coloured garments carving exquisite masterpieces, or happy apprentices dancing round the maypole or distributing the Christmas ale, then he is a hundred miles away from the point at issue. The case for the Guild has nothing to do with the romance of medievalism; nothing whatever.

The theory of a Guild, as distinct from socialism as generally defined and capitalism as at present practiced, is simply this: The men working in a particular trade remain independent tradesmen; in the sense that they are independent and therefore up to a point competitive. Each is working for himself, with his own capital or machinery, and in that sense each is working against the others. But each has entered into an agreement with the others, that he will not compete past a certain point or work against the others in certain unfair and forbidden ways. In other words, there is a competition, but it is a deliberately limited competition; or, if you will, an artificially limited competition. The object is perfectly simple: that it should remain a competition, and not merely turn into a combine. Capitalist competition, which started avowedly as unlimited competition, has only been running freely for about a hundred years, and everywhere it has turned into a combine. I use the word combine as a polite convention; for, of course, we all know that it involves no equality of combination. The true story of the thing is that when all the shops are let loose to compete anyhow and everywhere, by any method good or bad, one shop swallows all the rest. To speak more rightly and worthily, one man swallows all the rest. It is very often, by the nature of the competition, the worst shop and the worst man.

Now the Guild method is no more medieval than it is modern, in so far as it is a principle apart from time. The best proof is that it does still exist in a practical profession with which we are all acquainted. The doctor, the ordinary general practitioner, whom most of us know and to whom many of us owe our lives is a typical example of the member of a Guild. He is not a socialist official; he is not a state servant; he is an example of private enterprise. That is to say, he owns his own lances and stethoscope; he has to buy his own practice; he does in a certain degree compete with the men of his own trade.

But he is forbidden to compete with them by certain methods; he is forbidden to drive another doctor out of his practice by certain expedients of self-assertion or self-advertisement; he has to observe towards his fellow-doctor a certain respect and consideration. He has to do this because he has joined a Guild or confraternity, which exists for the maintenance of the members of his profession as a whole. Its definite and deliberate policy is to keep all the doctors in existence, as far as possible, and *prevent* one of them destroying all the rest. Once it is admitted that a man may use any methods of advancement and advertisement, the chances are that about twenty honest doctors will be swallowed up by one quack.

We know this is what has happened in journalism and in commerce, and in any number of other things. It is also to be noted that the other side of the old Guild idea, which balances this idea of preserving the small man in independence, the idea of testing him as to his claims to such independence, is also true of the modern doctor, as of the medieval Master. It is often regretted that Trade Unions do not insist, as did the Guilds, on a standard of workmanship and finish.

They cannot do so under modern conditions, because they exist to contend with another and specially modern evil. But it is quite true that, before the Guild protected a man from unfair competition, it examined him in the mastery of his craft; and all that obviously corresponds to modern medical examinations and medical degrees. Now a man may quite reasonably disapprove of this system, just as I, in my own opinion, quite reasonably approve of it. He may say quite truly that it has evils of its own. He may say quite tenably that in his view those evils outweigh the good. But his attitude is neither true nor tenable if he pretends that the case for this social system is a mass of romantic rubbish about the perfect beauty of the Middle Ages. He is simply making a fool of himself when he talks of the method by which all the most modern surgery is accomplished and all the most novel medical theories advanced as if it were a mere fantastic dream of bringing back falconry and tilting-armour.

The guild is a thing that man has done and man can do; but it is also a thing that man can perhaps do better. It is not ideal; in that sense it is something much more than ideal. It is impossible in the sense that the bulk of the business world would call it an impossibility, if it had not been a fact.

The nineteenth century had no notion that there could be a fellowship of tradesmen like that of tradesunionists. It did more than deride such a notion; it ignored it. It could not conceive commerce as anything but a competition of capitalists. It is true that since then capitalism has been too much for the competition. It is true that by this time the process has ended in a combination of capitalists that amounts to mere monopoly. But that is a modern alliance for the destruction of small shopkeepers, not the medieval alliance for the protection of them. Anyhow, the industrial civilization no more dreamed of guilds than of gargoyles. It was selfish on principle but I should be very sorry to ignore its virtues as blindly as it ignored all the medieval virtues.

To illustrate what I mean, I will leave on one side all these medieval superstitions that I am supposed to like, and take the sort of modern successes that I rather definitely dislike. I will take an example out of that very Victorian capitalist industrialism which I regret, but to which I should still try to be fair. Take such a case as this. A Frenchman or foreigner of some kind is said to have visited England in the Victorian time, and to have been asked what had struck him as most notable. The foreigner replied that what had really struck him as wonderful was the simple inscription on a huge block of public buildings, a hospital: "Supported by Voluntary Contributions." The facts, so far as they go, are valid and vivid; and they are an answer to anybody who says that a country *cannot* raise volunteers or raise voluntary subscriptions.

Now it would be quite possible to pick a great many holes in a merely patriotic or optimistic version of that fact; but it would still remain a fact. A scholar of great erudition might come upon the traces of a little-known nineteenth century record bearing the curious name of "Pickwick," and giving an account of the medical students in hospitals, which would be the reverse of reassuring to the patient awaiting dissection, which would be quite bloodcurdling glimpses of a barbaric age. Or even if he turned to more strictly scientific facts and records, he might find much to justify the same view. There would be any amount of evidence, in the experiences of people working among the poor, of the hospitals being regarded with popular suspicion or alarm. Then the critic might go carefully through all the tabulated names on the subscription lists and show how in many cases the charity was not really virtuous, and in some cases not even really voluntary.

In short, he would manage to find a very large number of flaws in the hospital and the hospital subscription list, considered as an ideal. But the Frenchman was not admiring it as an ideal; he was admiring it as a reality. The fact that he was talking about really *was* a fact; that people had tried to support an enormous building and an elaborate institution entirely by voluntary subscriptions, and had succeeded. If it was his experience that other societies could only work with the State, it was a relevant remark to say that this was done without the State. If anybody said: "You cannot build a hospital by voluntary effort," there would be a great big building to contradict him. You can explain that building in detail by many stories other than the story that it was built by angels or just men made perfect. But you cannot explain away that building by any stories at all.

Now what is true of the big building called the hospital is also true of the big building called the guildhall, and of the whole story of the guilds. A man, even a learned man, might see all sorts of faults in the guild. But I do not particularly want him to see merits in the guild. I want him to see the guild. I want him to see the guild exactly as the Frenchman saw the hospital. I want him to see a great big social fact as the other saw a great big solid building; as something notable and new, in that it is different from what he is accustomed to assume. I do not want him to see it as something perfect, or even at this stage as something pleasing. I want him to see it as something possible which many would have called impossible. If anybody says: "Trade cannot be organised except on the modern theory of unlimited competition," he will henceforth answer: "Yes, it can be organised quite otherwise, whether or no it ought to be."

If anybody says: "Commerce cannot have any outcome except what we call capitalism," he will henceforth answer, "It can." People might have proved on paper that tradesmen would never limit their free competition with each other; as in the other case people might have proved on paper that rich men would never give up enough of their money to make a hospital; but he would know better. That is what may rightly be called being educated; whether by traveling in other ages like the medievalist, or traveling in foreign countries like the Frenchman. That recognition of real institutions, managed by methods with which we are unfamiliar, that power to watch the workings of things which we should have supposed would not work, is exactly the one thing that is always lacking in those who jeer at the mediaevalist as if he were a mere romanticist. It is in the most exact sense enlightenment; it is the broadening of the mind.

Composite essay from *Illustrated London News*, January 5, 1929, and December 6, 1924

A Distributist Banking System

"There has arisen in modern life a literary fashion devoting itself to the romance of business, to great demigods of greed and to fairyland of finance." —G.K.CHESTERTON

BY JOHN MÉDAILLE

HOW TO MAKE MONEY

SOMEWHERE, SOME WIT OBSERVED THAT THE CRIME OF ROBBING a bank is nothing compared to the crime of starting one. Henry Ford found our system of money creation so appalling that he said if people understood how it worked, there would be a revolution before breakfast. What did Ford find so repugnant? Simply this: before you sign the mortgage to buy your home, the note to buy your car, or the credit slip at McDonald's to buy a hamburger, the money to buy the home, the car, or the burger does not exist; it comes into being in the very act of borrowing it. In other words, the banks create money, and they create it as interest-bearing loans.

The popular notion of banking is that we deposit money with them and they lend it out at interest to share some of the profits with us. Nothing could be further from the truth. The banks do not lend your deposits; these they keep as reserves against losses and for day-to-day cash needs. Rather, the banks lend out a multiple of their deposits as loans, through what is called *fractional reserve banking*. If you deposit $100,000 with the bank, they use that as a reserve to create $900,000 of new loans. This $900,000 suddenly "appears" in the economy as new money in the form of credits against which checks may be written.[1] Nearly all of the money in the United States is created by the banks as loans; that is to say, money creation has become a private monopoly of the banks.

THE IMPOSSIBLE CONTRACT

When all money is interest-bearing debt, then each new issue of money (that is, each new loan) requires a further issue of debt to repay the first note, because while the first loan injects the principle into the economy, it does not inject the money to pay the interest. For example, a $1,000 loan at 10% simple interest for a year requires a repayment of $1,100. But while the loan creates the $1,000, it does not create the $100 to pay the interest. Paying the interest presumes that someone else borrows the $100 and sets it loose in the economy. But the second loan requires a third in the amount of $10, which requires a fourth of $1, and so on. This creates an impossible contract in which there is never enough money to repay loans without making more loans. The higher the rate of interest, the more "impossible" is the contract.

Again, the first loan can never be fully liquidated without an infinite number of future loans; every new loan requires an infinite series of further loans. The practical effect is that a continual extension of credit is built into the economy, whether or not the economy—that is, the real economy of goods and services—needs the funds. Sooner or later the needs of the real economy and the financial economy must diverge, with a credit crisis as the result.

Money is a representation of the circulating wealth of a nation, that is, the goods that are for sale at any given time. We do need both the finance and money creation services that the banks supply. An expanding supply of goods requires an expanding money supply, and finance is necessary, because there is always a gap between the sowing and the harvest, between opening up a production line and the sale

---

[1] Dorothy Nichols and Ann Marie Gonczy, *Modern Money Mechanics: A Workbook on Bank Reserves and Deposit Expansion* (n.p., The Federal Reserve Bank of Chicago, 1992), pp. 7-12.

of a product, a gap that must be financed for business to proceed. But do we need banks in their present form to supply us with new money? When the banks create new credits, they do not create any new wealth; they merely create the power to command existing stocks of wealth. To illustrate this point, compare a bank loan with the case of a farmer who borrows some seed-corn from his neighbor. The borrowed corn represents his neighbor's work and wealth, and no one would deny the lender the right to demand at harvest time not only the return of his corn, but some additional corn as well in reward for his labor (which the corn represents) and for the risk he took.

But suppose that instead of going to his neighbor, the farmer goes to the bank. Unlike the neighbor, the banks have neither corn nor money to lend. Rather, they "lend" credits, which they themselves create, credits that have the power to command the wealth of other men. These credits represent no work, but only the power of the legal monopoly that we have given to the bank. Yet, the financial power that the monopoly represents will be greater than the power of any of the farmers, because the farmers can only create wealth through their work, whereas the bank can create a simulacrum of wealth by pressing a few buttons on the computer, and create it a lot faster than the farmers can create corn; the men who make real wealth cannot compete with the men who manufacture, *ex nihilo*, financial wealth.

Further, the banks have a tendency to create too much money in good times, thereby driving inflation, and too little in bad times, choking off a recovery and driving deflation. The great trick in issuing money is to ensure that the amount issued accurately reflects the stock of goods and services, which the money represents. Since this stock varies from day to day, the supply of money can never be perfectly matched to the supply of goods. The best method is to ensure that money is largely lent for productive purposes. But the banks can increase their profits by providing consumer loans (e.g., credit cards) or loans for financial speculation. Hence, they generally create more money than new production requires, while at the same time, creating an institutional bias for speculation and consumerism.

MONEY AND COMMUNITY

All this leads to the question, "If the banks shouldn't create money, who should?" Something is money if I can easily use it to purchase other things. This tells us who should have the power to create money: anyone who produces goods and services for which the money can be exchanged. In one sense, every producer does have this power, for when a merchant extends credit to his clients, he creates money to that extent, money backed by the goods he offers for sale. Airlines create money in the form of airline mileage credits, and grocers in the form of store coupons. But most businesses do not want the trouble or risk of issuing their own money, and they prefer to defer the privilege to some public power to create a currency that can purchase anything that is for sale. Nevertheless, it is important that businesses and communities have the right to create their own money. Indeed, the right of money creation is a right of any goods-producing community.[2] Note that I said "community" rather than "government." The government is a community, and hence has the rights of a community, but it does not have these rights exclusively, or it displaces all other communities. Federal governments take to themselves a monopoly right of money creation (which monopoly they then delegate to the banks), but it is not necessary for them to do so. Since the government can declare its own currency the only acceptable one for the payment of taxes, and since we all pay taxes, their currency will always have preeminence as long as it remains sound.

A DISTRIBUTIST MONEY SUPPLY

How would a Distributist money system work? Let's look at a national system, since that is most important today, but bear in mind the principles apply to any community. The first thing a supply of new money represents is a conscious decision by the government. The government issues its own money to fund capital projects, such as roads

---

[2] The town of Wörgl experienced a revival after its issuance of local currency during the 1933 Great Depression of Austria. See Alex Von Muralt, "The Wörgl Experiment with Depreciating Money," *Reinventing Money*, (1934), http://www.reinventingmoney/worglExperiment.php.

or dams. Presumably, these projects help to create new wealth, and the goods for sale grow with the new money. Further, the federal government may act as banker to state and local governments, lending them money for their capital projects for an administrative fee.

Note that the new money is created by the government, not borrowed from private parties with the power to create credit at interest. Hence, there is no increase in the national debt, no passing on to our children the expenses that we ourselves incurred. The federal bank may also lend money to the private banks at a modest interest, so that they in turn can combine it with their depositors' money and disperse it to businesses and entrepreneurs. In return, the bankers would have a right to participate in the profits gained from the money they lend. This also increases both the money supply and the supply of goods, which back the money. Further, it gives the public treasury a way of participating in the commercial growth of the country and decreases the need for direct taxation.

It may happen, and likely will from time to time, that governments will issue too much money, causing inflation. However, in such cases, the cause of the inflation will be well understood and the responsibility will be easily established. Those who had the responsibility for creating too much money (or too little) will have both the knowledge to fix the problem and the incentive to do so.

What ultimately disciplines any currency is the presence of other currencies. If people suspect that a given currency is going bad, they will cease dealing in that currency and demand payment in alternate currencies. It is the very freedom to create any currency that guarantees all currencies.

The current money system saddles us, and our children, with absurdly high debts and high taxes, since the interest on the debt must be paid with taxes. But worst of all, it enshrines *usury* at the heart of our economic system. By usury, I mean *wealth without work*; the banks create no wealth and provide no work, but are entitled to returns they have not earned. There is an almost comic absurdity about borrowing from an entity that has no money, only a monopoly of power we the borrowers have given them. And it is even more absurd to have to pay interest on this debt. Further, such a system both guarantees periodic collapses and grants the people who cause these failures the power to virtually blackmail the state into "rescuing" them with generous drafts from the public purse. Money—and economics—is not a "neutral" science; bad ethics equals bad economics; bad morals equal bad money. Usury and monopoly are examples of bad morals and bad economics.

Henry Ford was right: we do need a revolution before breakfast—a Distributist revolution.

John Médaille is an adjunct instructor of Theology at the University of Dallas, and a businessman in Irving, Texas. He has authored the book The Vocation of Business, *edited* Economic Liberty: A Profound Romanian Renaissance *and recently released the successful book,* Toward a Truly Free Market: A Distributist Perspective on the Role of Government, Taxes, Health Care, Deficits, and More.

THE PARTICIPATIVE ECONOMY

BY PHILLIP BLOND

"Politicians will not make a land fit for heroes to live in. It is heroes who make a land fit for all the other poor people to live in; even such poor little people as the politicians." —G.K.CHESTERTON

THE ECONOMY THAT WAS DESTROYED IN MEDIEVAL EUROPE WAS a Catholic economy. And in part what I want to suggest to you is that a Catholic economy is what we actually need today.

Because both secular forms of liberation we've been promised—in the United Kingdom and in the United States, from the Left and from the Right—have been disastrous. Let me tell you why.

I'm building here on the perspectives of the great Edwardian Catholic thinkers, Hilaire Belloc and G.K.Chesterton. According to Belloc the real change from the medieval economy is that both modern socialism and capitalism dispossess. Socialism dispossesses the worker for the sake of the general good, capitalism dispossesses for the sake of the monopolizing capitalist. So you now have two systems of dispossession.

The post-war welfare state settlement is nothing other than the left-wing acceptance of the dominance of monopoly capitalism. In Belloc's *The Servile State*, he talks about how people who think themselves radical have accepted welfarism, pursued by the state, as a means to buy off their legitimate demands for a share of the wealth. So in Belloc's thesis, what you have on the Left is a commitment to a servile relationship via welfare, and on the Right you still have a commitment to monopoly accrual. And indeed you could probably argue that this is true of Keynes.

This collusion between Left and Right has in fact been mirrored in our own day. What we have is the Left producing monopolies, transferring them to the Right, producing monopolies again. You have state protection of expropriating markets.

Therefore the real task and the real future is to invent a new economic and social model. Part of that must be a civic conservatism. By conservative I mean the notion of widely distributed property and assets for all, which is a distributist thesis (it could in fact be either a left or right wing thesis).

I also maintain the older liberal critique of neoliberalism, namely, that markets have tended to monopolies because the price of entry to them is set so high that you end up with modal monopoly dominance. By modal monopoly I mean a model of monopoly that extends beyond whether an individual company has undue market influence to the larger question of whether a certain mode or way of doing business constitutes a cartel.

For example, the great housing crash is primarily the result of the absorption of all local, regional and national systems of credit into one form of global credit. The world's financial system lacked the firewalls needed to separate local from national and international capital. Unduly reliant on one source of credit supply, the residential asset market collapsed when this supply was compromised. The housing bubble was just the last and most notable piece of neoliberal speculation to burst.

In the meantime, the big banks were dedicated to generating price fluctuations and asset bubbles and then exiting before their demise. This strategy of market manipulation deployed enormous amounts of capital in speculative arbitrage (just five U.S. banks had control of over $4 trillion of assets in 2007). This market was far from the thousands of small investors envisaged by classical free-market liberals.

So a civic economy based on local economies based on widely distributed ownership in turn based on new models of association and productivity is really the post-capitalist future.

I want to suggest three ways to move forward: economic, political, and social.

First, we must acknowledge that the whole of our free-market economy has been captured by the Chicago School. Because we're only focused within competition law on price utility as the interpreter of what would be a good outcome, the bigger your company, the cheaper you can deliver goods. So we pursue monopoly in the name of freedom and asset capture in the name of wealth extension. What we have produced as a result, from the Right, is a whole ideology of competition but no competitors. We've created a condition in which large businesses dominate—via a rigged market of rent-seeking capital—in an economy that cuts off for the majority the path to mobility and prosperity.

What do you do for people who aren't that clever, or that well positioned, or that rich, but who are hard-working? Well, it's permanently low wages for you—and for your children, and your children's children. You say you would like to open a store or a business, to have some financial autonomy? Well, we can't have that. The truth is, we can't create a situation in which you could prosper because you can't compete—you can't bully suppliers, you can't cross subsidize, you can't access the supply chains that are already controlled by the new monopolies, so you can't capture the price utility that those big concerns can. (No matter that the corporate model is subsidized by various tax breaks.) Consequently, there is no route out for many of those in the bottom half of the population.

Until we can change that economic structure, we cannot break the law. So staying within the private sector, we need to adopt an older liberal model and broaden it with a Catholic, distributist account of the notion of various plural senses to give human beings a chance at a stake in the world. An economy not wedded to a single market model susceptible to the winds of global finance could spread wealth throughout the sectors, creating a resilient and plural economy capable of self-sustaining in the face of the collapse of one segment.

I believe in the free market, but we haven't had a free market. In a brilliant paper, the head of monetary stability at the Bank of England, Andrew Haldane, recently asked why the speculative economy has done so well. Because the state has taken all the risks. Capital will always seek the highest return, and if you look at the rise of the state and the way it has legislated the banking sector, it has essentially (through deposit, capital, and liquidity insurance) taken on the risk of investment banking activity. Investment bankers can take any risk and not pay any price. Because of this, all capital is centralized. Why would you go to Wisconsin to open a smelting plant when you can get a much safer and higher return in Wall Street or the City of London because you are engaging in the highest return activity at a risk premium covered by the taxpayer? The most you can lose in high finance is your original stake, and sometimes not even that, as there seems no limit to what the state will do for finance capital. If you add up all the debt in the U.K.—personal, state, and corporate—it comes to 468 percent of Gross Domestic Product. This could mean 10 to 20 years of de-leveraging—a generational economic contraction. There's nothing free about that.

Along with the private sector being captured by big capital, the public sector has been captured by the big state. The public sector should be broken up—not privatized out, so that big-money interests could essentially gain the difference between the wages of those in the public sector and the wages they were prepared to pay, but turned into employee-owned co-ops. Let's have worker buy-outs instead of multi-leveraged management buyouts that game both stakeholders and workers. Let them de-layer and de-managerialize their own professions, and let them have a stake and deliver the service they've always wanted.

In terms of public assistance, I argue for a power of budgetary capture. Millions of welfare dollars are spent, yet all that ever does is make recipients passive. Ordinary people, recipients of public largesse, can't in any way create the associations and culture that can be part of their own renewal. So why not allow citizens' groups to take over government budgets and run them for themselves? Imagine women bonding together because they don't want to see their children fall into crime and degradation. In giving these people power over their own communities with the public money that has been subsidizing rather than transforming their lives, we will be giving the poor capital. And if they can gain access to the market, they might really create the free economy that everyone has been claiming but no one has been delivering. Then we'll have a situation in which the state won't regulate the small and the intermediate out of existence, a situation in which people can genuinely compete.

In the political realm, we have to admit that democracy doesn't work particularly well, mainly because it's hugely centralized and substantially captured by vested interests. We need to turn it upside-down—a doctrine of radical democratic subsidiarity that would allow local associations both to select and vote for their own candidates. We can't do that in the current political settlement. It's too locked; But if, like budgetary capture, we had a democratic capture, we could send democracy back to the streets. If we could ally that political economy with actual democracy, we could really have bottom-up associations and render the central state increasingly superfluous.

This sort of subsidiarity isn't a fetishization of the small. It's a belief in the most appropriate, and that can even be large transnational corporations. I don't, for example, believe in a localized nuclear industry. In addition, there will always be a role for the state as a kind of ultimate guild or virtue culture that can step in when things go wrong. In that view, it's not Robert Nozick's night-watchman state nor is it the centralized state of the Fabian socialists. The state becomes a facilitator of the sort of outcome it wants, but it has to be agnostic as to how people realize that outcome. And only if the outcome isn't being realized—for instance, if poor people aren't being educated—should it step in.

Finally, the real recovery has to come in civil society itself. Society should be what rules, what regulates, what is sovereign. Both the state and the market must be subservient to renewed civil association. This requires a restoration of social conservatism that recognizes the claim of the common good over the free agency of the individual. Rather than being a reactionary force that makes war on minorities or vilifies one-parent families, it should, for example, promote the understanding of the family as a feminist institution that because of its reciprocity and mutuality liberates both men and women to pursue the ends that most of them want, which is human flourishing, and children. It should also reach beyond the family to restore the social square. Placing people in relational matrices recreates for those who don't have a nuclear family the possibility of a civic and extended one.

In Britain, there's a part of Birmingham called Castle Vale that has had no government money. But they drove from their streets the drug dealers, the prostitutes, and the criminals. They took complete control of their area purely through social capital and self-organization, and all the indices of crime and violence dropped to rates unseen by any sort of state action. By having that social capital, they were able to capture political and economic power.

This is the essence of the Western liberal tradition: the rise of association—a state that isn't dictated by the oligopolies of the market and the central government. The task of a radical conservative politics is to recover this: the middle life of civil society. Villages should run villages, cities cities, and neighborhoods their own streets and parks. Additionally and most importantly, a transformative conservatism must take on the rampant individualism of the self-serving libertarian, not least because an individualism that undermines all social goods by denying a virtue-binding code and moral belief is not a conservative philosophy. On the contrary, extreme individualism is a leftist construct and should be recognized and abandoned as such.

The future is there to be gained, both for us in the United Kingdom and for Americans. It is the politics of the middle, the life of the civic, and the empowerment of the ordinary. It is to be hoped that a radical conservatism embraces this opportunity and creates and facilitates this future for us all: free association and a self-organizing citizenry producing the norms and the universals that alone license a civic state, a plural society, and a participative economy.

Phillip Blond is an internationally recognized political thinker and social and economic commentator. He is the director and founder of the award winning public policy think tank ResPublica and author of Red Tory: How Left and Right have Broken Britain and How we can Fix It, *which sought to redefine the centre ground of British politics around the ideas of civil association, mutual ownership and social enterprise. His ideas have influenced the agenda around the Big Society and have helped to redefine British politics.*

DISTRIBUTISM, THE COMMON GOOD, AND THE REJECTION OF TOTALITARIANISM

BY PHILIPPE MAXENCE

"A Catholic does not complain of there being a County Council or a Post Office, because recognized government has a right to rule; because social order itself has a natural and even a divine authority. But mere money has not even the smallest human authority."—G.K.CHESTERTON

CCORDING TO THE WISDOM INHERITED FROM THE ANCIENTS, especially Aristotle, the purpose of politics is to pursue the common good, which is not only the good of society as a whole, but also the good of all its parts. St. Thomas Aquinas further developed this teaching and wrote that, "[God] is the universal cause of all goods"[2] and "the common good of the many is more divine than the good of the individual."[3]

The classical philosophical approach does not divorce the common good, as the real purpose of the social and economic spheres, from the political. To say the end of society or of the economy is the production of goods and riches is false. Rather, both are subject to the good of society as a whole and both should be measured by how well they provide for the common good. As such, our purpose is not limited to the sum of material goods, by nature perishable and incapable of perfecting man and society. Although to some degree, it may be necessary to own a refrigerator, car, or DVD player, it would be hazardous to

[1] Translated from the French by Richard Aleman and Inez Storck.
[2] *In I Ethic.*, lect. 2, Marietti, n. 30.
[3] St. Thomas Aquinas, *Summa Theologiae* II-II Q. 31 Art. 3.

THE HOUND OF DISTRIBUTISM

imply that these material goods are essential to the common good. Any society merely producing material goods and finding in them its *raison d'être* would be a cold world, empty of social relationships and political bonds; a world of unbridled greed constantly pursuing an unrestricted possession it can never fully attain.

THE ECONOMIC ILLNESS

By extracting the concept of "good" (and hence "common good") from the notion of material wealth, the modern world undermined itself. Following the Renaissance, a period Chesterton aptly called "the relapse," our haunted minds have been tormented by the reductionism governing our actions and practices. To his credit, John Maynard Keynes clearly explored the implications of this divorce:

> "For at least another hundred years we must pretend to ourselves and to everyone that fair is foul and foul is fair; for foul is useful and fair is not. Avarice and usury and precaution must be our gods for a little longer still. For only they can lead us out of the tunnel of economic necessity into daylight." [4]

Such an outlook, contrary to all morality, can only justify itself by making the pursuit of wealth the pinnacle of human life. With this approach to man, by elevating economic activity to the critical and determining cause of individual and social existence, the descent to individualism was inevitable. Here the enrichment of the individual precedes the enrichment of society, as do the daily worship of the gods which for Keynes are greed, usury, and precaution. The abandonment of any perspective of the common good reduces the ends of man and society to the sole pursuit of material goods (or, to use modern terminology, self- interest) but it also attempts to destroy man's own nature, which is profoundly social and not exclusively economic. What follows is the closing-in of the individual on himself under the pretext of acquiring more and more material goods.

---

[4] "The Future," *Essays in Persuasion*, 1931.

The Canadian philosopher Charles de Koninck's book, *On the Primacy of the Common Good Against the Personalists*, defined such a world as a "society consisting of persons who love their private good above the common good, or who identify the common good with the private good, ...a society not of free men, but of tyrants...who lead each other by force...." [5]

One need not look far and wide for this world in our books and amongst our utopian philosophers. This world strangely resembles liberal society, which extends its global hegemony by removing all traditional societies and all the virtues necessary for "living well together," in order to serve the priority of economic production and the totalizing reign of technology.

SOCIETY IN REVERSE

The modern world of liberalism leads to the incoherent paradox of wanting to create a society with only individuals, a view the Belgian Thomist Marcel De Crote coined "dissociety," a society made up of individuals and the state. Marcel De Corte remarks correctly that, "The modern state lacks an underlying society; it arises from the dissociety it dominates. It is accountable for a contradictory task...building a society with elements that refuse to submit to the common good of all, according to the secularized Christianity that is their religion. It is wedged between the monolith crushing man and the anarchy claiming to deliver him by the slaying of his social nature. The refusal of one automatically generates the adoption of the other, and the adoption of the other automatically reaffirms the first...The almost immediate result is either the strengthening of the state machine or death. Each time the Roman Empire collapsed under the pressure of a greater individualism destructive of the common good, it consolidated its state machinery and turned into an anthill in which exhaustive and paralyzing regulations replaced a vanished social instinct."

---

[5] Translated by Sean Collins in *The Aquinas Review*, vol. 4, 1997 p. 25.

From the onset, distributists critiqued how the twentieth century produced the terrible choice between socialism, which devours the human for the benefit of the state, and liberalism, which completely annihilates society, leaving only isolated individuals. If socialism distorted any true notion of the common good by radically separating it from the good of the human person, capitalism claimed to elevate the individual good to the level of the common good by continually and violently reshaping the nature of man. As noted by Charles De Koninck, the root of these evils is the same:

> "This desire for the common good is in the singular itself. Hence the common good does not have the character of an alien good—*bonum alienum*—as in the case of the good of another considered as such. Is it not this which, in the social order, distinguishes our position profoundly from collectivism, which latter errs by abstraction, by demanding an alienation from the proper good as such and consequently from the common good since the latter is the greatest of proper goods? Those who defend the primacy of the singular good of the singular person are themselves supposing this false notion of the common good."[6]

RESPECT FOR THE NATURE OF MAN

The Distributist proposal follows an unwillingness to accept the false choice between a liberalism destructive of man's social nature on the one hand, and the inhumane anthill of state socialism on the other. Instead, Distributism aims at a society of free men pursuing the common good of each and all within the family and community, ordered to a truly common, universal and extrinsic good, which is God. Thus, the power of Distributism: the purpose of society and hence of man, is not primarily the production of wealth or collective servitude. It is about allowing men to achieve their purpose, to live in political camaraderie, to practice the virtues, and to achieve happiness and contemplation, which is the highest good in man according to Aristotle in his *Nicomachean Ethics*.[7]

---

6. *On the Primacy of the Common Good*, p. 18.
7. Aristotle, *Nicomachean Ethics,* Book X.

To achieve this, the Distributist revolution is foremost in respect for the nature of man. Unlike the modern perspectives of liberalism and collectivist socialism, the Distributist views man as born into a mini-society called the family, which Chesterton defined as "the anarchist institution *par excellence.*" Because of its nature, the family owes nothing to human artifice and nothing to the state. It is the foundation of freedom and responsibility because, as Chesterton pointed out, "it is based on love, not fear." Men learn to become men within the family not only as individuals but also as social beings. To feed his family a man must work and produce wealth, thereby entering into a working community acutely aware of its own laws and its own purpose. "Destroy the Guild and you destroy the natural classification of men," wrote Chesterton.

PRIVATE PROPERTY AND THE
UNIVERSAL DESTINATION OF GOODS

But this law of work and professional organization also requires another fundamental element: the private ownership of the means of production. St. Thomas Aquinas believed that it was "lawful that man possess private property" and it was even "necessary to human life."[8]

Property is necessary for human life. But, as the Church has always taught and distributists emphasize, this right is not absolute since it must also be directed toward the common good. According to St. Thomas, the "temporal goods which are divinely given to man, are his as to the ownership, but as to the use of them, they belong not to him alone but also to others who from them are able to be supported out of that which is superfluous to him."[9] Following in the steps of Leo XIII, Pope John Paul II reaffirmed: "Christian tradition has never upheld this right as absolute and untouchable. On the contrary, it has always understood this right within the broader context of the right common to all to use the goods of the whole of creation: *the right to private property is subordinated to the right to common use*, to the fact

---

[8] St. Thomas Aquinas, *Summa Thelogiae* II-II Q. 66 Art. 2.
[9] St. Thomas Aquinas, *Summa Theologiae* II-II Q. 32 Art. 5.

that goods are meant for everyone."[10] In his own words, Chesterton added, "Property is merely the art of the democracy. It means that every man should have something that he can shape in his own image, as he is shaped in the image of heaven. But because he is not God, but only a graven image of God, his self-expression must deal with limits; properly with limits that are strict and even small."[11]

TOTALITARIANISM, ECONOMIC VIOLENCE

Based on a society of free men living in their natural communities and concerned with the common good, the principles of Distributism firmly reject the very roots of totalitarianism and do not consist in an arbitrary extension of political policy. This heinous abuse of the purpose of political policy sacrifices the common good to the good of the individual under a regime of tyranny. As shown by the philosopher Claude Polin, totalitarianism is distinguished in that it consists in a power that is "the expression of the economic infrastructure." Totalitarian society expresses the absolute domination in everything and everywhere of *economism*, evidenced by Marxist-Leninism and, in its own way, the racism of Hitler's National Socialism.

For its part, liberalism is fundamentally unable to respond because it sees in economic society that which enables man to end his historical alienation in order to achieve personal freedom. Or, at least, the economic sphere is unable to meet this expectation because it always runs up against the tension between the desire for equality in modern societies and inequality born of economic activity.

Unlike its communist and Nazi ancestors, totalitarianism in modern economic society imposes itself not through bloody violence, but by the voluntary self-regulation of its members, who see the wickedness of this world and the certainty that it is impossible to escape from it. Market-driven, consumerist, and materialistic free-market economic society is imposed by totalitarian violence, and Distributism was born

[10] Pope John Paul II, *Laborem Exercens* §14.
[11] G.K.Chesterton, "The Enemies of Property," *What's Wrong with the World* (San Francisco: Ignatius Press, 1994).

and is developed today precisely against this typical modern violence. Distributism is determined to rebuild the economic sphere in society, as Karl Polanyi explained, so that it does not encompass the entirety of human existence or impede the search for the common good.

Philippe Maxence is editor-in-chief of L'Homme Nouveau, *the French Catholic newspaper, and president of Les Amis de G.K.Chesterton Society. He is the author of* Pour le réenchantement du monde: une introduction à Chesterton, L'Univers de Chesterton, *and several other books.*

DISTRIBUTISM AND MARXISM

BY DONALD P. GOODMAN III

"I do not object to Socialism because it will revolutionize our commerce, but because it will leave it so horribly the same." —G.K.CHESTERTON

TOO OFTEN DISTRIBUTISM IS ACCUSED OF BEING A SPECIES OF Marxism, when in reality it's hard to imagine a proposition farther from the truth. Distributism has little in common with Marxism beyond the fact that it's not capitalism; sadly, that fact is sufficient for many capitalists to attack Distributism as a brainchild of Engels and Lenin. But Distributism specifically opposes *all* the other primary tenets of Marxism; indeed, it could be accurately described as the anti-Marxism, fundamentally opposed to the most significant points of Marxism.

Marxism is primarily associated with three basic tenets. First, its critique of capitalism; second, its philosophical background of dialectical materialism; and third, its brand of proletarian revolution leading to collective ownership, considered as the abolition of private property. Various forms of Marxism—Leninism, Trotskyism, and so forth—differ according to details, but any system that does not embrace these three fundamental precepts cannot accurately be called Marxism. Distributism, it will be seen, can only be described as adhering to one, and even then only tenuously; it is thus so different from Marxism that equating the two, or even ascribing a real relation between them, is at best philosophically myopic.

The first fundamental precept of Marxism, its critique of capitalism, does share some vague similarities with Distributism's critique of the same. Marx held that capitalism involves the domination of the bulk of the workers (the proletariat) by a minority (the owners, or the bourgeoisie). Marx opposed the *commodification* of labor, as Distributism opposes it; he held that it rendered the worker politically as well as economically powerless, with which Distributism will partly agree. However, at that point the similarity ends.

Distributism's critique of capitalism does, like Marxism, begin with the observation that capitalism concentrates productive property into the hands of the few. However, Marx's objection to this fact is not Distributism's objection. Distributism argues that the ownership of the means of production by the few makes economic independence and political influence by the many non-owners impossible, or at least unreasonably difficult; the solution to this is to encourage the wider distribution of productive property among the people. As G.K.Chesterton famously noted in *The Uses of Diversity*, "Too much capitalism does not mean too many capitalists, but too few capitalists." Marx, on the other hand, held that even the few private owners of productive property in capitalism are too many; the means of production should not be owned by anyone, but should rather be owned only by the state, making not only most but *all* of the people non-owning workers. In other words, Distributism's complaint against capitalism is that the means of production are owned by too few; Marx's is that they are owned by too many. While Distributists and Marxists can both stand together in disapproving of capitalism, Distributism disapproves it for the right reasons, Marxism for the wrong ones. This is, as noted above, a vague correspondence in one of the essential elements of Marxism, but it is hardly enough to equate the two theories.

Second, Marxism is based on a philosophical outlook called *dialectical materialism*. In brief, dialectical materialism holds that human history is basically the story of class warfare. Society gradually struggles upward through different stages of development, from the slave societies of antiquity, through the feudal societies of the Middle Ages, to the capitalist societies of Marx's day. Inevitably, in each stage the proletariat gains more and more freedom and brings mankind closer and closer to the ultimate goal: the proletarian revolution, the abolition of private property, and the establishment of the communist society, in which the state will simply "wither away" because its coercive force is no longer needed. This history is *materialistic*; there is no God, no abstract principle guiding it. It simply *is*, a fact of nature, the societal equivalent of Darwinian evolution. Religion is false, the "opiate of the masses"; it is just another tool of the bourgeoisie, futilely attempting to prevent the inevitable communist revolution.

Distributism is precisely the opposite of this. It is based on religion and arises out of the philosophical and religious principles argued throughout the Christian era, and first authoritatively by Pope Leo XIII in his encyclical *Rerum Novarum*. It acknowledges no inevitable progress in history; indeed, Chesterton mocked the very idea in *The New York Times Magazine* as "prefer[ing] Thursday to Wednesday because it is Thursday." History will not help the workers; the workers must help themselves, guided by the principles of social life established by the Creator. The state will not, as in Marx's utopian nightmare, simply "wither away"; rather, the state is an essential part of human society, which will always and must always be present in that society, guiding all the subsidiary corporations and individuals within that society toward the common good. This unity of goal of all members of society, individual and corporate, goes by many names, most recently solidarity; it fundamentally rejects the notion that different parts of society should be at war with one another, instead insisting that all parts of society are members of the same body politic and must work for the same end. It is hard to imagine a vision of society, of history, and of the genesis of social theory more at odds with Marx's than Distributism's.

Finally, Marx advocated a proletarian revolution to overthrow the current system of ownership of the means of production and to socialize ownership. Distributism has nothing in common with such a program. While Distributists have advocated many different ideas in many different places for transforming capitalist societies into just ones, those ideas all have two things in common: they are *gradual* and they are *peaceful*. There is no sudden revolution, no barricades, and no violence;

there is the conscious transformation of society peacefully, through the rational action of the members of society themselves. The notion of solidarity briefly described categorically excludes anything like Marx's proletarian revolution. Once again, it's difficult to conceive of a system more opposed to Marxism than Distributism is.

It is *not* difficult, on the other hand, to imagine a system that conforms in many particulars to Marxism. Indeed, we can name it: capitalism. Like Marxism, capitalism ensures that the bulk of society will be composed of workers laboring for a wage, unlikely to ever become the owners of productive property. Like Marxism, capitalism ensures that the bulk of these workers will never have any significant political power, because they will never have the economic independence that will grant them an influence in the political process even remotely similar to that of the owners of productive property. Like Marxism, capitalism ensures that society is strictly defined into two classes, those who control the use of productive property and those who don't. Like Marxism, capitalism ensures that those who belong to the first group have the bulk of power, including power over those who belong to the second.

One of the greatest of the early Distributists certainly said it best, in his aptly titled work *What's Wrong with the World*: "I do not object to Socialism because it will revolutionize our commerce, but because it will leave it so horribly the same."

Donald P. Goodman III is a practicing attorney in the Commonwealth of Virginia, a graduate of the William and Mary School of Law and of Christendom College with a degree in history and a minor in classical languages.

MAKE YOUR BACKYARD A FOREST GARDEN

BY BILL POWELL

"If we were really besieged in this garden, we'd find a hundred English birds and English berries that we never knew were here…. I bet you've never examined the premises! I bet you've never been round at the back as I was this morning…"— INNOCENT SMITH, IN *Manalive*, BY G. K. CHESTERTON

IMAGINE YOUR BACKYARD WAS A MINIATURE FOOD FOREST. IN THIS forest, you could find apples, grapes, plums, and pears, figs, kiwis, oriental persimmons, flowers, herbs, lettuce, mint, strawberries, blackberries, blueberries, raspberries, mushrooms, and even a small pond or two. How much space do you think you'd need for all that? In Greensboro, North Carolina, Charlie Headington gets all that and more—from *one-tenth of an acre*.

"Three acres and a cow," runs the old Distributist mantra. Today, you're lucky if you have a backyard. So what can you do with just a backyard? More than G.K.Chesterton ever dreamed.

Take a long look at that backyard. Do you have any ground? Do you have any sun? That'll do.

"Three acres and a cow" remains a good motto for food self-sufficiency. Just because you can't produce *all* of your food on your own land, you can still produce plenty. You can't farm in the average backyard. But what you can do is *permaculture*. You can make your backyard the most productive and loveliest place you know with incredibly low-maintenance.

Permaculture means "permanent agriculture." It is the opposite of today's farming.

In contemporary farming, you focus on the product. Take a businessman who wants to sell eggs. That's all he thinks about—eggs—a single vision, like some mystic in the desert. And to build that vision, he makes a desert. He clears a space, and raises endless rows of cages, each shrunk with scientific precision to the absolute minimum space in which a hen can breathe. More hens mean more eggs.

Those hens get hungry and thirsty, so the businessman buys water and feed. Millions of eggs need to be delivered, so he buys trucks. Hens get sick (breathing the indoor stench of their own excrement all day can't help), so he buys antibiotics. And so on. In the short term, he can sell a dozen eggs for two bucks, and still make a profit, because he sells by the truckload. He has *major output*. Problem is, he requires *major inputs* from outside his land. The slightest glitch in his supply of water, feed, trucks, antibiotics, or cheap labor—any one of them—and the entire system collapses. He never noticed the system in the first place. He only wanted eggs.

Permaculture is *system design*. You start with the system. Instead of imagining millions of eggs, you look at the actual land. What system is already there? How much rainfall does it get? What plants will the soil support? What could you use the wind for? You look at the natural inputs, the resources you get for free.

You'll need some outside inputs, of course, but the less outside inputs you need, the more stable your system.

Back to our backyards. If you've ever tried to plant an annual garden, you've also discovered the most expensive input it needs: you. Your time. Your work.

Many people do manage to have annual gardens in their backyards. Maybe you're one of them. Gardens have advantages over livestock. They can't escape and trample the neighbor's petunias. They can survive a little longer without a drink. And unlike cows, pigs, and chickens, gardens are almost never illegal.

But annual gardens are still a lot of work. Every year, you do the same digging, planting, and worrying. Some people are great at it; others find that the slightest little thing, whether it's a virus or a vacation, will wipe the garden out.

So I propose a new project for the aspiring Distributist with a small backyard: the *forest garden*.

Think about the forests in your life. How much maintenance do they require? Do you see rangers anxiously weeding among the trees? Does the forest die if you forget to water it? Doesn't it seem like trees will grow practically anywhere, even on the smallest strip?

This insight still startles me. For most of my life, I thought of plants mainly as food, and farming mainly as work. Without huge tractors, or at least constant weeding, we could never wrest food from the miserly earth. Meanwhile, all that time, as I was growing up, and mainly being shuttled back and forth along I-95, what flourished along the highway shoulders, unplanted, and unweeded?

Trees. Plain, ordinary, drought-surviving trees. *Perennials*. Permanent plants.

Now, the skeptic might note that if I had leapt from my parents' car into this overlooked Eden, my feasting would have consisted mainly of acorns and those maple seed helicopters. So we come to the *garden* in "forest garden." If you want food, you need to plan your little forest.

I don't mean an orchard. An orchard is usually a whole lot of one kind of fruit tree, a lot of grass and poison ivy, and that's it. Orchards are great in their way. But a real forest has far more than just trees: shrubs, bushes, ground cover, and animals—it's a whole system of different creatures that flourish together. Your forest garden will be the same way. You may have a few animals, like chickens. You can definitely have bushes. Bushes may not sound so exciting, but some bushes grow blueberries. Others grow raspberries or blackberries. There's also room for herbs and other small plants, both in shady spots and, especially while the trees are growing up, sunny spots. Perennials are best, but you can make room for annuals like tomatoes and peppers if you like. And for the shady spots, there are all these interesting plants that are practically unknown. Shade-tolerant plants tend not to focus on fruits (though paw-paws do well), but you can get edible roots, tubers, greens, and more.

How much work will it be? If you plan your forest garden right, maintenance will be a lot less work than you think. I began with Charlie

Headington's forest garden, and the long list of crops he gets from his 0.1 acre backyard. Guess how much work he does on it? About 68 hours *per year*—ten hours a week for a couple weeks in spring, and another couple weeks in the fall. Then, during the growing season an hour a week, mostly for the annuals. I don't know about you, but to me, 68 hours a year sounds like a steal. And on top of that, his backyard is a gorgeous little forest, with different nooks and spots to relax in.

What's the catch? Setting it all up.

This may be a good time to reveal that I myself do not yet have a forest garden. I'm currently working through the second volume of *Edible Forest Gardens*, the definitive, intimidating, expensive, but amazing and readable two-volume set by Dave Jacke and Eric Toensmeier.[1] The art of backyard forest gardens isn't something you get as a kid with history and geometry, and there's a lot to learn. Setting up a forest garden is a big job. Trees won't plant themselves—well, not where you want them.

The hardest part is learning and designing before the spade hits the grass. You could just buy a bunch of fruit trees and pop them around the yard. And if you go out and do that, let me know, because that's splendid, and a million times better than nothing. But I want to get this right. If I just throw in some trees, they might not all fruit so well. Maybe I didn't think to plant "insectary" flowers that would attract the pollinating bees at the right times. Maybe I should have spent the first year or two building the soil fertility with ground covers (good thing some ground covers also offer edibles). Or maybe I put a fast-growing tree to the south of a slow-growing tree, and in five years, my slow tree will get shaded out.

There is a scary side of forest gardens. Mistakes are in *years* and so are the benefits. You have to make a big investment of time and money up front, and you won't see serious returns on the trees for four or five years. But those four or five years are going to go by anyhow, aren't

---

[1] For more information, you may wish to start with the *Edible Forest Gardens* site: http://www.edibleforestgardens.com/about_gardening.

they? If you already have an annual garden, why not think ahead, and combine it with a forest? You'll still have plenty of space for your annuals. And after a few years—wow! Plus, many of the smaller perennials, plants you may not even have heard of yet, will offer edibles sooner.

And if you've been scared off from gardening because of the extra work, this is a perfect fit. You don't commit to a lifetime of work. Instead, you do a big one-time project of learning, planning, purchasing, and planting. Then you luxuriate in a lifetime of low-maintenance fruit, nuts, berries, greens, edible roots, and herbs.

Who needs three acres and a cow? All you need is a backyard.

Bill Powell is the owner of Wineskin Media, a graphics design company in Front Royal, Virginia. He has designed book covers for notable authors such as Mark Shea, Warren Carroll, Race Mathews, and Brad Birzer.

DISTRIBUTISM
& MUTUALISM
The Convergence

BY HON. DR. RACE MATHEWS

"In as far as the machine cannot be shared, I would have the ownership of it shared; that is, the direction of it shared, and the profits of it shared." —G.K.CHESTERTON

CO-OPERATIVES AND OTHER MUTUALS ARE THE ROCK ON WHICH the universality and practicability of Distributism has from its inception rested. Mutuals expand the horizons of Distributism beyond small businesses, individual craft-workers and smallholder farms to encompass the ownership of the larger enterprises from which inevitably the majority of workers in an increasingly urbanised world derive their livelihoods. Chesterton wrote presciently in his *The Outline of Sanity* in 1926: "Even my Utopia, would contain different things of different types holding different tenures."

> There would be some thing nationalised, some machines owned corporately, some guilds sharing common profits, and so on, as well as many absolute individual owners, where such individual owners are most possible… Even while we remain industrial, we can work towards industrial distribution and away from industrial monopoly… we can try to own our own tools… In as far as the machine cannot be shared, I would have the ownership of it shared; that is, the direction of shared, and the profits of it shared.[1]

---

[1] G.K.Chesterton *The Outline of Sanity*, (London: Methuen and Co., 1926), pp. 108,151,148.

As noted by America's foremost Distributism studies scholar, Dermot Quinn: "Co-operatives were essential to the Distributist ideal. They combined ownership, labour for profit, reward for initiative, a degree of self-sufficiency, elimination of waste (as in the duplication of equipment or use of unnecessary middlemen) and a strong commitment to reciprocal self-help." [2] In the great complex of worker owned manufacturing, retail, financial, civil engineering and agricultural co-operatives and associated entities, businesses that the Basque priest Don Jose Maria Arizmendiarrieta established at Mondragón in the Basque region of Spain as in those of Northern Italy, Mutualism and Distributism have achieved a joint apotheosis. Were the original Distributists alive today, evolved Distributism as exemplified by Mondragón might well astonish them, but it is unlikely that they would be displeased.[3]

Mutualism preceded Distributism but stemmed from the same roots. Their respective forefathers faced comparable problems of endemic unemployment, underemployment, poverty and inequality which—in kind if not in degree—strikingly resemble those which the economies of the developed world have increasingly over the last forty or so years experienced, and which the Global Economic Meltdown has massively exacerbated. Then, as now, governments could offer no effective alternative. The times gave rise instead to the philosophy of Mutualism, which Distributism in its turn has so incomparably informed and enriched.

Mutualism should be understood as our acting in concert with one another to achieve objectives that are unachievable for us in isolation from one another—to become in the immortal words of the great Canadian Distributist, Fr. Moses Coady, "masters of our own destiny." Coady wrote:

---

[2] Dermot Quinn "The Historical Foundations of Modern Distributism" in *The Chesterton Review*, Vol 21, No 4, November 1985, p. 464.

[3] For a detailed account of the Mondragón co-operatives, see Race Mathews, *Jobs of Our Own: Building a Stakeholder Society: Alternatives to the Market and the State*, Irving, Texas (New York: The Distributist Review Press, 2009), Chapters 9 and 10.

"We start with the simple things that are vital to human living and move on up the scale to the more cultural and refining activities that make life whole and complete. Through credit unions, co-operative stores, lobster factories and sawmills, we are laying the foundations for an appreciation of Shakespeare and grand opera." [4]

Co-operatives and other mutualist bodies are almost always formed as means of enabling their members to acquire necessities such as otherwise would be unavailable or unaffordable for them. For example, the Rochdale Pioneers—the twenty-eight cotton workers who founded a co-operative store in Toad Lane in Rochester in 1884, and thereby launched the British consumer co-operative movement—were responding to a pressing social need for affordable access to such household requisites as food, fuel and clothing.

Credit co-operatives, now known generally as credit unions, were a response to the need for affordable carry-on loans for smallholder farmers, and later for affordable consumer finance. Friendly societies were initially a response to the need for access to affordable funerals, and, later, for unemployment benefits, sickness benefits, and medical and hospital care. Access to affordable life assurance was offered by mutual life assurance societies, as was access to affordable home loans by building societies.

Processing and marketing co-operatives met a pressing social need on the part of farmers to capture value added to their produce beyond the farm gate. Worker co-operatives—the precursors of Mondragon—were a response to the need for labour to hire capital rather than capital labour, and so for workers to be the owners of their jobs and workplaces. Trade unions were originally mutualist bodies or co-operatives, formed by employees in response to the pressing need for fair working conditions and a just price for their labour.

The usefulness of all these institutions, and the validity of their mutualist principles, is evidenced by their worldwide following. For

---

[4] M.M. Coady, *Masters of Their Own Destiny: The Story of the Antigonish Movement of Adult Education Through Economic Co-operation* (Antigonish, Nova Scotia: Formac Publishing Company, 1980), p. 68.

example, the membership of credit co-operatives affiliated with the World Council of Credit Unions (WCCU) is in excess of 44 million. Co-operatives affiliated with the International Co-operative Alliance (ICA)—the world umbrella body for the co-operative movement—currently total more than 650 million members. Taking into account the worldwide membership of friendly societies and building societies, Mutualism is a movement numbering more than a billion. Add to this the policyholders or mutual life assurance and the number is still more impressive. Mutualism rivals in its following many of the world's major religions. Mutuals adhere to a common set of principles, as set out, by the ICA and in slightly different words by the WCCU. The ICA statement reads:

> "A co-operative is an autonomous association of persons united voluntarily to meet their common economic, social, and cultural needs and aspirations through a jointly-owned and democratically-controlled enterprise. Co-operatives are based on the values of self-help, self-responsibility, democracy, equality, equity and solidarity. In the tradition of their founders, co-operative members believe in the ethical values of honesty, openness, social responsibility and caring for others. The co-operative principles are guidelines by which co-operatives put their values into practice: 1. Voluntary and Open Membership 2. Democratic Member Control 3. Member Economic Participation 4. Autonomy and Independence 5. Education, Training and Information 6. Co-operation among Co-operatives 7. Concern for Community." [5]

The strength of Mutualism stems from the ownership by members of the means of remedying the problems which cause them to come together in the first place. In as much as members are both the owners and customers of their businesses, there is a competitive advantage stemming from what theorists characterise as "the agency

---

[5] International Co-operative Alliance, Statement of Co-operative Identity, at http://www.ica.coop/coop/principles.html.

problem"—namely, "the difficulty in all but the simplest relationships, of ensuring that the principal is faithfully served, and the agent is fairly compensated." In a nutshell, the mutual and its members being one and the same have no incentive to exploit one another.

The downside is in the dual nature of mutuals as having the attributes of both businesses and social movements. As in other social movements, the typical lifecycle of a mutual falls into three stages, constituting a "generation-degeneration process." There is, in the first instance, a utopian stage where the vision and commitment of the founders energise their followers and enable the mutual to begin; secondly, a stage where the mutual assumes a more formal and institutional character in order to more effectively go about achieving its objectives, albeit usually at the expense of a diminution in the involvement of members in the conduct of its affairs, and, finally, a stage usually referred to as the "system stage" where bureaucracy takes over, and the survival and well-being of the organization assumes precedence over whatever purpose it was originally intended to serve. In the absence of high levels of member involvement and participation, the mutual becomes for all practical purposes indistinguishable from its commercial counterparts, and vulnerable in turn to being taken over and looted by predatory demutualisers.

What follows logically is that mutuals must be sufficiently flexible to adapt to changing needs and circumstances. They must be able to recognise when the needs for which they were established no longer exist, are less pressing, or are being met on favourable terms by other businesses and agencies. The need is for them to constantly reinvent themselves and re-target their resources so as to respond to new needs or those that are being experienced more widely or with greater urgency. In this way they avoid becoming what is referred to technically as "frozen" mutuals.

Reinvention in no sense means that, for example, credit unions necessarily should cease to be providers of affordable consumer loans, but rather that perhaps radically innovative additions to their product mix should be adopted as changing opportunities and obligations may dictate. That mutualist bodies are fully capable of re-inventing themselves in the face of changing needs and circumstances is evident from the example of a notable U.S. co-operative that was formed originally in the nineteen-thirties in response to a pressing social need for affordable hygienic home milk deliveries. When corporate dairies in due course offered a comparable service at a comparable price, the co-operative re-invented itself as a provider of affordable eye testing services and spectacles. When optometric corporations in their turn arrived on the scene with comparable services and prices, the co-operative re-invented itself for a second time, and is currently a major supplier of accommodation and support services for older people, with condominiums throughout the United States.

A further example is afforded by the great Desjardins credit union federation in Canada. The original Desjardins credit union was founded in Quebec at the turn of the century, in response to the need of low-income households for affordable carry-on loans to tide them over in emergencies from one pay day to another, and so avoid borrowing from so-called "pay day lenders" and other loan-sharks at interest rates up to and exceeding 100%.

What had, by the nineteen-fifties, become the Desjardins credit union federation than re-invented itself to meet the need of post-war households for affordable personal loans for consumer durables such as furniture, floor-coverings, white goods and cars. Faced as they have found themselves in the nineteen-eighties and beyond with a no less pressing need on the part of their members for jobs, the Desjardins credit unions have again re-invented themselves, as a source of capital for local and regional economic development.

No such transformation crowned what was initially the spectacular success of the quintessentially Distributist Antigonish Movement, effectively the first attempt in the English-speaking world at a large-scale application of Distributist principles, that Coady and his fellow priest Fr. James Tompkins established in the early nineteen-thirties in Nova Scotia. The glory of the Antigonish Movement, and the tragedy of its inability to transcend the "generation-degeneration" process, is attested to in an eloquent passage by Coady's biographer, Michael Welton. It reads:

"For an evanescent historical moment, the Antigonish Movement captured the imagination of the world. Journalists, liberal-minded religious leaders, papal authorities, eastern seaboard intellectuals, professors, theologians, social reformers, wild-eyed dreamers, co-operative leaders and innocent youth came from far and wide to witness 'the miracle of Antigonish'. Hard minds and doubting hearts were transformed by the credit unions and co-op stores springing up in communities with previously unremarkable histories. Antigonish, now a rural town like so many others, graced by malls and fast-food outlets, glowed with a radiant light in the 1930s and 1940s." [6]

If Antigonish ultimately asked more of consumer co-operation and credit unionism than they were able to deliver, that in no way detracts from the energy its adherents devoted to their cause, nor from the short-to-medium term alleviation of endemic poverty, the enhancement of human dignity and the restoration of hope that they accomplished, and the inspiration and encouragement they afforded for others after them and afar off.

It remained for Father Arizmendiarrieta, to finally bring to fruition the convergence of Distributism and Mutualism that Mondragón so triumphantly exemplifies.[7] Arizmendiarrieta gave practical effect to the fundamental Distributist truth that only work and the ownership of productive property were so central to the lives of ordinary people as to provide the foundations on which an enduring Distributist social order could be built. The essentials of the Mondragón story are simple. What began in 1956 as a handful of workers in a disused factory, using hand tools and sheet metal to make oil-fired heating and cooking stoves, has now become the seventh largest business group in Spain, comprising 260 individual co-operatives. Annual sales increased between 2006 and 2007 by 12.4 to some $20 billion, and overall employment by 24 percent, from 83,601 to 103,731. Exports accounted for 56.9 percent

---

[6] M.R. Welton, *Little Mosie from the Margaree: A Biography of Moses Michael Coady* (Toronto: Thompson Educational Publishing Inc, 2001), p. 253.

[7] For a detailed account of the Mondragón co-operatives, see Mathews 1999, op cit, Chapters 9 & 10.

of industrial co-operative sales, and were up in value by 8.6 percent. Mondragón's Eroski worker/consumer co-operatives now operate some 2,441 retail outlets, ranging in size from petrol stations and small franchise stores to supermarkets and shopping malls, in locations that now extend beyond Spain into France and Andorra. Mondragón co-operatives now own or joint venture some 114 local and overseas subsidiaries.

All worker-members of the businesses have an equal say in their governance of their co-operatives on a one member/one vote basis, and share on a proportionately equal basis in the profits or losses. The key Distributist objective of a sustainably widespread distribution of property has been achieved by the co-operatives, in as much as members have property of four kinds: firstly, ownership of their jobs; secondly, direct personal ownership of capital held for them in individual accounts that supplement their generous superannuation entitlements on retirement, and earn additional income for them through interest to which they have regular access; thirdly, a shared ownership of the assets of their co-operatives such as buildings, equipment and reserves; and, finally, a further shared ownership—albeit less direct—of the unique secondary support co-operatives in which the primary co-operatives are major stakeholders.

The convergence of Distributism and Mutualism at Mondragón gives rise to a query. Might not it now be time for Distributists to cease talking primarily to one another and seek wider audiences and strategic alliances? Might not a brighter future for Distributism lie with active partnerships such as might be forged with, among others, credit unions and other mutualist bodies?

The Hon. Race Mathews is a former Australian academic, federal MP, state MP and minister, municipal councillor and chief of staff to Labor Party leaders in the federal and state parliaments. He has written and spoken widely on politics, political history and public policy. Dr. Mathews is the author of Jobs of Our Own: Building a Stakeholder Society: Alternatives to the Market and the State.

DISTRIBUTIST EDUCATION

BY RYAN GRANT

"The moment men begin to care more for education than for religion, they begin to care more for ambition than for education." —G.K.CHESTERTON

WE ARE OFTEN TOLD MORE FUNDING IS NEEDED FOR EDUCATION and that we are not investing enough in our schools. The United States, however, spends more money per child than any other country in the world and performs poorly in overall performance.

The solution is the perpetual growth of regulation of schools and federal money per student. When the results fail to impress, more money is spent, and rather than support education in a proper sense, the consequence for the student not meeting the government's set target knowledge levels is to be "left behind"—of course, we cannot have anyone neglected on the road to educational utopia. Further laws requiring more standardization and stricter oversight are put in place in order to make certain everyone is going in the same direction, despite all the talk of diversity and free thought the educational establishment prides itself on. Although a certain degree of standardization is necessary, this ought to vary according to the real needs of the individual, the family, and local society, not according to the arbitrary determinations of the state.

There is an emphasis on math and science now paramount in all discussion of education. The arts, literature, Latin, logic, and philosophy belong to the patrimony of the culture from which we inherited our civilization; they are the handmaiden to math and science that help to form the whole individual toward his final end. We have made the gross mistake instead of minimizing the arts for the sake of math and sciences. Everything is reduced to practicality, love of learning has evaporated, and increasingly, what is produced, is a technocratic group of people who consider themselves superior to the previous generation because they have the Internet and an iPod. Unfortunately, the same teachers and students who enjoy the material superiority of modern man probably could not work out the propositions of Euclid, who lived 2,300 years ago.

In this we see the divorce of education from tradition as something handed down, without which there is no science, there is no math, literature, or any other subject. Throughout his ministry St. Paul declared, *Tradidi quod accepi*: "I handed down what I received." The divorce of tradition from education also brings the divorce of a coherent philosophy concerning the purpose of education. We see this in the dogmatic assertion that the Church must be so separate She cannot be mentioned in a state school. As Chesterton put it:

> "Given the modern philosophy or absence of philosophy, education is turned against itself destroying that very sense of variety and proportion which is the object of education to give... the moment men begin to care more for education than for religion, they begin to care more for ambition than for education. It is no longer a world in which the souls of all are equal before heaven, but a world in which the mind of each is bent on achieving unequal advantage over the other." [1]

The concept of society has fallen out completely from the school environment, and now it is focused on the needs of the individual only in the sense of what kind of comfortable white collar job he might be able to attain. "What college are you going to?" or "Well, if you want to go to college you need to take these classes." "You could do that

---

[1] *The Collected Works of G.K. Chesterton: Illustrated London News*, 1929-1931.

but you won't get into a good college." A certain level of excellence and achievement in basic things is necessary for a functioning educational system, but after a certain level of knowledge, which ought to be common to the majority of men in society, the traditional focus of education shifted to what the individual could *do* and educating him in like fashion. He might be apprenticed to a trade and put in a position at a young age to provide for himself when he is older by owning his own labor. Students who did not fall into this category still received a good education in many of the basic arts and sciences so that when he went to university he could enter any of those fields. Our educational system at present, however, is worn out, overtaxed, and underperforming. It is focused on material ends for the purposes of tax contribution and not the eternal end for which the individual himself is journeying. As Pius XI noted in *Divini illius magistri,* education neglecting man's final end is no education at all. The state's educational system has fallen into what Chesterton once called "the madness of bigness." In an attempt to be large enough to meet all needs, it has become mean and narrow; the real needs and the future of the individual student are left out of the equation.

In their educational systems, ancients and medievals concentrated on studies of grammar, rhetoric, and logic so they could explore the world around them. Arithmetic and geometry followed because they taught delightful truths and were useful for everyday life. Algebra was unknown to them, yet today's student with years of algebra under his belt is the same grocery clerk unable to figure out the change without the use of a register. Do algebra and calculus reveal truth and arouse wonder, or are they merely problem-solving techniques that train students to think and respond like computers? In general it seems as though it is the latter, which should not surprise us because that is the overall attitude of society and the increasingly common function of the worker within the framework of big business.

The numerous teaching orders such as the Christian Brothers, the Jesuits, and armies of Immaculate Hearts or Sisters of Mercy filled thousands of positions in private education helping to keep costs manageable for the average family. By replacing these orders with lay faithful, the increasing cost of salaries, health care, legal fees and other expenditures, have made running parochial schools expensive, if not cost prohibitive. Furthermore, parochial schools have often followed the demise of the state school by adopting the same curriculum and the same textbooks "dumbing down" education for the sake of nurturing student self-esteem.

Another possibility is for parents to run their own curriculum. What happens when they do? Scorn generally follows, with visits from social services, criticism from friends and neighbors, and there is, of course, media reaction. Homeschooled students tend to perform better on standardized testing and score very well. But even homeschooling has its pitfalls. Not every parent is competent to school well and in a world of two-income families, finding the time to homeschool can be difficult.

A homeschooling cooperative alleviates these time-constraints and also cuts the expenses of boarding or private school. Homeschooling co-operatives can function in this way, with a handful of teachers versed in subjects that provide elementary education while tailoring their services to the needs of growing children. In fact, homeschooling cooperatives are capable of serving as outsource to public or private schools without recourse to vocational education.

This practice harkens back to classical and medieval civilization, and provides opportunities for students at the discretion of their parents. In both cases, education was something handed down like an apprentice-ship. Charlemagne's ideal was to establish common education through the monasteries, which became the bedrock of medieval society and local medieval economies. Lacking Greek slaves (happily) in the case of the Romans, or monasteries in the case of the medievals, associations of accredited teachers could cut right through the "system" to pass on the educational patrimony of western civilization to the next generation.

This Distributist approach to education has additional advantages. Students in an educational cooperative offering the training and/or ap-prenticeship in mechanics, utilities, construction, or computer science, are attractive to many existing businesses seeking apprentices. These men and women can be trained, while in school, in exchange for free labor and the prospect of a job following graduation. Within the wider social outlook of Distributism, for the rebuilding of local communities and government, these opportunities would both buttress and improve the mission of small, local and sustainable business models.

Any solution, however, hinges upon the recovery of direction and common sense in society, and that depends almost entirely on the restoration and preservation of the family, and the recovery of religion in the state. *Religio* in Latin, shares the same root with the word *legio*. Referring to the Roman legions, it means to bind together, or yoke together. Religion, as classically understood, is the whole basis for constituting society. Pope Leo XIII emphasized this point when he taught in *Sapientiae Christianae*:

> "By nature parents have a right to the training of their children, but with this added duty that the education and instruction of the child be in accord with the end for which by God's blessing it was begotten. Therefore, it is the duty of parents to make every effort to prevent any invasion of their rights in this matter, and to make absolutely sure that the education of their children remain under their own control in keeping with their Christian duty, and above all to refuse to send them to those schools in which there is danger of imbibing the deadly poison of impiety."

Pius XI continues this point when he taught in *Divini illius magistri*:

> "It is paternal instinct, given by God, that thus turns with confidence to the Church, certain of finding in her the protection of family rights, thereby illustrating that harmony with which God has ordered all things. The Church is indeed conscious of her divine mission to all mankind, and of the obligation which all men have to practice the one true religion; and therefore she never tires of defending her right, and of reminding parents of their duty, to have all Catholic-born children baptized and brought up as Christians. On the other hand so jealous is she of the family's inviolable natural right to educate the children, that she never consents, save under peculiar circumstances and with special cautions, to baptize the children of infidels, or provide for their education against the will of the parents, till such time as the children can choose for themselves and freely embrace the Faith."

Politically, some may argue that Distributist educational reform would never work and cannot be done, but naysayers also told Bishop John Hughes in the nineteenth century that he could not enact Catholic school reforms in New York. Yet, Hughes advocated for Catholics to vote for candidates that would support public school reform and allow the establishment of parochial schools, which Catholics did. The third party candidate lost that year, but because Catholics had supported him, the Democratic candidate also lost. Small communities do have the ability to influence large outcomes and it starts at the basic level: the family and the education of children.

Ryan Grant is a native of eastern Connecticut. He received his bachelor's degree in Philosophy and Theology at Franciscan University of Steubenville, and also studied at Holy Apostles Seminary. He currently teaches Latin in Post Falls, ID where he resides with his wife and two children.

To Our Hopeful Posterity

BY RICHARD ALEMAN

"We have formulated questions to be addressed to Parliamentary candidates. We think that something can be done through Parliament to make small ownership easier to gain and to hold. But we are not a Party, and our main effort must be always outside Parliament." —G.K.CHESTERTON*1*

L IVING IN A WORLD DOMINATED BY CONVENTIONAL POLITICS, Distributism promises to challenge trends toward centralization of political power and economic globalism. Around the world, faith in common currencies, central banking, free trade agreements, and the mass production system—a distinctive feature of capitalism and socialism—is crumbling, as discontent over taxpayer bailouts of finance, rising unemployment, and the license given to mega-corporations over the needs of the masses is provoking protests.

The Left and Right wings of our political establishment are running out of answers and appear disinterested and incapable of meeting the challenges of the 21st century. It is becoming obvious that any perceived differences between conservative and progressive positions are differences of degree rather than of kind. Conservatism and progressivism are liberal, revolutionary philosophies with conservatives only appearing to be "conservative" by comparison. Social Liberals, that is, progressives, desire an ethical economy while resisting moral scrutiny of personal selfishness. Economic Liberals, that is, conservatives, shield the family from personal selfishness while rebuking any attempts to rein in economic selfishness. The cost of this schizophrenia is too much to bear, with unenviable consequences for the poor and the middle class, as individualist and collectivist policies dig us deeper into social and economic disaster.

Families struggling to keep their jobs or forced to borrow to pay mortgages, health care bills, and their children's education are watching their homes foreclose, their firms ship overseas, and their wages reduced to arbitrary "industry standards," while the gap between rich and poor tripled in the past three decades.[1] The market is working, but only for a few people. The reality for most is the credit card swipe, which has replaced wage increases in an effort to supplement our acquisitive economy.

Our national debt is increasing steadily with no serious production base to pay it back.[2] The trade deficit in the United States has exploded to $45.6 billion as companies continue to relocate to India and China in order to lower wages, avoid regulations, cut taxes, and fire or hire at will. Companies are making a killing and cities like Detroit, once admired industrial marvels, are becoming ghost towns.

It is myopic to suggest our problems are only economic given the social crisis facing the family. In the United States, "Sunday Laws" stressing the importance of family life and religious observation have mostly dissolved with little opposition. Half of all marriages end in divorce and 62% of all women continue to use some form of birth control to prevent pregnancy. Although abortions have declined in the past few years, 53 million unborn children have been stripped of their lives since the Supreme Court decision of Roe vs. Wade. Overpopulation myths and family "planning" campaigns are successfully convincing families to terminate life and target poor, minority women under the facade of class or gender equality. Indeed, the productive home with its central role in society, its education, its tools, its garden, and its entertainment is replaced with misogyny, feminism, sexual disorientation and, "a monumental economic disaster that is not the result of inflation or

---

[1] Center on Budget and Policy Priorities, http://www.cbpp.org/cms/?fa=view&id=3220
[2] Approximately $15 trillion as of this writing.

recession, but of the devaluation of children." [3]

A conversation about the social burdens we are passing onto the next generation is long overdue. As our nation increasingly becomes post-industrial, we can no longer afford to ignore the cost of depleting the world's resources, look the other way as slave labor replaces our manufacturing base, or dismiss the connection between moral decline, economic decadence, and political sterility.

While no social system is perfect, Distributism offers "an economic system which will place fewer obstacles for fallen humanity to put first things first, to put material goods in their own proper place and value other things more." [4] To put things in their proper perspective, "The family dates from the foundations of the world. Property is its buttress. The first is essential to any society at any moment: the second is essential to its health." [5] The family is the fundamental unit of society and should be defended, while ownership of property and its right use allows man to improve his condition, because "men always work harder and more readily when they work on that which belongs to them, nay, they learn to love the very soil that yields in response to the labor of their hands, not only food to eat, but an abundance of good things for themselves and those that are dear to them." [6] Property is personal. With it man can call something his own, he can work with his hands and reap the fruit of his labor, save, and direct himself toward the exercise of virtue. Property comes with responsibility, limits, and the provisions necessary to care for as many of his family's needs as reasonably possible.

However, man is not an island. He cannot provide for all of his needs and he cannot provide for all of his ends. Man is not simply an individual, but a person, a social animal who cannot be virtuous without

---

[3] Dale Ahlquist, "The Basis of Civilization," *The Distributist Review*, February 10, 2011, http:// distributistreview.com/mag/2011/02/the-basis-of-civilization/.

[4] Thomas Storck, "A Distributist Looks at Capitalism and Socialism," *The Distributist Review*, November 8, 2010, http://distributistreview.com/ mag/2010/11/a-distributist-looks-at-capitalism-and-socialism/.

[5] Harold Robbins, *The Sun of Justice*. Newman ePress, August 3, 2011 (Kindle edition). Robbins was editor of the Catholic Land Federation's publication, *Cross and the Plough*.

[6] Leo XIII, *Rerum Novarum* §47.

society. Because individuals cannot oversee the common good without a natural ruling authority that properly has "God for its Author," [7] men naturally create governing authorities so that through law the state can order itself and the "sufficiency of bodily goods, whose use is necessary for virtuous acting." [8]

Thus, it would be a mistake to describe Distributism as a form of economic personalism, as if the solution to institutional injustice is the pursuit of personal gain and individual self-interest. Individual choice cannot substitute justly ordered structures. Abortion and contraception cannot be eliminated by choosing them out of existence, nor will the destruction of small business by behemoth conglomerates cease if we frequent the mom and pop. Yes, we should foster a virtuous society and start by making the right choices, whether by opening accounts at credit unions, growing our own food or buying fresh staples from the local farmer. Indeed, we should use our vote and our money to cultivate a civilization of love and not breed a culture of death. We should also, however, recognize that law should facilitate man's eternal ends, not impede them, and so work toward structural changes to solve injustice is necessary because systematic problems require systematic solutions.[9]

To gain influence and political strength, political action committees (PACs) should be formed to support candidates and to write policy proposals. Although state, local, and federal regulations vary, Distributist political action committees could operate as issue advocacy groups challenging social or fiscal referendum, raising and dispersing funds for the purposes of furthering association goals, and supporting candidates embracing initiatives congenial with Distributist core issues. Not only would this group screen new leadership, it would pressure incumbents to adopt Distributist policies at the local and state levels by gathering support for its agenda, releasing information about candidate funding

---

[7] Leo XIII, *Immortale Dei* §3.

[8] St. Thomas Aquinas, *De Regno*, Lib. 2 Cap. 16.

[9] Hilaire Belloc's masterful *An Essay on the Restoration of Property* is a brief blueprint for the political establishment of the Distributive State, in which local government partner with citizens to create opportunities for the widest distribution of property.

sources and voting records to the community. As local, independent, and conventional party candidates seem more responsive and flexible to alternatives than mainstream partisan leadership, the D-PAC could successfully help Distributism rise from the bottom-up.

Although some PACs operate under the umbrella of policy institutes, D-PACs would be local and grassroots, with large and small team sizes cooperating with other groups across the country. Advisors from various sectors would make up core teams consisting of educators, farmers, urban planners, economists, political scientists, organizers, clergy, and others passionate about improving community life. Practical outlines and manifestoes will vary according to local, regional, and national interests. For instance, to stimulate small business development, tax incentives and grants could strengthen the native economy and help develop family-owned businesses and cooperative firms, neighborhood micro-credit programs, and local currency programs. Guilds may be the recipients of these tax measures to help reinvigorate craftsmanship and other trades, while restrictions on the production or sale of Genetically Modified Organisms would go far to help the small farmer compete regionally and provide local consumers with healthier, organic foods.

D-PACs can also work up "back-to-the-land" schemes to plant the decentralization of our economy and encourage new opportunities outside of our concentrated cities. Using the example of historic and existing land projects such as the Catholic Land Association of Great Britain, the Guild of St. Joseph and St. Dominic, and Peter Maurin Farm in the United States,[10] these models may encourage the unemployed, families, and groups to cooperatively own farms or raise non-farming enterprises like houses of hospitality, arts and crafts guilds, and so forth.

If the common man is forced to tighten his belt so will government. Candidates should argue in favor of eliminating unnecessary spending and subsidies for out-of-town producers. The millions in taxpayer

---

[10] For more information on moving "back to the land," read G.C. Heseltine's *Town to Country: A Guide for Townsmen Who Seek a Living on the Land* published by Catholic Authors Press.

dollars thrown at developers of strip malls and big box stores could be saved and small sums could be offered to hundreds of small producers, companies with Employee Stock Ownership Plans, and cooperatives. D-PACS should also lobby for a cooperative spirit between local governments and religious-run services to help reduce the burdens or dependence on welfare programs, education, and other social services. Indeed, Christian hospitals, counseling centers, safe havens for pregnant mothers, adoption agencies, and shelters to feed the homeless have a long history of providing exemplary and free care. Allowing them to operate without intruding on their religious beliefs will help outsource and drastically lower the cost of government.

G.K.Chesterton's shrewd strategy to challenge "Parliament" while remaining outside of it may usher in what some have dubbed as "the Distributist moment." But our confidence rests in ordinary people doing extraordinary things. In the third millennium let us applaud the ubiquity of leadership, not from our politicians, but from our farmers, our shopkeepers and assembly workers, our sculptors, our parishioners, our teachers, and our parents who only wished to bequeath something better than what we've become and something more than what we have. Who are the distributists? We are the common men and women in pursuit of a new nation whose very foundation is built upon "what dreams may come, when we have shuffled off this mortal coil..." We are the voices of those who have come before us and the tender eyes of our hopeful posterity.

Richard Aleman, a native Spaniard, is the managing editor for The Distributist Review. *He is a contributing editor for* Gilbert Magazine, St. Austin Review's Ink Desk, *and* The Remnant *newspaper.*